THE POWER SERIAL RAPIST

ABOUT THE AUTHORS

Dawn J. Graney, Psy.D., is a practicing clinical psychologist with a specialization in forensic psychology. She is currently working at the Federal Medical Center in Rochester, Minnesota, where she provides mental health services to male inmates within the federal prison system. She received her doctoral degree from Alliant University/California School of Professional Psychology, School of Social and Policy Studies. Her areas of practice interest include working with mentally ill offenders, sex offenders, correctional psychology, and conducting forensic evaluations. Her areas of research interest include violent offenders, sexual predators, criminal victimization, and corrections related issues. Dr. Graney is also interested in researching the concept of victim selection in relation to crimes other than power serial rape. Her current research focuses on validating the power serial rapist victim selection typological model, applying it within clinical and law enforcement settings.

Bruce A. Arrigo, is Professor and Chair of the Department of Criminal Justice at the University of North Carolina–Charlotte, with Adjunct Professor appointments in the Public Policy Program and the Psychology Department respectively. Formerly the Director of the Institute of Psychology, Law, and Public Policy at the California School of Professional Psychology-Fresno, Dr. Arrigo began his professional career as a community organizer and social activist for the homeless, the mentally ill, the working poor, the frail elderly, the decarcerated, and the chemically addicted. Dr. Arrigo received his Ph.D. from Pennsylvania State University, and he holds a master's degree in psychology and in sociology. He is the author of more than (100) monographs, journal articles, academic book chapters, and scholarly essays exploring theoretical and applied topics in critical criminology, criminal justice and mental health, and socio-legal studies. He is the author, coauthor, or editor of seven (7) books; including, *Madness, Language, and the Law* (1993), *The Contours of Psychiatric Justice* (1996), *Social Justice/Criminal Justice* (1998), *The Dictionary of Critical Social Sciences* (with T.R. Young, 1999), *Introduction to Forensic Psychology* (2000), *Law, Psychology, and Justice* (with Christopher R. Williams, 2002), and *Punishing the Mentally Ill: A Critical Analysis of Law and Psychiatry* (2002). Dr. Arrigo is the founding and acting Editor of the peer-reviewed quarterly, *Journal of Forensic Psychology Practice.* He was recently named the Critical Criminologist of the Year (1999-2000), sponsored by the Critical Criminology Division of the American Society of Criminology.

THE POWER SERIAL RAPIST

A Criminology-Victimology Typology of Female Victim Selection

By

DAWN J. GRANEY, PSY.D.

Institute of Psychology, Law and Public Policy
California School of Professional Psychology — Fresno

and

BRUCE A. ARRIGO, PH.D.

Department of Criminal Justice
University of North Carolina — Charlotte

Charles C Thomas
PUBLISHER • LTD.
SPRINGFIELD • ILLINOIS • U.S.A.

Published and Distributed Throughout the World by

CHARLES C THOMAS • PUBLISHER, LTD.
2600 South First Street
Springfield, Illinois 62704

ISBN 0-398-07249-3 (cloth)
ISBN 0-398-07250-7 (paper)

Library of Congress Catalog Card Number: 2001044298

With THOMAS BOOKS *careful attention is given to all details of
manufacturing and design. It is the Publisher's desire to present books that
are satisfactory as to their physical qualities and artistic possibilities and
appropriate for their particular use.* THOMAS BOOKS *will be true
to those laws of quality that assure a good name and good will.*

Printed in the United States of America
RR-R-3

Library of Congress Cataloging-in-Publication Data

Graney, Dawn J.
    The power serial rapist: a criminology-victimology typology of
female victim selection/by Dawn J. Graney and Bruce A. Arrigo.
        p. cm.
    Includes bibliographical references and index.
    ISBN 0-398-07249-3 (cloth) – ISBN 0-398-07250-7 (pbk.)
    1. Rapists–Psychology. 2. Rape. 3. Rape victims. 4. Escobedo,
    Gilbert Hernandez. 5. Rapists–Texas–Dallas–Biography. I. Arrigo,
    Bruce A. II. Title.

HV6558.G73 2002
362.883–dc21
                                                2001044298

PREFACE

The Power Serial Rapist provides an in-depth, comprehensive, and integrated approach to understanding this sexual offender's victim selection process. Consolidating the criminological research on rape and the victimological literature on victims, this book deepens our knowledge about the offender, his victim, and the sexual crimes this rapist commits. *The Power Serial Rapist* systematically explores past victimization theories and models, mindful of their relative strengths and limits. Moreover, by selecting out the most salient and useful features of past victim selection typologies, this book develops a detailed assessment of what sort of individuals are likely victims and why.

Going well beyond the presentation of theory, *The Power Serial Rapist* examines the explanatory and predictive capability of the victim selection typology it proposes. To this end, the case of Gilbert Escobedo, the Ski Mask rapist, is thoroughly explored. After important background material on this sexual offender, past victimization models and theories are applied to the case for purposes of interpreting and explaining Escobedo's method of selecting victims. Moreover, the victim selection typology developed by the authors is also applied to the Escobedo case. The authors demonstrate where and how their own typology significantly advances our assessment of female victim selection for sexual offenders like the Ski Mask Rapist. The text concludes by reviewing the implications of the authors' model for purposes of future clinical treatment, criminal justice administration and policy, and ongoing research.

D.J.G.
B.A.A.

CONTENTS

THE POWER SERIAL RAPIST

Chapter 1

INTRODUCTION

THE SUBJECT OF INQUIRY

This book investigates power serial rapists and female victim selection with the intent of developing a conceptual typological model. Rape can be differentially defined, depending on the source of the explanation (e.g., a legal versus a psychological context). In general, however, the term rape refers to sexual penetration and/or a sex act (i.e., vaginal, oral, anal sex, as well as object penetration) performed forcibly and without an individual's consent (Holmes & Holmes, 1996; Holmes, 1991). According to U.S. Department of Justice statistics, based on the National Crime Victimization Survey (NCVS), there were 98,000 rapes and an additional 99,000 attempts in 1996. We note, however, that the information obtained by the NCVS comes directly from crime victims and is not validated by, or representative of, crimes accounted for by the police. Therefore, these numbers represent both reported and unreported rapes.

Many researchers believe that less than 10% of all rapes are reported to law enforcement officials (e.g., Holmes, 1991). This underreporting logically means that only a small percentage of rapists are ever apprehended for their crime. However, statistics from the Rape Relief Center in Louisville, Kentucky, suggest that each time a rapist is caught the person has typically offended approximately fourteen previous times (Holmes, 1991). Given these statistics, it is reasonable to argue that, in essence, most rapists commit serial sex crimes. This position notwithstanding, a clear and unambiguous definition of a serial rapist is difficult to identify in the literature.

For purposes of our research, the term "serial rapist" refers to an individual who has raped on two or more separate occasions and has had at least two different victims. We note that this definition distinguishes itself from rapists who commit a single offense with more than one victim or those who repeatedly victimize the same individual. The phrase "separate occasions" draws attention to individual acts of rape that, when assessed in total, represent a series of crimes committed by the same offender. Thus, the phrase "separate occasions" is not predicated on a specific span of time (e.g., isolated rapes that occurred over X number of hours, days, etc., by the same individual). Rather, our definition recognizes an offense as a separate occurrence in a series if two unrelated victims are raped either in separate structures (e.g., physical dwelling, public building) or within different time frames. In this context, then, the amount of time that transpires between the assaults is not a pivotal issue for conceptual or empirical inquiry.

Throughout this book the terms "power rape," "serial rapist," and "power serial rapist" are used considerably. To avoid any confusion, a brief discussion of these terms is warranted. Rape can be divided into several subcategories, according to common elements and/or characteristics of the rapist and the sexual assault. For example, these elements may focus on the manner in which the rapist approaches the victim, the level of violence the offender uses, or whether or not the individual uses a weapon during the assault. These subcategories also denote personal aspects of the rapist (e.g., motivation, sense of self-worth, feelings of adequacy). Consequently, the term "power rape" (or power rapist) refers only to one particular sexual offender or rapist subtype.

The various rape categories are described in detail in subsequent sections of this chapter and elsewhere throughout this study. However, as previously noted, the purpose of the categorizations is to provide a quick and easy reference regarding personal and assault characteristics of a particular rapist type. When the term power rape (or rapist) is used in this book, our intent is to refer only to those elements that are distinctive to that particular sexual offense or rapist type. Thus, although the term power rape does imply serial offending, its fundamental function is to provide readers with a simple term by which to describe a particular type of rapist and the person's sexual assault.

As we previously explained, the term serial rape refers to a number of sexual assaults committed by the same offender. The phrase serial rape does not, on its own, specify a rapist subtype. Rather, it serves only to describe the repetitive nature of the sexual offense. Although this project focuses specifically on the power serial rapist, we anticipate that our inquiry will yield additional and fruitful information on the crime of serial rape in general. Therefore, throughout this book, the term serial rape is relevant to and resonates for all types of serial sexual offenders and not just the power serial rapist. We note that the subsequent chapter (and section) on rape incorporates a great deal of research on the serial rapist in general; however, it is not applicable to the power serial rapist in particular. As we explain in Chapter 2, the research findings discussed are not germane to a rapist subtype. Finally, the term power serial rapist (or power serial rape) refers to those instances in which the offender repeatedly commits rape assaults.

WHY INVESTIGATE POWER SERIAL RAPISTS?

This study was principally conceived from and is based on the first author's presuppositions regarding serial rape and victim selection. These assumptions emerged several years ago during an undergraduate lecture in a criminology course. The instructor spoke about a serial rape case in a large metropolitan area in which each victim had been approached by the offender in a particular local park. An undercover female officer was then assigned to patrol the area. However, during the time the female officer was in the park (several days for a number of hours each day), the police officer was never approached by the assailant. Eventually, the rapist was caught, and the female officer did question him about why he never approached her in the park on the days she was there. The apprehended felon responded that he did in fact see her in the park each day; however, he could tell by the way she carried herself that she was not a victim.

This very provocative story led to a series of (research) questions for the first author, especially regarding the concept of victim selection and what offenders look for in potential victims. In addition, both researchers have always been fascinated by the crime of rape, given the frequency with which it occurs and/or is attempted and the very physical and emotional invasion it represents for the victim (e.g., Arrigo, 1993). Thus, learning something more about the offender's motivations and thought processes regarding this sexual offense–curiosities harbored by many social science investigators, forensic mental health practitioners, criminal justice professionals and the lay public–would arguably go a long way in satisfying our intellectual and practical interests. Accordingly, our decision to focus on the serial rapist stems from very personal feelings about this atrocity and a genuine desire to learn more about this crime. We believe that both explanations inform the implications of this study, explored at the end of the book.

We have offered some observations on why serial rapists are the focus of our inquiry. We have not, however, explained why we specifically examine the power serial rapist subtype. In general, the justification is methodological. Several comments along these lines are discussed in this chapter.

Before initiating this study, we assumed the following: (1) many serial rapists do make use of victim selection techniques; (2) because of the nature of their crime, power rapists rely on victim selection techniques to an equal or greater extent than other rapist subtypes (e.g., anger and sadistic types); (3) power serial rapists rely on both personal and situational (i.e., micro and macro) criteria in the selection of their victims; (4) power serial rapists are not always cognitively aware of factors that affect their selection processes (e.g., neighborhood structure, surveillability); and (5) because of the significant overlap between micro and macro-level factors, it is difficult to determine the extent to which particular factors contribute to the victim selection techniques.

According to Clinnard and Quinney (as cited by Knight, Rosenberg, & Schneider, 1985), typologies are "classifications which . . . attempt to specify the ways in which attributes or variables are empirically connected" (p. 33). The creation of our typological model on the victim selection process for power serial rapists stems from its potential to contribute meaningfully to both the study of victimology and the phenomena of serial rape. Victimology is the study of crime victims, their characteristics and behavior, and their relationships and interactions with offenders (Fattah, 1995). Victimology was first recognized as a branch of criminology in the 1940's when works such as Von Hentig's *The Criminal and His Victim* (1948) began to focus primarily on victims in the study of crime. Although victimology is increasingly recognized as a viable domain of inquiry in the criminological field, research on criminal victimization is evolving somewhat independently of its predecessor, given the seemingly difficult task of connecting victimization theories with current crime theories. The proof of this assertion is found among the scholarly periodicals principally anchored in the victimological (rather than criminological) frame of reference (e.g., *Violence and Victims, Journal of Interpersonal Violence, Victimology: An International Journal*).

Fattah (1991), a pioneer in victimology, argued that although criminology has traditionally ignored the role of the victim, victimology cannot make the same mistake by ignoring the role of the offender. His suggestion has been to study victim selection processes as one method for developing interactionist models of crime, focusing equally on the victim and the offender. Indeed, Fattah's doctoral dissertation investigated victim selection in cases of murder for robbery, exploring several notable aspects of the offended party and the assailant.

After Fattah's (1991) observations, we maintain that the development of our typological model will serve to further integrate victimological and criminological explanations of serial rape. Moreover, we contend that our conceptual typological exploration will help foster a synthesis of these intellectual perspectives for other crimes as well. We believe that efforts at integration in criminology and victimology will further legitimize the latter as a bona fide domain of scholarly inquiry and increase awareness regarding the significant contributions the discipline offers the field of criminology.

The premise of victim selection can be linked to the rational choice perspective, which is a recognized theoretical orientation in criminology (e.g., Cornish & Clarke, 1986; Clarke & Felson, 1993). Many researchers have discouraged the creation of any formal definition for the construct of rationality in this theory, given the debatable quality of such a definition (Newman, Clarke, & Shoham, 1997). For example, Opp (1997) stated that defining rationality is not as important as identifying the kind of reason and judgment that appropriately and accurately explains a particular crime. However, others have argued that this approach suggests that some criminals process and evaluate information in a strategic manner in order to make decisions concerning the commission of their crimes (e.g., Stevens, 1994). This criticism draws attention to the contentiousness inherent in defining rationality in the rational choice criminological perspective.

Empirical research on victim selection techniques, particularly with offenses such as rape, robbery, and burglary, has only recently been of interest to the field of criminology. However, as we previously indicated, early victim selection studies date back several decades (e.g., Von Hentig, 1948). The discipline of victimology views victim selection as an invaluable facet of victimization theory and practice (Fattah, 1991). Although some researchers have made attempts to construct theoretical models of victim selection, these early efforts have been limited either in approach or in number of selection factors. Fattah (1991) referred to these earlier models as either micro- or macro-level schemes, arguing that future initiatives would need to incorporate both.

Micro-level approaches view victimization according to individual characteristics or small group behavior. Macro-level approaches deal with more generalized victimization factors. For example, the typological approach, which is a micro-level model, is based on victim characteristics and was most popular during the early years of victimology. However, subsequent approaches such as the lifestyle model (Hindelang, Gottfredson, & Garofalo, 1978; Fattah, 1993; Felson, 1994) and the routine activity approach (Cohen & Felson, 1979; Felson, 1986; Felson, 1992; Clarke & Felson, 1993; Felson & Clarke, 1995) are macro-level oriented, focusing more on situational factors. By incorporating a breadth of criminological and victimological research on rape and victim typologies, the ensuing research lends itself to a more global and practical model than those that currently exist, providing a solid foundation for future empirical research.

Society views rape as one of the most traumatic criminal events an individual can endure. This is the reason that an abundance of research exists regarding the rape victim (Resmick & Nishith, 1997). Most of this scholarship focuses on psychological reactions or trauma after the sexual offense; however, there is far less research focusing on the victim before the crime. The dearth of scholarly inquiries regarding the rape victim as an agent in the commission of the offense makes victimization prevention efforts extraordinarily difficult to conceive and implement. This dilemma notwithstanding, both the disturbing nature of the crime and the staggering statistics pertaining to it necessitate social science efforts that further our awareness of the victim's role in the serial rape act. Accordingly, this book endeavors to address this research deficiency, mindful of identifying preventive measures.

We note that one inherent danger in presenting a victim selection typology is the possibility that some might misconstrue the model as attributing blame to the victim. Rape is a thoroughly atrocious and extremely invasive crime. It is one of the most physically, sexually, and psychologically violative acts one human being can inflict upon another. Indeed, the offense not only violates the body, but the soul as well. The emotional trauma experienced by the victim far exceeds the physical harm. The pain from the latter may be endured; the scarring from the former may never heal. Regardless of personal characteristics or situational factors, it is inconceivable to blame a victim for being raped. Many individuals often deny or discount the reality of a situation in order to protect themselves from feeling powerless; regrettably for some, it is easier to assign blame to a rape victim than to accept one's own fear of being raped.

With the preceeding observations in mind, the purpose of the proposed victim selection typology is not to attribute blameworthiness to rape victims or to instill fear in women. Rather, the intent behind the typology that we develop is to advance our understanding of the offender and the nature of the assailant's crime. Moreover, the purpose of our typology is to educate women about factors that may make them more vulnerable to victimization. We maintain that this very awareness and insight can assist potential (and past) victims in gaining (or regaining) a sense of self-efficacy.

IDENTIFYING OUR HYPOTHESES

This study attempts to discern whether or not power serial rapists use selection techniques and/or criteria when seeking out their victims. By relying on existing research from both the rape and victimology literature, we maintain that power serial rapists incorporate elements of victim selection into the commission of their crimes. Having substantiated our contention by analytically reviewing the pertinent research, we then ascertain the types of general and/or specific factors constituting the selection process. Relying once again on the existing scholarship in the field, we identify victim selection factors based on both micro- and macro-level theories of victimization as they relate specifically to elements of power rape. After this identification process, we then organize these factors into a conceptual typology of victim selection. Finally, to test the explanatory and predictive usefulness of our integrated criminology-victimology typology, we compare it with existing victimization models. This comparison is principally based on an assessment of how both the established victimization schemes and our own typology interpret and explain the case of Gilbert Escobedo, a documented power serial rapist.

SOME COMMENTS ON RESEARCH METHOD AND ORGANIZATION OF THE BOOK

Our efforts at theoretical synthesis (i.e., criminology-victimology integration) regarding victim selection for the power serial rapist endeavors to build on and extend the current typologies, thereby providing a stronger foundation for future empirical research. Arguably, these empirical inquiries will pave the way for the development of additional theoretical victim typology models. However, given the paucity of social science investigations on these matters (particularly for serial rape), a heuristic methodology is used in our study. Heuristics is an analytical process in which existing literature, research, and knowledge are used to uncover answers to questions, following empirical guidelines and reasoning.

Accordingly, we begin with a broad overview of the rape phenomenon. This section of Chapter 2 provides brief definitions and relevant research findings (including crime statistics) regarding the various types of rape that have been identified in the literature to date. Along these lines, the range of categories we canvass extends from marital rape to serial-stranger rape. We conclude this section by introducing the reader to the serial rapist. We then provide an in-depth assessment of this sexual offender, paying special attention to research findings substantiating the contention that this type of rape assailant uses victim selection techniques (e.g., Cornish & Clarke, 1986; Chappell & James, 1986; Stevens, 1994). We conclude our review of the pertinent literature on the subject by presenting and analyzing various rape typologies, including descriptions of the power serial rapist (e.g., Groth & Birnbaum, 1979; Knight & Prentky, 1987).

Although the first portion of Chapter 2 emphasizes the criminological literature pertaining to the rape phenomenon, the latter portion identifies and explores the relevant victimology literature. The victimology section begins with a brief overview of the movement, highlighting its origins, its evolution, and its impact to date in the social scientific community. In this context, we consider the extent to which victimology has been accepted and embraced by the field of criminology throughout the former's intellectual development. In Chapter 3, we examine victimization, victim selection, and the ideology underlying these concepts. We present research on victimization models and the selection process, along with an introduction to the various types of typologies currently found in the literature (e.g., Gottfredson, 1981; Hindelang, Gottfredson, & Garofalo, 1978; Cohen & Felson, 1979). In addition, the chapter systematically filters this information for purposes of identifying those dimensions and criteria integral to creating our own victim selection typology.

Chapter 3 reviews and critiques the existing victimization theories and models used to explain victim selection. We focus on both micro- and macro-level factors of victimization. For purposes of simplicity and accessibility, the respective theories are discussed separately. In addition, however, when necessary and appropriate, we explore how the individual theories and models are linked to and further our understanding of the act of power serial rape.

Chapter 4 addresses method, both as the source of critique and as the subject of our inquiry. Indeed, before creating our own victim selection typology, it is essential that we critique those victim typologies and victimization models currently found within the literature. In the first section of this chapter, we explain the purpose and method of our critique. In addition, we examine several examples of past inquiries. In the second section of this chapter, we conduct our assessment of the existing approaches. Along these lines, we comment on the relative strengths and weaknesses of the current victimization schemes. In the third section of the chapter, we present the method of inquiry for this study. In this context, we outline why heuristics is a preferred methodological approach, given our subject of analysis.

In Chapter 5, we present our own conceptual typology of victim selection for the power serial rapist. Key components contained within the criminological and victimological literature, systematically canvassed in previous chapters, will be selectively integrated. This theoretical synthesis forms the basis of our own typological model, incorporating a broad range of victim selection dimensions, criteria, and/or factors as applied specifically to the power serial rapist.

In Chapter 6, we present the case of Gilbert Escobedo, also known as the Ski Mask Rapist. According to the best available research, this sexual offender may have been connected to as many as 100 rapes between 1985 and 1990 (Swindle, 1997). Within this chapter, we examine how the existing victimization models further our understanding of the Escobedo case and compare these insights with the explanatory and predictive contributions generated by our own conceptual model. Several Appendixes are included to facilitate our understanding along these lines.

In Chapter 7, we tentatively explore the implications of our analysis for future forensic psychological practice, administration, and policy. In the context of therapeutic practice, we explore such matters as psychological assessment, diagnosis, victim treatment, offender treatment, and prevention. In the context of criminal justice administration and management, we consider such matters as offender profiling, tracking, and apprehension, as well as general crime prevention. In the context of public policy, we assess prospects for research impacting the law and community planning.

WHAT WE EXPECT TO FIND

By engaging in this study, information may be uncovered that will advance current knowledge about the power serial rapist and further substantiate the concept of victim selection. The combination of criminological and victimological scholarship—research insights at the core of our typological model—may shed new light on both the profile of the serial rapist in general and the offender's victim selection process in particular. We maintain that for purposes of this inquiry a broad range of dimensions, both micro- and macro-level, will be needed to create the most appropriate conceptual typology. Through our theoretical and integrative investigation, the discovery of the personal characteristics and situational factors most common among power serial rape victims may increase societal recognition regarding this offender's method of planning and crime commission. Indeed, the awareness of victim selection techniques and the applicability of these insights to real-life circumstances (e.g., the Escobedo case) can fuel interest in this area of forensic psychology, especially in relation to other types of (sexual) offenses. Overall, however, we hope that our efforts through this research project represent a viable conceptual model that will encourage future investigators to engage in more empirical studies, promoting the integrated contributions of criminology and victimology in social scientific inquiries.

Chapter 2

CRIMINOLOGY AND RAPE, VICTIMOLOGY AND VICTIMS

OVERVIEW

The following review of literature provides a necessary foundation on which to understand the conceptual model of the serial rapist victim typology. The scope of the research falls mainly under two broad categories: rape and victimology. The rape section is introduced with a brief historical overview on the emergence of rape awareness in American society. The feminist movement is emphasized as a key factor in raising social consciousness in cases of rape and as propagating sexual assault research, particularly beginning in the 1970s. The culmination of rape literature is then discussed based on a multidisciplinary view, highlighted with contributions from psychology, sociology, and criminology.

The reader is then introduced to the various categories of rape, including acquaintance, marital, stranger, gang, male-on-male, and female-offender types. Each category is described in terms of statistics and features, and further details are provided regarding the offender and/or victim. After the presentation of rape categories, we explain various rapist typologies. These are categorizations developed to describe rapists' motives, behaviors, and characteristics. The most frequently documented typologies are then discussed with details on each rapist category.

The review then focuses specifically on the serial rapist in an attempt to inform the reader of the various personal characteristics and assault behaviors that exemplify this type of offender. Considerable attention is given to a particular serial rapist study conducted by the Federal Bureau of Investigation to provide an overview of some of the most detailed information gathered regarding this type of offender. Finally, research concerning elements that differentiate between apprehended and unknown serial rapists is addressed.

The section on victimology begins with an overview of how the field originated and how it has evolved, particularly in relation to criminology. The difficulty in defining the study of victimology is raised by considering the various political and philosophical approaches that have been associated with the discipline. The differing roles of the humanistic and scientific orientations are also discussed. Finally, the importance of the victim-offender relationship in both the field of victimology and criminology is established.

RAPE

The History of Rape Research

Although a full historical analysis of the act of rape is far beyond the scope of this study, it is important to acknowledge that rape has existed since the earliest civilizations. Nevertheless, despite rape's interminable presence, the search for an understanding of such an act was barely addressed before the twentieth century. In Krafft-Ebing's study regarding sexual disorders, *Psychopathia Sexualis* (as cited in Brownmiller, 1975), he simply referred to most rapists as being "degenerate, imbecilic men." Even highly regarded theorists who followed, such as Freud, Adler, Jung, and Marx, had little or nothing to say regarding the phenomena of rape (1975.). It was not until the late 1960's and early 1970's that rape became a focal concern within the United States. This newly found interest was credited, in part, to the creation of the National Center for the Prevention and Control of Rape. This center, which was introduced as a bill in 1973 and established under the National Institute of Mental Health in 1975, was designed for the purpose of providing research and program development for both rape victims and offenders. However, it was the women's movement that was recognized as the dominant force in pushing the issue of rape to the forefront of national consciousness (Geis, 1977; Burgess, 1985).

Consciousness raising (CR) groups and public "speak outs" were used as organizing tools in the early years of the women's movement.

The CR groups provided many women a safe environment in which to share their previously unspoken and personal stories regarding rape. However, the "speak outs," although often a source of humiliation, also provided women an opportunity to break the public's silence (Burgess, 1985). It was in the context of these groups and "speak outs" that Susan Brownmiller came to realize her own ignorance and fear of rape. It was that realization that later compelled her to write *Against Our Will* (1975), which represented one of the major feminist statements of the time (Chappell, Geis, & Geis, 1977).

Going beyond her extensive historical analysis, she openly challenged the country's racial attitudes, institutional powers (i.e., slavery, prison, and war), and libertarian philosophies that surrounded the crime of rape (Brownmiller, 1975; Chappell et al., 1977). Brownmiller's position was that ". . . a feminist analysis approaches all prior assumptions, including those of the great, unquestioned liberal tradition, with a certain open-minded suspicion, because all prior traditions have worked against the cause of women. . ." (p. 390). Although the feminist perspective has maintained an undeniably strong presence in the rape literature, it is only one facet of an extensive body of theory and research.

A Multidisciplinary Approach

Chappell, Geis, and Fogarty (1974) presented a bibliography of forcible rape literature that was later updated by Feild and Barnett in 1977. However, in addition to the amended bibliography, Field and Barnett also included an outline detailing contributions made by various disciplines and specific areas of research. The three main disciplines noted included psychology, sociology, and criminology, with focuses on areas such as the offender, the victim, rape laws, medicolegal aspects, and police investigation (Feild & Barnett, 1977). Other researchers have also noted the variety of approaches used in investigating the rape phenomena (Groth, Burgess, & Holstrom, 1977; Burgess, 1985; Hazelwood, Reboussin, & Warren, 1989). Rape research in the field of psychology has focused on both the victim and offender. Victim research is often concerned with clinical aspects such as the psychological effects of the rape and treatment issues. A noteworthy example is the work of Burgess and Holstrom (1974) and their description of the "rape trauma syndrome." However, other researchers have investigated numerous topics from victim resistance in a rape assault (Ullman, 1998) to the effect of victim characteristics on perceptions of rape (Macrae & Shepherd, 1989).

The offender research has focused more on the motivations of rapists and the development of rapist typologies. In fact, it was the cumulative work of numerous psychologists, sociologists, and criminologists, in establishing the importance of power and dominance within the crime of rape, that assisted in the creation of such typologies (*see* Groth et al., 1977). Studies such as those of Groth et al. (1977), and Prentky, Cohen, and Seghorn (1985) made significant contributions in this area. However, as more is learned about characteristics of the offender, studies are also being undertaken to investigate treatment possibilities for rapists (Polaschek, Ward, & Hudson, 1997).

As previously noted, in addition to the numerous advances made through psychological rape studies, other academic fields have also contributed to forcible rape research. Sociological research examining rape is mainly focused on issues such as cultural context and societal values and attitudes regarding the offense (Burgess, 1985). Amir's *Patterns in Forcible Rape* (1971) was a "landmark sociological effort" toward understanding the crime of rape (Chappell et al., 1977, p. 19). The purpose of Amir's work was to uncover ". . . recurring patterns in which particular groups of people are found to commit a particular type of crime in particular types of circumstances" (Amir, 1971, p. xx). Deming and Eppy (1981) provide a systematic review of sociological literature and theory focusing on social structural determinants of rape and social reactions to the crime.

Finally, criminology has extended the rape literature through inquiry into such issues as the victim-offender relationship, dynamics of the assault, and law enforcement strategies. The victim-offender relationship has been of considerable importance to criminologists (Koss, Dinero, Seibel, & Cox, 1988). Authors of the National Crime Survey for the Bureau of Justice Statistics stated that "the nature of the relationship between victim and offender is a key element to understanding crime and judging the risks involved for the various groups in society" (BJS, 1984, p. 10). The concept of victim precipitation in forcible rape was introduced by Amir (1971), and although his explanation of the concept was not entirely well received, the importance of the role of the victim remained significant in criminological studies. For critiques regarding the treatment of rape in criminological literature, the reader is encouraged to see Wisan (1979) and Pitch (1985).

Categories of Rape

The term "rape" is often used in a generic manner, providing a nondescript reference to a sexually coercive behavior. However, the use of such a broad term elicits an equally extensive array of theories, images, beliefs, social responses, and so forth. To gain a fuller understanding of the dynamics of rape, it is necessary to divide the topic into more discrete categories. In reviewing the literature, there are arguably six predominate types of rape noted: (1) acquaintance (including date rape); (2) marital; (3) stranger; (4) gang; (5) male-on-male; and 6) female offender.

Statutory rape is not discussed, because it represents a legal construct more than a category of assault and also because the focus of this study is on *forcible* rape with *adult* victims. Conversely, statutory rape can occur in consensual relationships and must include a minor. Assaults involving children will also not be addressed again because of age specifications and the differing legal definitions of rape and molestation. Although some overlap exists between the categories that will be addressed, it is necessary to discuss each separately because of their distinct representation within the literature.

Acquaintance Rape

According to the Bureau of Justice Statistics for 1995 there was a total of 172,810 rapes and attempted rapes involving non stranger assailants (U.S. Department of Justice). More specifically in 24.5% of the cases the offender was a casual acquaintance, in 33.1% he was well known to the victim, and in 1.3% he was a relative (other than an immediate family member). Hickman and Muehlenhard (1997) defined acquaintance rape as an act in which the female victim is raped by "someone known to her, ranging from a man she has just met to a close friend or boyfriend" (p. 528). Their study examined the fears and precautionary behaviors of college women relating to acquaintance versus stranger rape. Although the results showed that women recognized acquaintance rape as more prevalent, they reported a greater fear of and took more precautions in relation to rape by a stranger (1977). However, the preexisting victim-offender relationship in these instances creates a unique context not found in stranger rapes.

First, acquaintance and/or date rapes occur under circumstances in which a consensual sexual relationship could possibly exist. Also, acquaintance rapes are more likely to be seen as the result of misperception or miscommunication than are stranger assaults (Bechhofer & Parrot, 1991). Nevertheless, although there was a greater fear of stranger rape, both stranger and acquaintance rapes were seen as equally traumatic (Hickman & Muehlenhard, 1997). Acquaintance rapes more often involve repeated victimization by the same offender, particularly when the offender is a family member. Also, those raped by an acquaintance were less apt to report the incident or seek crisis services compared with those raped by an unknown assailant (Koss et al., 1988).

Marital Rape

Marital rape is essentially a category of acquaintance rape; however, because of the level of intimacy already established between the victim and offender, marital rape deserves independent attention. In 1995, six percent of rapes were perpetrated by the victim's spouse and 1.3% were by an ex-spouse (U.S. Department of Justice). It was not until 1977 that the first social science article appeared regarding marital rape (Burgess, 1985; *see* Gelles, 1977). This form of sexual assault was slow in receiving attention, because many early rape laws defined rape as an act involving intercourse by force or threat and without consent with a woman other than one's wife (Burgess, 1985). Russell, in her book *Rape in Marriage* (1982), preferred the term *wife rape* to emphasize that it was women, not spouses in general, who were suffering this type of offense.

According to Groth and Birnbaum (1979), there may be several underlying reasons for marital rape besides a refusal of sex. These explanations may include (1) sex equated with power; (2) sex equated with love/affection; (3) sex equated with virility; (4) sex equated with punishment; and (5) sex as a measure of marital success. Assaults perpetrated by a victim's husband tend to be significantly more violent than rapes involving other forms of acquaintances. In fact, violence is also significantly greater for rapes by other family members (Koss et al., 1988).

Similar to victims of acquaintance rape in general, wives are less likely to report such incidents than are those who are attacked by strangers. Revealing or seeking help for an assault by an acquaintance declines directly related to the level of intimacy between the offender and victim (1988.). A common misconception has been that marital rape is somehow less traumatic than other forms of rape, however, this is not necessarily the case. Whereas a women who is attacked by a stranger may have general concerns about her physical safety, a woman who is assaulted by her husband often suffers a deeper trauma by losing trust in her most intimate relationship(s) (Burgess, 1985).

Stranger Rape

In contrast to offenses in which the victim and offender have some level of familiarity, stranger offenses are those in which there is no previous association. Although stranger violence represents a smaller portion of total violence than offenses between known individuals, stranger violence often causes greater aftereffects and is one of the most terrifying forms of victimization (Riedel, 1993). Statistics show that approximately twenty-five percent of rapes are committed by strangers (U.S. Department of Justice, 1995). Stranger rape is reportedly a greater cause of fear among women than forms of acquaintance rape, and it also elicits more precautionary behavior in women (Hickman & Muehlenhard, 1997).

Perhaps one of the most terrifying aspects of a stranger assault is that it can be an arbitrary attack that often makes victims or potential victims feel they have little or no control in preventing the situation (Riedel, 1993). Research findings by Koss et al. (1988) showed that stranger rapes tend to be more violent than acquaintance rapes and were more likely to involve multiple offenders. Also, victims of stranger rapes were more likely to report the incident and seek professional help. This finding may be due in part to the victim feeling more like a "legitimate" victim and having greater recognition of the event as a sexual offense (LeBeau, 1987a, p. 310).

Gang Rape

As previously stated, stranger rapes are more likely to involve multiple offenders than are other forms of rape. These multiple offender assaults are called gang rapes, or pair rapes if there are only two perpetrators (Groth and Birnbaum, 1979). The Bureau of Justice Statistics estimated 32,480 multiple offender rapes and attempted rapes for a one year period (U.S. Department of Justice, 1995). However, overall these types of offenses are relatively less common. In a study by Groth and Birnbaum (1979) of 348 men, only nine percent of cases involved multiple offenders. Of these incidents, eighty percent were pair rapes and twenty percent were gang rapes. Most multiple offender rapes involve a single victim (1979) and the victim tends to be in the same age range as the assailants, with offender ages ranging from as young as ten years to the mid-thirties (Holmes, 1991).

It is believed that most incidents of gang (or pair) rape are attempts by men to confirm their masculinity. However, motives, such as power, and group dynamics also contribute to the assault (Groth & Birnbaum, 1979; Holmes, 1991). Often, there is a single offender who tends to lead the group and is usually the first, and sometimes the only, offender to actually rape the victim. This individual seeks control, not only of his victim, but also of his cohorts. These cohorts will then take part in the sexual assault, or assist in restraining the victim, to maintain their acceptance by others and confirm their masculinity as well (Groth & Birnbaum, 1979).

The form of gang rape described is not uncommonly associated with images of prison rapes. In a study of a Midwestern state prison system, including men and women, it was found that twenty percent of inmates had been forced into some form of sexual contact against their will at least once. Of these individuals who were targets of forced intercourse (anal, vaginal, or oral), one fourth of the cases were gang rapes (Johnson, Johnson, Rucker, Bumby, & Donaldson, 1996). Although studies of sexual assault in prison settings are relatively few, these types of studies conducted in the 1970's lead the way for recognition of male-on-male sexual assaults (Scarce, 1997). Brownmiller (1975) stated that prison rape:

> is an acting out of power roles within an all-male authoritarian environment in which the younger, weaker inmate . . . is forced to play the role that in

the outside world is assigned to women. . .it is often the avowedly homosexual youths . . . who fall victim to the most brutal of prison gang rapes.
(p. 258)

However, while Brownmiller investigated the act of male-on-male
rape through social denotations, other researchers sought to uncover
information regarding the more psychological dynamics of the assault
(Scarce, 1997).

Male-on-male Rape

Groth and Birnbaum (1979) believed that male-on-male rape, like
most others types, was not motivated by sexual desire. Instead they
cited the following as underlying causes for these attacks: (1) conquest
and control; (2) revenge and retaliation;(3) sadism and degradation;
(4) conflict and counteraction; and (5) status and affiliation. Hodge
and Canter (1998) believed male sexual assaults could be divided into
two categories: heterosexual and homosexual. Heterosexual assaults
more commonly involve strangers and tend to be motivated by the
need for domination and control. Heterosexual assaults on males
also account for most of male victim gang rapes. In fact, sixty-six percent of the gang assaults reported in the Hodge and Canter study
involved heterosexual offenders, and seventeen percent of these were
considered gay-bashing incidents. Motivation for this type of offense
was compared with Groth and Burgess' (1980) category of sadism and
degradation (1980).

In contrast, the homosexual offender tends to rape someone known
to them, and the assault often involves more psychological than physical control. It is estimated that approximately five to ten percent of
reported yearly rapes involve male victims, with gay men being
raped at a higher rate than heterosexual men (Scarce, 1997).
According to a presentation by King (as cited in Scarce), male-on-
male rapes generally involve men who are acquaintances and are
more likely to involve weapons than rapes of females. Although men
may experience a recovery process (physically, psychologically, sexually, etc.) similar to women, male rape victims tend to experience a
greater sense of self-blame, shame, and guilt, in the aftermath of the
assault. (1997).

Female-perpetrated Rapes

Although male-on-male rape is less commonly investigated than offenses with female victims, another area of rape that has received even less attention is the female perpetrator. Findings from the Johnson et al., (1996) prison study indicated that only two percent of inmates reported assaults by a female perpetrator, whereas an additional five percent included a male and female cooffender. Although the sexual assault of one woman by another (without a male accomplice) may be more common in prison settings, in other environments the female offender may assist a male assailant in obtaining, restraining, or assaulting a victim. In cases in which a man is raped by a woman, there are usually two or more female offenders (Groth & Birnbaum, 1979).

A number of psychological and social factors may account for the paucity of research in this area. First, although the use of forced sex can be an expression of anger for men, women are more likely to express anger or dissatisfaction by withholding sex. In addition, few women have the necessary levels of physical strength or aggression to complete the rape act. Second, men are less likely to reports assaults by females. This may be due to social beliefs that may make it difficult to sustain such an allegation, for example, that rape is equivalent to sex and all men are "ever-ready and indiscriminate in regards to sex" (1979, p. 188).

An Introduction to Rapist Typologies

The categories of rape discussed thus far have placed emphasis on the victim-offender relationship, with additional distinctions made by gender and number of assailants. However, rapists can also be categorized according to the motivational intent and dynamics of their offense (Groth & Hobson, 1983). Early research from a variety of disciplines established that fact that rape was more than an act based on sexual desire, and issues relating to power and dominance became focal (*see* Groth et al., 1977). Grounded in research and theories regarding motivations of rape, researchers as early as the 1950s made attempts to create rapist typologies. An extensive review of all existing rapist typologies is beyond the scope of this study. Therefore, the following review is an adaptation from a review by Knight and colleagues (1985) that focuses on the more well-documented and/or substantiated typologies in the literature.

Guttmacher and Weihofen's Typology

Guttmacher and Weihofen (1952) proposed one of the first rapist typologies, which introduced the following three rapist subtypes based on offense motivation: (1) true sex offenders–motivation for the offense was seen as sexual needs related to "pent-up sexual impulse(s)" or latent homosexuality; (2) sadistic rapists–motivational force was seen as aggression which exceeded or was in addition to sexual aims, plus a particular hostility to women; and (3) aggressive offenders–motivation was related more to general criminality (Guttmacher & Weihofen, 1952; Knight et al., 1985).

Kopp's Typology

Kopp (1962) devised a typology of two rapist types based on whether the offense behavior was consistent or inconsistent with the offender's personality characteristics. Offenses of the type I rapist were seen as being inconsistent with the individual's character. These offenders were generally seen as accommodating to gain acceptance and warmth from others. Therefore, their offense behavior was often a cause of considerable guilt and concern for the rapist. The type II offender, however, was described as more psychopathic or antisocial and thus lacked concern or guilt for his actions (Kopp, 1962, Knight et al., 1985).

Gebhard, Gagnon, Pomeroy, and Christenson's Typology

Gebhard, Gagnon, Pomeroy, and Christenson (1965) developed a seven-category typology of "heterosexual aggressors against adults" that was based primarily on aggression factors relating to the offense. The seven rapist subtypes included (1) assaultive offender–perpetrates unnecessary violence in excess of that needed to complete the sexual assault; (2) amoral delinquent–has a general disregard for rights of others and views forced sex on a woman as legitimate; (3) double-standard rapist–views forced sex as acceptable with sexually promiscuous women (similar attitude as the "amoral delinquent" only in regard to a particular type of woman and not women in general); (4) explosive type–offense violence is sudden and atypical from offender's general nonaggressiveness; (5) drunken offenders–offense aggression is possibly related to intoxication; (6) offenses related to mental deficiency; (7) offenses involving a mix of the preceding categories (Gebhard et al., 1965; Knight et al., 1985).

Despite limitations to Gebhard et al.'s typology, it was noted as an important contribution to the field because it was based on a large database that, unlike earlier typologies, permitted frequency estimates of the rapist subtypes (*see* Knight et al., 1985).

Massachusetts Treatment Center Typologies

It was not until the 1970's that additional work on rapist typologies began to evolve. Cohen and colleagues (1969, 1971, & 1980) introduced their rapist classification systems, followed by the presentation of Groth et al.'s (1977) typology. Both classifications were founded on the early typologies, and each included offender motivation and personality as mainstay factors. Furthermore, both studies were based on similar samples (i.e., rapists at the Massachusetts Center for the Diagnosis and Treatment of Sexually Dangerous Persons). Nevertheless, each research group formulated the typologies separately, and there are some important distinctions (Knight et al., 1985).

Cohen, Seghorn, and Calmas' Typology

Cohen, Seghorn, and Calmas (1969) focused on the motivational factors of sex and aggression in rape, which is similar to the early typologies of Guttmacher and Weihofen (1952) and Gebhard at al. (1965) (Knight et al., 1985). The proposed typology of Cohen and his colleagues included four rapist types described as follows

1. Compensatory rapist–underlying offense motivation is primarily sexual, with aggression being limited to only that which is necessary to accomplish the sex act. Sexual fantasy and high sexual arousal are components of this offense. This rapist is considered socially inept and uses the offense to minimize his feelings of inadequacy. He may often misinterpret or distort his

victim's response and believe she is being sexually gratified or he may ask the victim to verbally validate his sexual performance.

2. Displaced aggressive rapist–underlying motivation is aggression and anger towards women. The act is often explosive and brutal, and the sexual behavior serves only to degrade the victim. This offender may maintain the appearance of social adequacy; however, he has difficulty relating to women and anger associated with a significant female in his life may be displaced onto an unknown victim.

3. Sex-aggression-defusion type–motivation for this offense is the eroticism of violence and aggression, which may be necessary components for sexual arousal. These assaults are particularly sadistic, and aggressive acts may be focused on sexual areas of the body; however, the feeling of anger is absent. This type of rapist commonly displays more psychopathic characteristics or behaviors or severe psychiatric disturbances.

4. Impulsive rapist–motivation for the offense is a general antisocial personality or lifestyle. This offender is seen as more predatory and impulsive and may commit a rape in the process of another felony. Although this offender may not show empathy for his victim, he also does not set out with the intention of purposively harming her. Aggressive and sexual aims are not necessary components in this type of offense (Cohen et al., 1969; Knight et al., 1985).

In a follow-up study, Cohen and colleagues (1971) emphasized that rapists may in fact be more continuously distributed, rather than discretely classified, along the discriminating dimensions (Prentky, et al., 1985). On the basis of the motives of sex and aggression, as well as the undifferentiated cases of sexual sadism, Cohen and colleagues (1971 & 1980) proposed a clinical classification of rape. Although this classification was not intended as a typology, it is important to include these categories in the rape typology section so that the reader may understand how the conceptualization of rapist subtypes has continually evolved.

The rape classification included the following four categories:

1. Aggressive aim rape–the sexual assault is a primarily aggressive act. The sexual behavior is only in service of the aggression and is meant to humiliate and defile the victim. Violence

may range from simple assault to, on rare occasion, a victim's death. When aspects of sexuality are present, they are in the extreme forms such as biting, cutting, or tearing to the genitals. The victims are most often strangers, and the assaults occur most frequently in the victim's home. However, the offender often experiences feelings of concern for the victim after the assault and may attempt to make some sort of restitution.

2. Sexual aim rape—this form of sexual assault is only a means through which to complete the sexual act, otherwise there is relatively little violence. These offenses most often take place outdoors and the victims are almost always strangers. However, these victims are usually not happened on by accident, but instead have been followed after being noticed by the offender. Sexual fantasy is an important component in this offenders' assaults.

3. Sex-Aggression defusion rape—the sexual assault is influenced by both aggressive and sexual motivations and involves a strong sadistic component. The offender has no ability to experience sexual excitation with some form of violence. The degree of sadism may vary; however, in extreme and rare cases, the assault may be in the form of a lust murder. In these cases, mutilation and excessive brutality occur before, during, and after the victim's death. Most often the violence is used to sexually arouse the offender and then after the rape there is no further aggression. These offenders may also project their own sadism onto their victims and perceive the victim's resistance as part of her own sexual excitation (Cohen et al., 1971).

4. Impulsive rape—neither sexual impulses nor aggression are dominant factors in this form of assault. This type of offender is most closely associated with antisocial personality disorder, and the rape is more often an impulsive, spontaneous act to gratify the offender's needs. The victim is chosen simply because she is available, and the assault may occur during the commission of another crime (e.g., a robbery). Any degree of force or aggression is goal directed and is used only as a means by which to gain control over the victim.

Groth's Typology

A significant limitation to the typologies presented thus far is that they were based predominantly on data regarding only the offender (*see* Groth et al., 1977; Chappell et al., 1977). However, Groth et al. (1977) created the clinical rape typology, including rapist subtypes, based on comparative accounts from both victims and offenders. The study was based on data obtained from 133 convicted rapists and 92 adult rape victims. The rapist data were collected from assessments at the Massachusetts Center for the Diagnosis and Treatment of Sexually Dangerous Persons, whereas victim data were obtained from rape victims treated at the Boston City Hospital. The assaults recounted by victims and offenders were congruent in time, but unrelated.

Analysis of the data revealed that there are three components present in all cases of forcible rape: power, anger, and sexuality. It is these three elements that compose the clinical rape typology. Although all three components are interrelated, Groth and his colleagues found discernible patterns in which either power or anger was the dominant motivational force. Therefore, rape was considered a "pseudo-sexual" act in which sexuality was merely the means by which to express anger or power (Groth et al., 1977, Groth & Birnbaum, 1979). The motivational factors that characterize Groth et al.'s typology are, therefore, a significant distinction from Cohen et al.'s model, which focuses predominantly on aggression and sexuality (Knight et al., 1985).

Power Rape

Based on the clinical rape typology, power rape is an assault in which power is the underlying motivational force and the offender seeks to control his victim. Although he may gain control of his victim through means of intimidation or aggression (e.g., verbal, physical, or presence of a weapon), his intention is not to harm his victim but to possess or conquer her sexually. The purpose of the rape is to reassure the offender of his sexual adequacy, to reestablish his sense of identity, and to defend against feelings of worthlessness or rejection. However, because the rape is a test of his competency, the rapist may feel a mixture of anxiety, excitement, and the anticipation of pleasure.

The assault is most often premeditated, and the victims tend to be within the offender's age range or younger. He may have fantasies in which the victim gives into her sexual pleasure during the rape and, thus, during the actual assault he may inquire about the victim's sexual past or ask for verbal reassurance about his performance. Because his assaults do not live up to his sexual fantasy, the rapes often become more compulsive as the rapist seeks the "right" victim (Groth et al., 1977; Groth & Birnbaum, 1979; Groth & Hobson, 1983).

Types of Power Rapists

Power-assertive Rapist

There are two rapist subtypes that fall under the category of power rape: the power-assertive rapist and the power-reassurance rapist. The power-assertive rapist has a sense of entitlement regarding rape and women and views the assault as an expression of masculinity and dominance. Although he may outwardly seem confident about his abilities and identity, his rapes are actually an indication of his feelings of inadequacy (Groth et al., 1977). This rapist often approaches his victim openly (e.g., picking up a hitchhiker); however, once she is in his control he will then turn aggressive and attack. He is often verbally demeaning to his victim during the assault and demonstrates little concern for her welfare. He may also subject the victim to repeated assaults in the time frame of the rape. This rapist tends to rape when he feels he "needs" a woman. The power-assertive rapist is the second most common rapist found in profiling cases involving the FBI (Hazelwood, 1995). For a real-life account of a power-assertive rapist, the reader is encouraged to see Neff (1995).

Power-reassurance Rapist

The power-reassurance rapist commits his assaults in an attempt to overcome doubts regarding his virility and adequacy. His purpose is to control the victim to the point that she cannot reject him, thereby bolstering his sense of self-worth (Groth et al., 1977). This type of rapist often selects his victims through voyeuristic activities and tends to attack in the victim's home while she is alone or sleeping. This type of rapist is the most common found in stranger assaults. During the assault, he may exhibit "pseudo-unselfish" behavior (e.g., apologizing to his victim) and, therefore, has been called a "gentleman rapist" (Hazelwood, 1995, p. 161). He may also attempt to contact his victim (either by phone, mail, or in some instances, in person) after the rape. The assaults tend to be short in duration, and the timing and consistency of subsequent rapes are contingent on the success and reassurance gained from previous attacks (Hazelwood, 1995). For a real-life account of a power-reassurance rapist the reader is referred to Swindle (1996).

Anger Rape

The second category in Groth et al.'s clinical typology of rape is anger rape. The underlying motivation of this type of rape is anger, rage, or hatred. The purpose of the assault is to degrade the victim, which is vindicated on perceptions of rejection or perceived wrongs by women in his life. Force and aggression are used in excess of that which would be necessary to control the victim, and the assault often involves physical violence to all parts of the body. The rapist's attacks may be sudden (i.e., without premeditation) or performed in a manner similar to the power-assertive rapist, and females older than the perpetrator are often targeted. This offender receives little satisfaction from the sexual component of the assault and typically views the sex act as repulsive. Instead, the experience for him is based on intense anger, degradation, and brutality, to such an extent that the victim may fear for her life. These types of assaults tend to be more sporadic and are often triggered by life circumstances, particularly difficulties with women (Groth et al., 1977; Groth & Hobson, 1983).

Types of Anger Rapists

Anger-retaliation Rapist

The two rapist subtypes incorporated under the anger rape category include the anger-retaliation rapist and the anger-excitation rapist. The anger-retaliation rapist uses rape as a form of revenge, and his aim is to punish and degrade women (Groth et al., 1977; Hazelwood, 1995). This type of assault is often impulsive and is triggered by extreme emotion, thus the anger and rage displayed during the attack can seem almost frenzied. In some instances this behavior can lead to unintentional death of the victim (Groth & Hobson, 1983). The assault is relatively brief in duration; however, the offender uses extreme levels of force and may use weapons of opportunity, particularly his feet and fists. He is also both verbally and sexually selfish. His attacks often result in a release of tension, therefore, subsequent rapes may be sporadic and based on the degree to which his anger reemerges. This is the third most common rapist type found in rape cases submitted for FBI profiling (Hazelwood, 1995).

Anger-excitation Rapist

The anger-excitation rapist has eroticized violence and aggression. Therefore, his purpose in raping is to receive pleasure and excitement from watching the suffering of his victims through physical and emotional pain and torture. This rapist's ultimate goal is to bring the victim to complete submission. Of the power and anger rapists discussed thus far, the anger-excitation rapist exhibits the highest level of offense planning and preparation (e.g., weapons, travel routes, bindings), except for the selection of his victim. Although she may meet certain criteria necessary to fulfill his fantasies, she is typically a stranger. This rapist, like the power-assertive rapist, often approaches his victim and interacts with her until he is able to get her within his immediate control. These assaults are brutal and often result in the victim's death. The victim may be kept for several hours or days and subjected to suffering, which may include bondage, being bitten, and/or having objects inserted vaginally or rectally. There seems to be no pattern to these types of assaults, and they are the rarest form of rape.

The rapist typology originally introduced by Groth et al. (1977) has since been adapted and modified by other researchers for application and study purposes. For example, Hazelwood and Burgess (1995) noted that in dealing with referred rape cases, the FBI relies upon the rapist typology developed by Groth et al. (1977). The decision to use that particular typology was based on the classifications having been derived at empirically and the accuracy of the classifications when compared to with past FBI cases. The only minor modification made was in the explanation of the "style of attack" for the various rapist types (Hazelwood, 1995). The term "style of attack" will be discussed subsequently; however, it generally refers to the method in which the offender approaches his victim before the assault.

Groth and Hobson (1983) also made adaptations to the original typology; however, the underlying premises such as motivational intent and offense dynamics remained unchanged. The most significant modifications noted were the inclusion of the sadistic rape category in place of the *anger-excitation* subtype and the removal of the term *anger-retaliation* for the more general classification of *anger* rapist (the category of power rape and the two rapist subtypes, *power-assertive* and *power-reassurance*, were unchanged). Although some terms may have been renamed, the underlying descriptions and key characteristics of each subtype remained.

The preceding rapist typologies suggest that there is substantial agreement among researchers regarding those factors that are important for differentiating between rapist subtypes (Knight et al., 1985). However, it was not until the work of Prentky and colleagues that substantial work was done on measuring the reliability and validity of a rapist classification. For purposes of their validation study, Prentky, Cohen, and Seghorn (1985) chose the rapist typology as devised by Cohen et al. in 1969 because they believed it was "the most inclusive and descriptive clinical classification system in the extant literature" (Knight et al., 1985 7.45).

Prentky et al.'s first attempt to revise the taxonomy (which became identified as the Massachusetts Treatment Center: Rapist Typology [MTC:R2]) resulted in eight subtypes. The model resulted from the creation of a three-tier decision tree for classifying rapists, which included the following factors: (1) the meaning of aggression in the offense; (2) the meaning of the sexuality in the offense; and (3) the amount and quality of impulse control in the life history of the offender (Prentky et al., 1985). Decision A, regarding the meaning of the aggression, included either instrumental aggression or expressive aggression. In instrumental aggression the degree of force does not exceed that which is needed to gain the victim's compliance. However, in the expressive type the aggression is more uncontrolled and the sexual acts are in service of hurting or humiliating the victim.

Decision B, regarding the meaning of the sexuality, includes compensatory, exploitative, displaced anger, or sadistic types. The compensatory type uses the sexual behavior as an expression of sexual fantasy or as a means to fulfill nonsexual needs (e.g., reduce tension associated with or redress a fragmented sense of self). For the exploitative type the sexual behavior is impulsive and of a predatory nature, often determined by situational factors more than sexual fantasy. For the displaced anger type the sexual behavior is an expression of rage displaced onto the victim; however, there is often no sexual meaning in the assault itself. Finally, the sadistic type uses sexual behavior to fulfill sexual-aggressive fantasies in which there is an undifferentiated relationship between the two drives.

Decision C, based on low or high impulsivity, examines the lifestyle and history of the rapist to determine the overall degree of impulsive behavior. Some characteristics associated with low impulsivity may include individuals who are introverted, withdrawn, underachievers, or those who react impulsively only to situational factors. Characteristics of high impulsivity may include individuals who are hyperactive, display more antisocial personality traits, or who demonstrates a more impulsive and aggressive way of relating to the world in general.

Prentky, Cohen, and Seghorn's MTC:R2 Typology

On the basis of these various decision factors, the resulting eight subtypes of the MTC:R2 included: (1) Instrumental aggression, sexual compensation, non-impulsive lifestyle; (2) Instrumental aggression, sexual compensation, impulse control problem; (3) Instrumental aggression, exploitation, nonimpulsive lifestyle; (4) Instrumental aggression, exploitation, impulse control problem; (5) Expressive aggression, displaced anger, non-impulsive lifestyle; (6) Expressive aggression, displaced anger, impulse control problem; (7) Expressive aggression, sexual aggressive (sadistic), non-impulsive lifestyle; and (8) Expressive aggression, sexual aggressive (sadistic), impulse control problem (For an in depth description of each subtype, *see* Prentky et al., 1985).

Knight and Prentky's MTC:R3 Typology

Although the MTC:R2 yielded acceptable reliability, Knight and Prentky (1990) decided to test the validity of the revised system. Using an identified method for testing typological schemes in deviant populations (*see* Knight & Prentky, 1990), they validated and further refined the MTC:R2 to create the MTC:R3. Although the methodols and analyses used to revise the typology are beyond the scope of this

review, it is important to note some of the more prominent areas in
which changes were made. First, the distinction between instrumental
and expressive aggression in the MTC:R2 was reconsidered because
of insufficient levels of reliability and validity. It was also found that
social competence, which was a neglected construct in the previous
revision, emerged as a significant factor that helped to identify distin-
guishable subtypes within the compensatory, exploitative, and displaced anger types. Additional deficiencies were found within the
exploitative type which could actually be subdivided into three more
homogeneous subgroups. Finally, the differentiation between the displaced anger and sadistic types were not a prevalent as once thought
(1990).

Based on their analyzes and revisions, Knight and Prentky proposed
the MTC:R3, which includes the following four summary categories
with a total of nine subtypes:

1. Opportunistic–the sexual assault is most often an impulsive,
   unplanned, predatory act, in which situational circumstances
   serve as antecedent factors. The act involves little anger or
   aggression (other than that needed to control the victim), but
   rather serves to fulfill a need for immediate sexual gratification.
   This category consists of two subtypes including those offenders low in social competence (type 1) and those who are high
   in social competence (type 2).

2. Pervasively angry (type 3)–the sexual assault is motivated by
   undifferentiated anger. Serious physical injury, up to and
   including death, characterize this assault. However, the rage is
   not sexualized, and there seem to be no preexisting sexual fantasies.

3. Sexual–the sexual assault is influenced by the presence or preoccupation with sexual or sadistic fantasies. These fantasies
   may include features of aggression, dominance, needs, felt
   inadequacies, or coercion. The sexual category consists of two
   types, including the sadistic and nonsadistic groups.

   The sadistic group includes two subtypes: the overt sadistic
   type (type 4) and the muted sadistic/ high social competence
   type (type 5). Both sadistic types show no differentiation
   between sexual and aggressive drives. For the overt type the
   sadism is manifested in the physically damaging behavior that
   takes place during the assault. For the muted type the sadism

is either carried out symbolically or in fantasy, but is not acted out behaviorally.

The nonsadistic type also includes two subtypes: the high social competence group (type 6) and the low social competence group (type 7). For the nonsadistic types, their sexual fantasies do not include the sexual-aggression synergism. In fact, they display less aggression in both sexual and nonsexual contexts compared with the other offender types. Their sexual fantasies and behavior generally include a conglomeration of sexual arousal, distorted cognitions regarding women, and inadequate feelings regarding their masculinity.

4. Vindictive—the sexual assault of this offender type is generally related to a pervasive anger focused exclusively on women as evidenced in their behavioral patterns. Aggression and physical injury are used to degrade the victim; however, the aggressive component of the sexual act is not eroticized. The vindictive type can also be divided into two subtypes: low social competence (type 8) and moderate social competence (type 9).

Focus on Groth's Power Rapist

This study's conceptualization of a serial rapist victim typology will be predicated on the category of power rape as described by Groth and colleagues (1977 & 1983). Therefore, this study's typology will be applicable to only those cases concerning a power serial rapist. Several reasons exist for the exclusion of the other rape typologies and rapist subtypes (i.e., anger and sadistic). First, as exemplified in the review of the rape typologies, a number of distinctions exist between various rape offenders and their assaults. Consequently, it would be difficult, if not impossible, to create a victim typology which would reflect the various aspects of all the rapist categories. Even if such a typology were devised, it would be so encompassing as to provide little predictive power. Therefore, the most useful victim typology will be one that focuses on the motivations and offense-related aspects of a specific rapist type.

Second, there are dynamics of anger and sadistic rape that lead to their exclusion from this study. The nature of an anger rape offense does not particularly allow for the conceptualization of a victim selection typology because of the impulsivity and lack of premeditation relating to this type of assault. In contrast, sadistic rape is a highly premeditated and planned assault; however, this may not necessarily apply to selection of the victim. Regardless, the category of sadistic rape was eliminated from this study because of the overlap in the literature of the sadistic rapist and the serial murderer (*see* Holmes, 1991; Holmes & Holmes, 1996). Because of the brutality and sadistic nature of the offense, it is not unlikely for victims of sadistic rapists to be killed. In fact Holmes and Holmes (1996) point to the eventuality of the sadistic rapist killing if he is not apprehended. Therefore, because of the potential overlap of offender characteristics and offense dynamics between the sadistic rapist and the serial murderer, the sadistic rapist category was eliminated to maintain specificity with the victim typology.

Finally, the rape typology described by Groth et al. (1977) is the method of rapist categorization adopted by the FBI. As previously noted by Hazelwood (1995), the decision to adopt that particular typology was based on Groth et al.'s use of empirical data and reliability of the rapist subtypes as demonstrated through FBI case files. This is significant because little validation work is done with most rapist typologies. In addition, it is anticipated that this victim typology will be a useful tool for law enforcement officials involved in serial rape cases. Therefore, basing the victim typology on a categorization of rapists used by a large law enforcement entity may increase the typology's acceptance and legitimacy by other law enforcement officials.

Also, there is a higher prevalence of power rape noted in the cases that are referred to the FBI for consultation (1995). In addition, the power-reassurance rapes in particular were the most commonly observed stranger assaults, which is a focus of this study. However, one final reason for selecting the same rape typology as incorporated by the FBI is that the conceptual victim typology is being created to apply specifically to serial rape cases. Because the FBI is consulted by local law enforcement agencies in particularly difficult rape cases (i.e., serial rapes), it seems logical to use a rape typology that is used for such investigations.

The Serial Rapist

The following research results are relevant to serial rapists in general and are not specific to the power serial rapist (unless otherwise noted). However, the subsequent information will help inform the reader of the nature of serial rape offenses and characteristics of serial rapists overall. A serial rapist, or serial offender, is one who commits two or more offenses before apprehension (LeBeau, 1987a). Recall that for the purpose of this study the term "serial rapist" refers to an individual who has raped on two or more separate occasions and has had at least two different victims. As recognized previously, there is the hypothesis that all rapists are potential serial rapists, and perhaps the only distinction is that those who repeatedly offend are more adept in alluding apprehension. Conceivably, it is for this reason that serial rapists represent one of the greatest investigative challenges for law enforcement personnel (Hazelwood & Burgess, 1987).

NCAVC Serial Rapist Study

Because of the potential number of victims and the fear generated within communities, local law enforcement agencies often dedicate an immense amount of time and manpower to investigate serial rape cases. The Federal Bureau of Investigation, which often provides training and/or support to law enforcement agencies in these cases, assigned members of its National Center for the Analysis of Violent Crime (NCAVC) to conduct research on the serial rapist from a law enforcement perspective (1987). For purposes of the NCAVC study, a serial rapist was defined as someone who had committed ten or more rapes. Overall, there were interviews with 41 incarcerated male serial rapists who had committed 837 rapes with an additional 400 attempts. Because of the vast number of offenses, when responding to interview questions the rapists were asked to answer in regard to their first, middle, and last rapes only.

Characteristics of Serial Rapists

Although the study findings revealed a significant amount of information about the serial rape offender, the data that will be reported here are only those that prove most relevant to present inquiry. Of the serial rapist sample, eighty-five percent of respondents were white, twelve percent were black, and only two percent Hispanic. Their mean age at the time of their first rapes was 21.8 years, at the middle rapes was 25.8 years, and at the time of their last rapes was 29 years. More than fifty-four percent of the participants reported having generally stable employment histories and seventy-one percent had reported being married at least once. It was found that sixty-one percent of the rapists had a high school diploma or GED, and twenty-two percent had an associate or bachelors degree. Of the rapists who had been previously institutionalized, fourty-six percent were in a correctional facility, whereas twelve percent were in a mental facility. Furthermore, of those who had committed previous sexual assaults, thrity-seven percent were previous rapes only, eight percent were sexual nuisance offenses only, and fourty-two percent had committed both types of offenses. In addition, thirteen percent had charges of such crimes as breaking and entering and burglary. Interestingly, seventy-six percent also reported sexual abuse or observing disturbing sexual acts as children.

Study interviewers also provided some personal impressions of the serial rapists. Most of the serial rapists were described as well-groomed individuals and articulate speakers. They reportedly had little difficulty becoming acquainted with people; however, the offenders did admit to eventually wanting to dominate their relationships. To the outside observer they would appear as an achiever; however, they tended to be impulsive and often had difficulties. Overall, they liked to maintain an "image" through their appearance, behaviors, and possession, but according to study interviewers, there was "a sense of inadequacy, immaturity, and irresponsibility" regarding the rapists (Hazelwood & Warren, 1989a, p. 14).

It was found that most of the serial rapists (fifty-five to sixty-one percent) premeditated their attacks. Although comparable data were not available, it was postulated that premeditation was characteristic for these offenders. It was stated that perhaps the level of planing was due to their preference for this type of crime and also responsible for their ability to avoid apprehension (Hazelwood & Warren, Feb. 1990). Therefore, respondents of the NCAVC serial rape study were also asked to provide information regarding preoffense-related behavior and victim information for 123 rapes (focusing only on the first, middle, and last rape of each offender).

Victim-related Findings

Across the three rapes specified it was found that eighty to eighty-eight percent of the victims were strangers, ninety-eight to one hundred percent were women, approximately ninety-two percent were white, and fifty-eight to seventy percent were between the ages of 18 and 33 years. Furthermore, seventy-nine percent of the victims were alone at the time of the assault and fifty percent of the rapes took place in the victim's home (Hazelwood & Warren, 1989b). It is interesting to compare the rapist's victim selection techniques to some of their adolescent and adult criminal behaviors. Many of the rapists reported using voyeuristic behaviors in the selection of their victims and to learn their victims daily patterns (e.g., work hours, sleeping hours, roommates). This is significant because sixty-eight percent of the rapists reported beginning window peeping in childhood or adolescence.

Voyeurism is considered a nuisance sexual offense, because there is no physical harm done to the victim and therefore it is not considered a serious sexual infraction (Holmes, 1991). Collectively, rapists in the NCAVC study were responsible for more than 5,000 nuisance sexual offenses (Hazelwood et al., 1989). Nevertheless, some researchers are beginning to consider nuisance offenses from a more serious perspective, because many dangerous sexual offenders have histories of voyeurism and other such activities (Hazelwood & Warren, 1989b; Holmes, 1991).

The serial rapists also reported several incidents of entering their victims' homes when no one was present to familiarize them with the environment. The purpose of entering the victim's home before the assault can serve many functions. Examples include learning the layout of the house and individual rooms to work more effectively in the dark, searching for any possible weapons, items of value the rapist may want, or looking for clues as to roommates, spouses, etc., who may also live in the home (Swindle, 1997). Entering the victims home ahead of time in her absence is also noteworthy, because the most common nonsexual offense for the serial rapists was breaking and entering and burglary (Hazelwood & Warren, 1989a). This type of information regarding the behaviors before the offense can be important clues to law enforcement during investigations of serial rapists at large

Regarding specific victim selection criteria, victims were chosen for their availability and location more than for any other reason (ninety-eight percent and sixty-six percent respectively). The other three criteria that were dominant included the victim's gender (95%), age (66%), and race (63%). Overall, this information indicates that victims' were chosen for vulnerability more than personal characteristics or symbolic reasons (Hazelwood & Warren, 1989b). The purpose of this investigation is to gain a greater understanding of those factors (personal, situational, environmental, etc.) that make a victim a more vulnerable target. Although most of the serial rapists in the NCAVC study cited availability and location as prominent victim selection factors, the study at hand will endeavor to determine what makes some victims and locations more prime for victimization.

Victim Approach Styles

Hazelwood and Warren (1990) also used the data obtained from the NCAVC study to describe behavior during and after the sexual assaults. One aspect investigated was the manner in which the rapists approached their victims. According to the researchers, three basic styles of approach are used by rapists, which are indicative of various means of selecting, approaching, and overcoming a victim. These approaches include the "con," the "blitz," and the "surprise" styles. It is important to note, however, that other researchers have distinguished between approach styles using somewhat different terminology and descriptions (Burgess & Holstrom, 1974; LeBeau 1987a & 1987b). For example, Burgess and Holstrom (1974), who essentially began the differentiation of attack styles, described only two approaches: the "blitz" and the "confidence" attacks. According to their descriptions, the "blitz" and "surprise" attacks described by Hazelwood and Warren would both be incorporated under the "blitz" attacks described by Burgess and Holstrom. Nevertheless, for purposes of the following review only the terms and descriptions used in the NCAVC study will be used.

THE CON APPROACH. The con technique involves the offender being able to approach and interact with women in an open manner (e.g., conversing or asking for directions). However, once the victim is within the offender's control, he suddenly becomes more aggressive and the assault ensues. The power-assertive rapist or anger excitation rapist (Groth et al., 1977) is an example of the type of rapist who use the "con" approach (Hazelwood, 1995). This approach was used by the serial rapists for twenty-four percent of first rapes, thirty-five percent of middle rapes, and fourty-one percent of last rapes.

THE BLITZ APPROACH. In the blitz approach the offender directly and physically attacks the victim to obtain control. This type of approach relies on physically overpowering the victim and is more likely to result in victim injury. The "blitz" style of approach is exemplary of Groth et al.'s (1977) anger retaliatory rapist (1977). The blitz approach was used by twenty-three percent of the serial rapists for first rapes, twenty percent for middle rapes, and seventeen percent for last rapes.

THE SURPRISE APPROACH. The final style is the surprise approach, in which the rapist attacks the victim while she is sleeping. This approach is based on the presumption that the rapist had preselected his victim and had knowledge of her daily routines (e.g., hours of sleeping, when victim is alone). Threats or presence of a weapon may be used to maintain control of the victim; however, actual injury is uncommon. An example of the "surprise" approach would be the attack style of Groth et al.'s (1977) power-reassurance rapist. The surprise approach was used by fifty-four percent of serial rapists for first rapes, fourty-six percent for middle rapes, and fourty-four percent for last rapes.

Additional Offense-related Behaviors

Hazelwood and Burgess (1987) stated that how the serial rapists maintained control of their victims during the assault depended on the motivation for the attack and/or resistance by the victim. The most common methods of control in rape, and the use of these methods by the serial rapists in the study, include physical presence (eighty-two percent to ninety-two percent); verbal threats (sixty-five to eighty percent); display of a weapon (twenty-nine to fourty-four percent); and physical assault (twenty-seven to thrity-two percent). Minimal or no physical force was used by seventy-five to eighty-four percent of the study respondents and it was found that for most rapists (92.9%) the amount of force did not increase over subsequent assaults.

During the assaults the most common sexual acts were vaginal intercourse (fifty-four to sixty-seven percent), oral copulation (twenty-nine to fourty-four), kissing (eight to thirteen percent), fondling (ten to eighteen percent), anal sex (five to ten percent), and foreign object penetration (three to eight percent). Despite the variety of sexual activities performed, most rapists reported relatively little sexual pleasure from the experience. In addition, thirty-five to thirty-nine percent of the rapists reported some form of sexual dysfunction over the course of their rapes. It was also found that during the assault most of the rapists (seventy-eight to eighty-five percent) only conversed with the victim in the context of verbal threats. However, though less frequently, other rapists reported conversations with the victim that were friendly, personal, inquisitive, manipulative, or degrading.

After the assaults, rapists participated in various post offense behaviors as well: fourty-four to fifty-one percent expressed guilt; twenty-eight percent followed the case in the media; twenty to twenty-seven percent increased in substance abuse; twelve to fifteen percent revisited the crime scene; and eight to thirteen contacted the victim. In general, most serial rapists do not change their offense-related behaviors over the course of their assaults (Hazelwood et al., 1989). Therefore, the type of information provided by the NCAVC study regarding offense behaviors (including before and after) can be instrumental for law enforcement personnel in tracking and apprehending serial rapists.

In an attempt to understand what factors affect differing rates of apprehension among various types of rapists, LeBeau (1987a) researched patterns of stranger and serial rape offending to distinguish between apprehended offenders and those who remained at large. Cases of stranger rape use more police resources than nonstranger cases; however, a stranger case involving a serial rapist intensifies investigative efforts. For purposes of his study, LeBeau identified three categories of offenders: (1) open unknown—number of rapes committed by the individual is unknown because a specific suspect remains at large; (2) single—one rape was committed before the offender's capture; and (3) series—two or more rapes were committed before the offenders capture. Data were obtained from 271 open unknown cases, 240 single cases, and 171 series cases. Using the crime scene data from these cases, LeBeau observed that the apprehended serial offenders tended to use repeated geographical patterns in their offenses. Therefore, he surmised that this patterning contributed to the apprehension of the series offenders.

LeBeau further analyzed the data to illustrate the general behaviors that differentiate the apprehended serial rapists from those at large. Two important sources of information that can assist apprehension efforts are the offender's style of approach and the number of distinct scenes in the crime. For styles of approach, LeBeau notes two that are relevant to stranger offenses. The first is the "capturing the victim" approach, in which the offender interacts with the victim in an open manner before the assault, such as conversing at a party or offering a hitchhiker a ride. The second style is the "blitz" approach, in which the offender attacks the victim without before interaction, such as attacking the victim in her sleep or while she is walking on the street. In the Hazelwood and Warren (Feb. 1990) study, the "con" approach would be similar to "capturing the victim," and the "blitz" and "surprise" approaches would both be incorporated under LeBeau's "blitz" style.

The distinct scenes of a crime (which LeBeau adapted from Amir's [1971] original crime scene typology) refer to the initial meeting place, the crime scene, and the after scene(s). This factor is strongly related to the geography of the offense because the more distinct number of scenes there are in the crime, the more geographical movement, or mobility, of the offender. Also, more scenes tend to indicate more interpersonal distance between the victim-offender relationship (LeBeau, 1987a).

Data analysis showed that both the open unknown and series offenders were very similar in regard to both approach style and mobility. First, the open and series offenders predominantly used the "blitz" style of attack (seventy-five percent and seventy-seven point three percent, respectively). The most common techniques used were "illegal entry" and the "kidnap-attack." Illegal entry refers to breaking into the victim's residence, whereas the kidnap-attack involves the offender attacking in an outdoor setting and applying immediate force to subdue the victim. Although LeBeau actually categorized ten approach methods, a complete listing is beyond the scope of this commentary. Therefore, to review the full list of method types and descriptions of each, see LeBeau (1987a, p. 316).

Statistically little difference existed between the open unknown and series offenders in regard to mobility. For both groups the two-rape scene was predominant; however, the open offenders were slightly more likely to engage in multiple rape scenes than the apprehended series offenders. The series offenders committed approximately 81.7% of two to three scene rapes, and approximately 18.2% of four to five scene rapes. In contrast, the open offender committed approximately 75.1% of two to three scene rapes, and 24.9% of four to five scene rapes. There was no statistical difference in distance between the groups regarding movement of the victim by the offender.

LeBeau (1987a) initially proposed that the more scenes involved in the rape, the more information the victim could supply in regard to the offense, and thus the greater the possibility of apprehension. The information provided regarding the open unknown and series offenders would tend to contradict this assumption. However, the distinct feature of the series rapist that may result in greater apprehension is his tendency to restrict his attacks to a small geographical area, which on average is one-half mile from previous attacks (LeBeau, 1987a). In contrast, open unknown offenders carry out their offenses in such a way as not to provide predictable information regarding their behaviors. One final difference that may affect apprehension is that the series offenders are more likely to commit a nonstranger assault in the course of their rapes than are open unknown offenders.

Rape Summary

The preceding review helped to inform the reader about the act of rape on an initially general level through a discussion of its history and an explanation of the types of rape identified in the literature. We then focused on more specific aspects of the rape phenomena (e.g., rapist typologies), which introduced the reader to personal and offense-related characteristics of the offender. We concluded the section by systematically discussing the serial rapist and familiarizing the reader with various components of this offender's personality and crimes.

We note, however, that to understand how such information can be used to conceptualize a victim selection typological model, it is necessary to understand several features of investigating the victim. This entails a deliberate focus on the discipline of victimology. Therefore, the following section will present the field on a variety of levels beginning with victimology's origination and history and ending with the establishment of the victim-offender relationship.

VICTIMOLOGY

The Advent of Victimology

Benjamin Mendelsohn has credited himself as founding the doctrine of victimology which was a gradual evolution from a 1937 study that he conducted during his profession as a barrister. His study consisted of a 300-item questionnaire, based on criminology and related sciences, that served as a method for scientifically studying the defense aspect of criminal cases. Although most questionnaire items focused on biological, psychological, and sociological characteristics of the defendant, personal and social information regarding the crime victims was also gathered (Mendelsohn, 1974). The results of Mendelsohn's study led him to conclude that the personalities of the offender and victim were parallel in nature (Schafer, 1974).

As a result of his findings, Mendelsohn published *Rape in Criminology,* which focused on aspects of the victim and victim-offender relationships in cases of rape (Mendelsohn, 1974). He later stated that the title *Rape in Victimology* would have been better suited to his work. Several years after that publication he also began a manuscript on victimology and communicated the concept at a state hospital in Bucharest on invitation by the Roumanian Society of Psychiatry (Mendelsohn, 1974). Mendelsohn advanced victimology as a distinct area of science and believed that it should be established as an independent field of study. He objected to the victim being studied as a corollary to the offender and thought that criminology and victimology should be separate disciplines (Schafer, 1974; Walklate, 1994).

The Relationship Between Victimology and Criminology

There has been scholarly skepticism and objection to Mendelsohn's distinction between victimology and criminology as separate sciences. Nagel (1974) analyzed the separation of victimology and criminology in contrast to the separation of criminology and penology from penal law. Penology is the "study of the reformation and rehabilitation of criminals and of the management of prisons" (Guralnik, 1980). Although it is incorporated under the study of penal law (that constituting criminal punishment), it is considered a special branch of science because it is also influenced by such disciplines as pedagogy and psychiatry (Nagel, 1974). However, the need to distinguish criminology from penal law was even greater because the relationship between the former and other sciences was even more extensive than that of penology and because the scope of criminology went beyond what was incorporated under penal law studies (Nagel, 1974).

Nagel argued that only if criminology dealt solely with the criminal would there be a need for a distinct area of study of the victim. Although classic criminology may have neglected the victim in interest of the offender, criminology has evolved into a science in which the importance of environment and relationships are central determinmates of crime. In fact, "in such a modern criminology of relationships, the victimological relationship is of such a paramount importance that there is no longer a need for a separate victimology" (Nagel, 1974, p. 14).

Despite Mendelsohn's introduction to the importance of the victim-offender relationship, the beginning of victimology as a recognized scientific area of study was not until Von Hentig's 1948 publication of *The Criminal and His Victim* (Drapkin & Viano, 1974). Von Hentig endeavored to understand crime in terms of "doer-sufferer" interactions and he believed that a "reciprocality" existed between the offender and victim. He also contended that the victim played a part in shaping the crime and criminal and that the relationship between the two was more complex than the mechanical definitions of the law suggested (Schafer, 1974). Unlike Mendelsohn, however, Von Hentig fostered the notion of victimology as a branch or subdiscipline of criminology in which the primary focus of study was the victim of crime (Nagel, 1974; Walklate, 1994). Yet despite the contributions of these early scholars and the increased interest and advances in victimology over the last few decades, victimology still remains a somewhat indeterminate concept.

Orientations in Defining Victimology

Miers (1989) stated that "victimology has too many voices to allow any coherence in its reported understanding of the world" (p. 17). Perhaps that is why there are so many interpretations of the field of victimology. Victimology has been described in terms of political and philosophical orientations. Although an elaboration of these individual views is beyond this scope of this inquiry, it is important to men-tion the various orientations distinguished within the field. However, this study is not identified with, nor intended to advance, any one position.

Political Approaches

Karmen (as cited in Walklate, 1994) identifies three political dimensions of victimology: the conservative, the liberal, and the radical-critical. The conservative position is concerned particularly with street crime; however, it also focuses on holding people accountable for their actions, encourages self-reliance, and emphasizes restorative justice. The liberal stance extends the conservative position by including other forms of crime. It focuses on helping the victim reestablish her life and advancing restitution and reconciliation as legitimate penal plans. Finally, the radical-critical view extends victimology to include all forms of victimization (not just criminal) and analyzes the criminal justice system, law, and the state as contributors to the construction of such suffering (Walklate, 1994).

Philosophical Approaches

Victimology has also been described by various scholars on the basis of dichotomous philosophical positions: the humanistic and the scientific approaches (Walklate, 1994). The humanistic approach is adopted by activists who seek to use victimology as a means by which to foster social change and advance the position of crime victims. However, the scientific approach embraces objectivity and empirical data as a means by which to understand victims of crime. The problem is that the two orientations foster very different views of the victim, therefore, complicating the way in which victimology is perceived.

The discomfort with intertwining these two positions within the field of victimology is that, much like with other social sciences, it is *assumed* that this area of study is based on traditional views of science and the scientist/"object" relationship, which will provide an empirical base of knowledge (Walklate, 1994). As Cressey (as cited in Walklate) stated, "the humanists' work tends to be deprecated because it is considered propagandistic rather than scientific, and the scientists' work tends to

be deprecated because it is not sufficiently oriented to social action"
(p. 57).

Fattah (1991) stated that to achieve the goal of applied victimology,
theoretical victimology must maintain scientific character and clearly
define the boundaries of the subject matter (i.e., criminal victimization). In other words, before efforts can be made to prevent or allevi-
ate the suffering of crime victims, action and policy must be first
grounded in empirical science, not politics or ideology (Fattah, 1991).
Such questions of empiricism and objectivity lead to another distinction in the study of victims: the positivist versus critical victimology
approach.

Positivist vs. Critical Approaches

Positivist victimology "assumes a consensus of norms and values
which readily allows us to identify victimization when it occurs . . . and
treats the process of victimization as a variable . . . based upon statistical or other empirical evidence" (Miers, 1989, p. 3–4). It is essentially based on three major concerns: (1) identification of factors in
individuals or their environment that contribute to nonrandom acts of
victimization; (2) a concentration on interpersonal crimes of violence;
and (3) identification of victims who may have contributed to their victimization (Miers, 1989).

In contrast, critical victimology believes that labeling an individual
as a victim involves a statement of values and questions the power and
authority from which these labels are derived. Furthermore, the factors that contribute to why some individuals who sustain injury are
labeled victims, and others are not, must be examined (Miers, 1989).
Essentially critical victimology is concerned with (1) the social processes by which individuals are labeled victims in place of examining only
personal characteristics; (2) the role of the victim in criminal processes; and (3) how various forms of victimization or suffering are desig-
nated as legitimate claims on society's legal, medical, and financial
resources, whereas others are not (Miers, 1989).

It should be stressed that the various political and ideological orientations that have been addressed thus far should not be construed as
discernible concepts. In fact Mawby & Walklate (1994) note similar
patterns between various scholarly interpretations of positivistic and
conservative victimology and also the humanistic and radical-critical

approaches. The importance of introducing these diverse positions is to emphasize the various ideas and concepts that influence the approaches to, applications of, and views on the developing discipline of victimology.

Establishing the Victim-offender Relationship

As previously stated, the relationship between the victim and offender has been a central tenet of both victimology and criminology alike. As early as the 1940's, researchers such as Mendelsohn and Von Hentig introduced the concept in association with victimology, whereas studies such as Wolfgang's (1958) *Patterns of Criminal Homicide* and Amir's (1971) *Patterns of Forcible Rape* were significant criminological contributions (Davis, Taylor, & Titus, 1997). Founded on a growing body of research, Fattah (1997) supported the contention that not only is there a link between victimization and offending but that the victim and offender are not mutually exclusive groups. He stated that "the roles of victim and offender are neither fixed nor antagonistic, but rather revolving and interchangeable" (p. 266).

Studying the victim-offender relationship in crime can serve multiple purposes: (1) to help reveal criminal motives; (2) to determine the existence or level of victim contribution; and (3) to assist in police investigations (Fattah, 1991). Nevertheless, examining the victim as a contributor to the crime has not always been favorably regarded. Victimology has consistently maintained the position that no victim is responsible for his or her misfortune. However, notions that criminal victimization was simply a matter of chance was thought to have been a reaction against criminologists' early attempts to attribute some active role to the victim (Fattah, 1997).

For example, in the 1970's the idea of crime as capricious was strongly asserted in relation to crimes against women, particularly sexual assault and domestic violence (Fattah, 1997). It was during this era that Amir introduced his concept of victim-precipitation (adapted from Wolfgang, 1958) in cases of forcible rape (Amir, 1976; Amir, 1971). Amir's use of the term "precipitation" did not foster a broad acceptance of his work, and it was later suggested that the use of the term "victim vulnerability" may have been prudent (Chappell et al., 1977). Nevertheless, feminist Brownmiller (1975) skillfully reworded Amir's basic tenets to help define the use of the concept:

> Victim precipitation is a new concept in criminology. It does not hold the victim responsible, but seeks to define contributory behavior in effect, an unlawful act has been committed but had the victim behaved in a different fashion, the crime in question might have been avoided. (p. 353)

The depiction of the blameless victim also served to advance conservative politicians' aims at making crime legislation tougher and also general changes in the way victims were treated by law enforcement and criminal justice entities (Fattah, 1997). In fact, Fattah (1992) stated that "the search for theory, characteristic of the early days of victimology, gave way to an obsessive preoccupation with policy. Gradually, rhetoric overshadowed research findings and disinterested unbiased scholarship was in danger of becoming eclipsed by political ideology" (p. 19). However, in light of the many advances that have since been made in regard to treatment of the victim, scholars have proposed that more current research make a "paradigm shift" and begin to refocus on the notion of the victim as an actor in the crime (Davis et al., 1997, p. 169).

Victimology Summary

The preceding review served has an introduction to the field of victimology, beginning with the origination of the doctrine based on the works of Mendelsohn and Von Hentig. The discussion then proceeded to define the relationship between the fields of victimology and criminology and focused particularly on the debate concerning whether the two disciplines should be considered distinct areas of study. Victimology was then described in terms of its various orientations, including the political, philosophical, and positivist versus critical approach. The purpose of considering these various perspectives was to present victimology as a somewhat equivalent domain of scholarly inquiry to its criminology counterpart, lending itself to multiple interpretations and investigations. The section concluded with a description of the victim-offender relationship, an important concept in both the fields criminology and victimology.

Chapter 3

MODELS OF VICTIMIZATION: ANALYSIS AND CRITIQUE

OVERVIEW

In this chapter the reader is familiarized with various victimological approaches to studying the victim. The use of the typological approach is addressed, including a review of early efforts that were developed to create victim typologies based on personal characteristics of the victims. The reader is then introduced to the micro- and macro-level factors of victimization. These factors are first defined and are then differentiated on the basis of what they have to offer victimological research. The micro-level section begins with a brief look at personal characteristics that are associated with a higher risk of criminal victimization. The section then focuses on those micro-level factors that have been identified as key elements in victim selection. Throughout the micro-level section, attempts are made to relate the given information specifically to the power serial rapist.

The final section outlines the macro-level theories with particular emphasis on the lifestyle model, the routine activities approach, opportunity theory, and the social ecology model. We note that the macro-level theories share many similarities and overlap to a large extent. For this reason, they are often referred to within the literature as variations on a single theme. However, in the macro-level section, each theory is discussed separately to familiarize the reader with these various approaches. Similar to our presentation of micro-level theories, when possible and appropriate, we attempt to link the macro-level theories to the act of power serial rape.

ANALYSIS: APPROACHES TO UNDERSTANDING VICTIMIZATION

The Typological Approach

Given the numerous factors that can contribute to victimization, it is too arduous a task to analyze the phenomenon without some attempt at categorizing or creating a typology. Although such classifications could be based on a variety of criteria (e.g., nature, degree, effects), Fattah (1991) established the *source* of victimization as his focus because he was interested in understanding specifically criminal victimization. Fattah substantiated selecting a specific criterion based on the fact that typologies, or classifications, are "by their very nature, arbitrary groupings subservient to the specific objectives of this researcher" (p. 5). This focus is also pertinent to the objective of the present study; that is, to uncover those factors that contribute to victimization specifically by the power serial rapist.

Silverman (1974) stated that a typology that attempts to identify determinants of increased susceptibility to victimization should emphasize categories that can be tested, such as through victim surveys. In addition, Sparks (1981) stated that unlike past victim typologies, which were primarily based on personality traits, more current attempts have focused on environmental and ecological elements and in some cases have involved model building. Again, the significance of such an approach is that the typology or model can potentially be tested by use of victim surveys. Although environmental and ecological factors have yet to be discussed, they are primary components of this study. Also, by taking a conceptual approach to creating the victim selection typology model, this study can serve as a basis by which to analyze existing victim survey data and possibly contribute to the creation of victimization theory.

The Creation of Victim Typologies

From the foundational ideas of victimology emerged the early victim typologies, which were based on biological, psychological, physical, and situational factors as determinants of victimization (Gottfredson, 1981). Silverman (1974) summarized and critiqued several conceptual typologies offered by early contributors in the field. Von Hentig, for purposes of his categorization, disregarded any legal distinctions between the "doer and sufferer" and created an eleven category typology based on biopsychosocial classifications of victims.

Von Hentig's (1948) Typology

Von Hentig's typology consisted of eleven categories based on biopsychosocial factors. Silverman's (pp. 55–56) summary of the eleven categories as they appear in *The Criminal and His Victim* (1948, p. 438) is as follows: (1) *The Young*–"The weak specimen . . . in mankind, is the most likely to be a victim of an attack"; (2) *The Female*– "Female sex is another form of weakness recognized by law"; (3) *The Old*–"The aging human being is handicapped in many ways"; (4) *The Mentally Defective and Other Mentally Deranged*–"The feeble-minded, the insane, the drug addict, and the alcoholic . . ."; (5) *Immigrants, Minorities, Dull Normals*–"An 'artificial disadvantage' is imposed on these three groups . . .The immigrant is likely to be poor and inexperienced . . ."; (6) *The Depressed*–". . . a disturbance of the instinct of self-preservation;" (7) *The Acquisitive*–"The greedy can be hooked by all sorts of devices . . .";(8) *The Wanton*–". . . cases of sexual assault or adultery where the female plays as much of a seducing role as the male"; (9) *The Lonesome and Heartbroken*–"These victims lower their defenses while they seek companionship"; (10) *The Tormentor*–". . . generally found in 'family tragedies';" (11) *Blocked, Exempted, and Fighting Victims*– ". . . an individual who has been so enmeshed in a losing situation that defense moves have become impossible or more injurious than injury at criminal hands."

Mendelsohn's (1956) Typology

Mendelsohn introduced a six-part typology based on the amount of guilt contributed to the victim. Schafer (1968), in his book *The Victim and His Criminal*, summarizes Mendelsohn's typology in the following manner: (1) The "completely innocent victim"–is seen as the "ideal" victim and refers to all children and those who suffer victimization while they are unconscious; (2) The "victim with minor guilt" and "victim due to his ignorance"–example is the woman who "provokes" a miscarriage and as a result dies; (3) The "victim as guilty as the offender" and the "voluntary victim"–includes various circumstances of suicide and euthanasia; (4) The "victim more guilty than the offender"–

includes the "provoker victim" who provokes someone to crime, and the "imprudent victim" who induces victimization; (5) The "most guilty victim" and the "victim who is guilty alone"–refers to the criminal who himself becomes a victim as a result of his criminal acts (e.g., being killed by someone in self-defense); and (6) The "simulating victim" and the "imaginary victim"–refers to individuals who mislead the criminal justice system to obtain a conviction against an innocent person (pp. 42–43).

Fattah's (1967) Typology

Fattah proposed a five-category typology based on sociological and psychological characteristics of victims. These five major types, as introduced in *Towards a Criminological Classification of Victims* (1967), are described by Silverman (1974, p. 57) as follows: (1) *nonparticipating victims*–these are individuals who maintain denial or repulsion toward the offense or offender and by no means contributed to the cause of the crime; (2) *latent or predisposed victims*–individuals who because of certain predisposed character traits are more likely to be victimized and are more likely to be victims of the same type of offense; (3) *provocative victims*–persons who are said to have provoked the offense as a result of either instigating the offender or creating a situation likely to lead to crime; (4) *participating victims*–these victims play their role during the commission of the crime by adopting a passive attitude, making the crime easier to commit, or by assisting the criminal; and (5) *false victims*–one who is truly not a victim of a crime or who is only a victim of his own actions.

Overall, although these early attempts may have been groundbreaking in understanding the role of victims in crime, Silverman described these typologies as either not exhaustive, not mutually exclusive, or poorly defined. However, use of the typological approach was popular in the beginnings of victimology. Parallel to the efforts of criminology to explain criminal behavior by means of an offender's personal characteristics or background, victimology followed a similar course of investigation by inquiring about victim's personal characteristics and behavior. For example, victimology's ideas such as proneness or vulnerability to explain criminal victimization correspond to criminology's notions of predisposition or propensity to explain criminal involvement (Fattah, 1991).

Defining Micro- and Macro-Level Factor Approaches

In attempting to identify those variables which contribute to victimization, researchers have investigated factors at various levels, ranging from the individual victim to the community at large. Although these various levels are consistent elements in criminological and victimological research, the terminology for such factors has varied across researchers. For example, Sampson and Lauritsen (1994) used the terms "individual," "situational," and "community" to describe the various levels of victimization factors. The individual level refers to individual characteristics that explain behavior and that are associated with victimization and offending. Situation-level risk factors are more broadly defined as those elements which "influence the initiation or outcome" of an event (p. 2). Sampson and Lauritsen also include analyses of victim-offender overlap and victim-offender relationships within the situational context. Finally, community level factors refer to community structures or cultures that may increase or produce differential rates of victimization.

Short (1990) used the terms "individual," "micro," and "macro" in referring to the various factor levels (p. 11). Short's use of the term "individual" is very similar to that described by Sampson and Lauritsen (1994). His use of the term micro-level, which corresponds with "situational," focuses attention on the interaction of the involved parties and unfolding of the events. Finally, the macro-level, that corresponds with "community," again involves the larger community structure and various social characteristics (e.g., residential mobility and population density).

However, to provide a more simplistic understanding of the various factors associated with victimization, the following discussion will rely upon the terms micro and macro as defined by Fattah (1979; *see also* 1991). According to Fattah (1979), the analysis of characteristics or small group behavior of victims is defined as a micro-level approach. The use of personal characteristics (e.g., attractiveness, vulnerability, and proneness) and behavioral characteristics that may have facilitated victimization (e.g., provocation or carelessness) are considered micro-level explanations (Fattah, 1991).

Macro-level factors consist of characteristics, lifestyles, and routine activities of a more general population (Fattah, 1979). This level incorporates various approaches, such as the lifestyle model, routine activities approach, and opportunity theory, that are considered more general explanations of criminal victimization. Fattah did not directly address the larger social structure (such as the previously described "community" level) in his macro-level definition. However, models and theories relating to larger social elements (e.g, social ecology, neighborhood structure, urbanization) will be described and analyzed within the macro-level section. Despite the general absence of such social and community factors, Fattah's description of both the micro- and macro-level approaches was chosen as a basis for the following in-depth review because of his in depth discussion of such factors as related to victim selection.

It should be noted that the distinctions between micro- and macro-level explanations are not absolute nor are the categories mutually exclusive. In fact, within the literature the models are sometimes treated as one in the same or simply as variations of the same concept . For example, the lifestyle model or routine activity approach could be described as either micro- or macro-level theories (Fattah, 1991). Although the current presentation of victimization delineates between the micro- and macro-level explanations, it should be emphasized that this delineation is artificial and is used for explanatory purposes only.

MICRO-LEVEL EXPLANATIONS

Personal Characteristics of Victims

Most information regarding risk of victimization has been obtained through the National Crime Survey (NCS) data. The NCS is an ongoing survey conducted by the Bureau of Justice Statistics which measures the extent of criminal victimization in the United States. The NCS allows for estimates of victimizations that are not officially reported to police and provides a means of determining prevalence of victimization for particular subgroups (Sampson & Lauritsen, 1994). In fact, it was the advent of victimization surveys that allowed researchers to determine subgroup probabilities in a way that official crime data had previously not permitted (Gottfredson, 1981). Hindelang's (1976) theft and assault research is a classic study using victimization surveys. His study included analyses of surveys from eight U.S. cities and provided an in-depth look at victim characteristics for a variety of crimes (e.g., personal, household, and business). Furthermore, his work offers a thorough overview of the development and methodological issues of victimization surveys. Although findings have changed somewhat since the work of Hindelang in 1976, the use of victimization surveys still shows that certain demographic factors are highly correlated with the risk of criminal victimization (e.g., Blazicek, 1979).

Some of the more common risk factors, which are relevant to this study, include age, sex, race, and marital status (Sampson & Lauritsen, 1994; Laub, 1997). However, it must be noted that these factors are correlated with risk of criminal victimization *in general* and *are not* crime specific. Because these factors have been identified as important elements in the study of criminal victimization, they will be introduced briefly. Nevertheless, the usefulness of these variables in creating a crime specific victim typology is somewhat limited. Thus, the appropriateness of each factor in regard to serial rape will be analyzed after each factor description.

Age

Age is one of the strongest and most important predictors of victimization (Hindelang, Gottfredson, & Garofalo, 1978; Laub, 1997). The NCS data has shown that there is an inverse relationship between age of the victim and risk of victimization (Laub, 1997). In other words, as a person increases in age, their risk of victimization decreases. Risk of victimization is highest for individuals under the age of 25 years. However, after 25 years of age the risk gradually decreases, and by age 65 the risk is approximately only one tenth of that for persons under 25 year old. This relationship is particularly strong for violent crimes including rape, homicide, and assault (Sampson & Lauritsen, 1994).

Based on the data obtained by Hazelwood and Warren (1989b) regarding characteristics of serial rape victims, certain age groups do seem to be at greater risk for this particular offense. However, the age groups that seem to be at higher risk for serial rape victimization differ from those age groups identified with a more general risk of victimization. Although the NCS data showed that victims under the age of 25 years were more likely to be victimized, the most common age range for the serial rape victims was between the ages of 18 and 33 years. According to the serial rape victim data, individuals under age 17 and above age 41 seemed to be at a lower risk. Therefore, although age does seem to play a factor in serial rape assaults, the ages of risk seem to differ somewhat from the age ranges identified for non-specific criminal victimization.

Sex

The NCS data have also shown a relationship between sex and victimization. It has been found that men are at a higher risk for victimization than women, particularly for the crimes of homicide, robbery, and assault. However, one obvious exception to this correlation is in cases of rape, in which women are at an overwhelmingly higher risk (Sampson & Lauritsen, 1994; Laub, 1997). Much like the NCS data, Hazelwood and Warren's (1989b) serial rape study indicated that serial rapists target women almost exclusively. However, because the devised victim typology is focused only on female victims, the differential victimization rates between men and women is irrelevant for purposes of this study.

Race

Race has been found to be associated with the risk of criminal victimization with blacks being at a greater risk than whites (Sampson & Lauritsen, 1994; Laub, 1997). U.S. Department of Justice statistics (as cited by Sampson & Lauritsen, 1994) indicated that blacks were five times more likely than whites to be the victims of homicide, and three to four times more likely to be the victims of rape and robbery. This differentiation has also been noted in cases of aggravated assault and burglary; however, whites have been found to be at a slightly higher risk for personal theft.

These data do not coincide with the results of the Hazelwood and Warren (1989b) serial rape study. In fact according to their data, white women represented eighty-eight to ninety-five percent of the serial rape victims, whereas black women accounted for only two to seven percent. It is interesting to note that of the serial rapists interviewed, eighty-five percent were white and only twelve percent were black. Furthermore, although white rapists did not cross the racial line and rape black females, the black rapists raped both black and white women (Hazelwood & Warren, 1989b). Therefore, based solely on these data, it would seem, that white women are at a higher risk for serial rape victimization than black women who are high-risk victims for rape in general.

Marital Status

Although less studied than the previous three demographic factors, marital status has also been found to be related to risk of victimization (Hindelang et al., 1978; Cohen, Kluegel, & Land, 1981). According to Department of Justice statistics (as cited by Sampson & Lauritsen, 1994) unmarried persons are at a greater risk for criminal victimization than are married persons. More specifically, those who have never been married are also at a higher risk than those who are divorced, separated, or widowed (in that respective order). Although overall the risk for unmarried persons is nearly four times higher than married individuals, the differential victimization rates for rape and robbery are not as pronounced between the married and unmarried groups.

Unfortunately, victim marital status was not available for any of the previously discussed serial rape studies. However, Laub (1997) noted that some of the risk associated with marital status may be accounted for by age. In other words unmarried individuals are more likely to be younger, whereas the lower risk divorced, separated, and widowed individuals are likely to fall into higher age categories. Nevertheless, regardless of age, married individuals are at the lowest risk for victimization (1997). On the basis of the assumed relationship between age and marital status, it may be possible to predict that most serial rape victims would be of an unmarried status considering the victim age range noted in the Hazelwood and Warren (1989b) serial rape study. Furthermore, it could be assumed that unmarried women are more at risk for serial rape than married women because of differences in guardianship and lifestyle.

Both guardianship and lifestyle are factors that will be explored further in subsequent sections. However, the reader should note that although the use of victimization surveys has indicated a link between personal characteristics of victims and rates of victimization, this link is based on correlation and not causation. Although personal characteristics alone may not be sufficient to explain one's becoming a victim, the interrelationship between these factors and the more macro-level factors (e.g., lifestyle) may provide valuable insight (Fattah, 1991).

Micro-level Victim Selection Factors

On the basis of a review of various studies that have examined victim selection in predatory offenses, Fattah (1991) identified five basic categories of selection factors used by offenders: proximity, accessibility, attractiveness, manageability, and the degree of risk the victim represents for the perpetrator. However, these five criteria can be incorporated within the three broader categories identified by Fattah to explain victimization by reference to personal characteristics of the victim: (1) attraction/repulsion; (2) proximity/distance; and (3) proneness/vulnerability.

Table 1 has been provided to assist the reader in conceptualizing the relationship between the various factors and to understand the organization of the material that follows. However, it is important to note that the following categories are not mutually exclusive. Therefore, various dimensions of the victimization factors may overlap and may work interdependently.

Table 1—Victim Selection Factors (as cited in Fattah, 1991)

Attraction/Repulsion	Proximity/Distance	Proneness/Vulnerability

Accessibility:
  temporal
  physical
 	
Manageability
		Proneness:
		  spatial
		  structural
		  deviance-related
		  occupational
		
		Vulnerability
		
		Degree of risk:
		  security
		  surveillability
		  danger
		  sanctions

Attraction/Repulsion

Attraction and repulsion are subjective selection criteria, and thus the features of these concepts can vary by offender and crime. The terms were originally derived from the animal kingdom in which the "universality" of attraction and repulsion led to the belief that they are, in some instances, instinctive (e.g., the natural antagonism between cats and mice) (Fattah, 1991). In terms of explaining victimization, however, attraction and repulsion refer to an offender's consideration of both the positive versus negative features and the potential rewards versus perceived risks of a particular target victim (Fattah, 1991). The term "attraction" is used most often in cases of sexual assault and property crime. For example, in sexual offenses the term may be used to describe the actual physical attractiveness of a victim, whereas in financially motivated crimes the lucrativeness of a business may be attractive to the offender (Fattah, 1991).

Repulsion is considered more instrumental in crimes of expressive violence (Fattah, 1991). Nevertheless, it is possible that repulsion could also play a key role in sexual offenses in which the primary motive is anger. For example, the anger-retaliation rapist, as described by Groth, commits his offense with the intention of punishing and degrading his female victim. Therefore, it is conceivable that a target who the offender perceives as "repulsive," in terms of her being the type of woman he disdains rather than in terms of physical appearance, would be a more likely victim. However, because this study focuses on the power rapist, and not rapes or other crimes of *expressive* violence, the remainder of this section will pertain only to the concept of attraction.

Accessibility

In addition to physical appearance, there are other characteristics of a victim that may be considered aspects of attractiveness, such as accessibility and manageability.

Accessibility refers to the ease with which an offender can access a potential victim. It is considered an attraction feature, because those victims that are readily accessible are considered more attractive targets than a less accessible victim, with all other things being equal. However, accessibility can be further divided into two categories: temporal accessibility and physical accessibility (Fattah, 1991).

TEMPORAL ACCESSIBILITY. Temporal accessibility refers to the actual time frame in which an offender has access to a selected victim. For example, an individual who wants to rob a store is limited to the hours in which the store is open. During nonbusiness hours, the store is no longer an accessible target for the robber. Regarding cases of serial rape, the reader may recall from Hazelwood and Warren's (1990) study that the surprise approach, in which the rapist attacks the victim while she is sleeping, is a common attack style of the power-reassurance rapist. Thus, in these instances temporal accessibility would refer to the hours in which the victim was sleeping or home alone. Therefore, times during which the victim was out of the house, awake, or in the presence of company would have made her temporally inaccessible.

PHYSICAL ACCESSIBILITY. Physical accessibility refers to such factors as location or layout of a potential crime area that may enhance or impede the commission of a crime. For example, the location of doors and windows on a home, and thus the ease of entering and exiting a dwelling, may be important determinants in cases of burglary. In addition, the placement of fences or hedges may make certain areas less visible to others and, therefore, a more accessible and attractive target. On the basis of these concepts and data regarding the serial rapist, physical accessibility is arguably an important factor of victim selection in power serial rapes.

For example, as previously discussed in Hazelwood and Warren's (1989b) study, ninety-eight percent of the rapists identified availability as a key victim selection factor, whereas sixty-six percent noted the importance of location. In fact, these criteria were considered greater determinants of selecting a victim than more personal characteristics such as physical appearance. The reader is also reminded that of the NCAVC study participants, thirteen percent had committed burglary or breaking and entering offenses (Hazelwood & Burgess, 1987), and sixty-eight percent reported voyeuristic activities (Hazelwood & Warren, 1989b). Furthermore, voyeurism was noted as a manner through which to select victims, and several rapists reported entering the victim's home during her absence to learn the layout of the dwelling, etc. (Hazelwood & Warren, 1989b; for a biographical example see Swindle, 1997).

These issues are relevant because location and layout are essentially important elements in both burglary and voyeuristic offenses. For example, Rengert and Wasilchick (as cited by Fattah, 1991) found that residential burglary victimization was related to the degree of access to the dwelling based on street design. Hindelang (1976) also noted access as a key determinant of target selection in burglary offenses. Because burglars and voyeurs alike rely on being unseen and having no personal contact with their targeted victims, elements of location or layout that contribute to such anonymity would be attractive features in victim selection. On the basis of the high percentage of serial rapists that perform both breaking and entering and/or voyeuristic activities, it is arguable that the factors involved in selecting these crime targets (e.g., physical accessibility) are also used in their selection of rape victims. This is particularly significant, because many serial rape cases occur in the victims' homes (Hazelwood & Warren, 1989b).

Manageability

An additional feature of attractiveness is manageability. This factor is particularly important in crimes involving face-to-face confrontation and may include determining the victim's likelihood of resistance, ease of intimidation, and the necessity of using force (Fattah, 1991). Manageability is such an important element of target attractiveness because the successful completion of a personal crime largely depends on the offender being able to maintain control of his victim. Chappell and James (as cited by Geis, 1977; and Fattah, 1991) reported that a key element in the contact situation was whether the targeted female was alone. In fact, ninety-six percent of the rapists in their study indicated this to be a primary consideration before the assault. This factor is related to Swindle's (1997) description of the serial rapist who would enter his victim's unoccupied home to search for indicators of her being married, having a roommate or children, and also to determine her access to any possible weapons.

The concepts of attraction and repulsion are highly relative terms and thus are limited in the extent to which they may explain victimization. Although they may be useful micro-level determinants as to why a *particular* victim was selected, these terms are more difficult to incorporate into macro-level explanations (Fattah, 1991). However, this study endeavors to relate macro-level factors (i.e., lifestyle model, routine activities, opportunity theory, and social ecology) to micro level determinants using categories such as attractiveness, which incorporate location and layout.

Proximity/Distance

Fattah (1991) describes proximity and distance in relation to the offender attempting to "get physically close to, but stay emotionally remote from, the victim in order to decrease the geographical distance while increasing the affective distance that separates them" (p. 258). Therefore, Fattah's focus is more on the psychological aspects of proximity and distance between the victim and offender than the greater spatial and geographical aspects as discussed in LeBeau (1987a & 1987b).

The underlying premise of these concepts is that hurting a victim at a distance, in which there is less personalization, is easier than doing so at close proximity (*see* Milgram, 1974). This is relevant to the present inquiry, which focuses solely on stranger rape, because as discussed in the serial rape section, eighty percent to eighty-eight percent of the cases involved victims and offenders who were strangers. Thus it could be contended, on the basis of the proximity/distance factors, that serial rapists *select* victims who are unknown to them to decrease their inhibitions or level of emotional discomfort associated with the rape act.

Fattah (1991) noted that proximity and distance may also explain why some sexual offenders attempt to calm or reassure their victims during the assault. Again, this is particularly relevant to this study because, as the reader may recall, the power-reassurance rapist is also known as the "gentleman rapist" because of his "pseudo unselfish" and apologetic manner during the rape. Interestingly, the power-reassurance rapist is also the most common in cases of stranger assaults (Hazelwood, 1995).

Proneness/Vulnerability

Although the terms "proneness" and "vulnerability" are often used interchangeably, some researchers suggest that there are subtle distinctions between the two concepts. For example, Reiss (as cited in Fattah, 1991) describes these differences based on the explanatory variables underlying each term. Victim proneness is based on personal, social, and behavioral characteristics of potential victims, in addition to the their relationship to the offender. However, victim vulnerability incorporates situations and characteristics of offenders, their networks, and behaviors, and their relationship to potential victims as explanatory variables. Reiss adds ". . . victim proneness models explain high risk of victimization . . . by victim behavior and relationships . . . vulnerability models are more offender oriented. . ." (p. 41).

Proneness

The concept of proneness is based on the notion that some individuals are simply more susceptible to negative occurrences than others. This idea, which is reflected in the phrase "accident prone," has long been accepted (Fattah, 1991). Some studies have drawn a parallel between victims of crime and accident victims, and it has been stated that available research supports the idea that some people are more victim-prone than others (Gottfredson, 1981).

For example, Keane and Arnold (1996) investigated the relationship between criminal victimization and accidents using the routine activities approach. The basis of their study were findings from victimization surveys in the United States, Canada, and Great Britain, and previous research that identified certain demographic and lifestyle characteristics as being associated with both crime victims and offenders and accident victims as well.

Keane and Arnold obtained their data from the Canadian General Social Survey in January and February of 1988 and included information on both accident and criminal victimization of individuals age 15 years and older. For purposes of their analysis, the crime categories included violent crime, theft of personal property, household crime, and motor vehicle theft. Accident responses were limited to those incidents that interrupted the respondents' normal activities for at least half a day. The total sample was 9,870 responses.

Overall, their findings were consistent with past research and indicated that certain demographic and/or lifestyle characteristics (e.g., male, divorced/separated, urban dweller) were common elements of increased likelihood to both criminal victimization and accidents (particularly those involving motor vehicles and sports)(Keane & Arnold, 1996). Therefore, these factors could be considered as increasing one's proneness to various forms of victimization.

TYPES OF PRONENESS. Proneness can be divided into four basic categories: spatial, structural, deviance-related, and occupational (Fattah, 1991). Deviance-related proneness focuses on the high risk of victimization for "socially deviant" groups (e.g., homosexuals), whereas occupational proneness relates to high-risk occupations (e.g., prostitute or bartender). However, the two categories that are most relevant to the present research are spatial and structural proneness.

SPATIAL PRONENESS. Spatial proneness refers to actual ecological factors (e.g., urbanization) that may contribute to an individual's likelihood of victimization. Because social ecology in relation to crime will be discussed at length in the subsequent macro-level section, it is unnecessary to elaborate on the concept at this time. However, by introducing spatial proneness as a potential personal characteristic of the victim and then again as a broader sociological factor, it should suggest to the reader the possible overlap and mutual influence between micro-and macro-level explanations.

STRUCTURAL PRONENESS. Structural proneness refers to social, or sociodemographic, elements that may contribute to varying risks of victimization. Three examples of structural proneness include being of young age, being female, and having a minority status (Fattah, 1991). Although youth and minority status are important considerations in understanding victimization, the only category that will be addressed is that of "being female", because it is most pertinent to a study examining female victim selection.

Many researchers, particularly feminists, have argued that the high incidence of female victimization is based on the socially derived power differences between men and women. Essentially, the powerlessness of women in American society is the result of historical, cultural, economic, and political factors that make women attractive, legitimate, and highly vulnerable targets (Fattah, 1991). Four main factors that contribute to women's proneness to victimization include: (1) women being perceived as less powerful than men; (2) economic dependency; (3) gender inequality; and (4) system inequality.

The notion of women being perceived as less powerful than men is actually based on the obvious fact that men are physically stronger than women. Therefore, women are anticipated to be more easily intimidated and more subservient (Gates, 1978). Economic dependency derives from the institution of marriage in a patriarchal society, which places women in a state of financial reliance on men (Fattah, 1991). Gender inequality is based on socially established gender roles that socialize girls for their "inferior role in the hierarchy of power and reinforces the values of a male sexist culture" (Fattah, 1991, p. 271). Finally, system inequality is described as the male-dominated criminal justice system, which perpetuates the injustices and prejudices against women (Fattah, 1991). Collectively these factors, among others, greatly contribute to women's victimization as a result of structural proneness.

Vulnerability

As previously discussed, there are subtleties that differentiate prone-ness from vulnerability; however, vulnerability is considered a dimension of proneness (Fattah, 1991). Being vulnerable may be a constant state for an individual; however, it may also be a temporary condition. For example, "ephemeral vulnerability" is considered a transient state that may last for days or months (e.g., being a college freshman), whereas "situational vulnerability" is based on an even shorter time period and may last for only a few hours (e.g., a state of intoxication) (Fattah, 1991).

Despite logical assumptions, there is not a positive linear relationship between vulnerability and victimization. Therefore, high vulnerability alone is not definitive of a high victimization risk (Fattah, 1991). As noted at the outset of the micro-level section, there is significant overlap between the personal victimization characteristics. Much like vulnerability is a dimension of proneness, other factors such as exposure, accessibility, and attractiveness, may also be considered dimensions of proneness and must be considered when determining a person's likelihood of victimization. Therefore, although an individual may be high on vulnerability, if she is low in regard to other dimensions, then victimization will be less likely.

Vulnerability was previously described as incorporating more offender characteristics and behaviors as explanatory variables, whereas victim proneness focused more on the personal and behavioral characteristics of the victim. A review of the following research will assist the reader in understanding the concept of vulnerability and its various dimensions; however, it should be noted that the distinctions between proneness and vulnerability as previously defined are not always clear.

Few studies have investigated victim selection on the basis of personal characteristics and related features; however, Stevens (1994) conducted a qualitative, grounded theory study of predatory rapists and victim selection techniques. He defined the 'predatory rapist' as an unknown male attacker who performed a sexual activity on a female without her informed or legal consent. His study consisted of sixty-one personal interviews with incarcerated predatory rapists. Although the number of admitted rapes varied by individual, it was estimated that approximately 319 rapes had been committed by the sample of men or an average of 5.2 rapes per subject. As data were collected, repetitive themes were incorporated into a "typology of target methods." The four categories that evolved were (1) easy prey (victims perceived as vulnerable); (2) attributes (victims appearance or job); (3) random/situational (no victim evaluation prior to attack); and (4) not sure.

Overall, the most common victim selection criteria noted was vulnerability. Some of the types of females perceived as most vulnerable included young girls, middle-class women, and those who worked in "helper roles" (e.g., nurses and teachers). However, it is interesting to note that some of the rapists identified very personal characteristics as clues to a female's vulnerability. For example, one rapist would go to food stores and watch for women who were "overly apologetic" if someone bumped into them. Apparently, several of the rapists indicated that those women who have been socially trained to be polite are easier prey, because they are often more submissive. Another rapist noted watching to see if the women walked on her heels rather than her toes to determine her level of physical fitness and thus her ability to put up a fight.

The theme of vulnerability, in combination with the theme of attributes, was also explored by Richards (1991) in her analysis of nonverbal communication and victim selection in sexual assaults. The basis of her analysis was a conglomeration of psychological and sociological research concerning sexual assault, self-enhancement, communication, perception, and impression formation. Essentially, when the environment is visually perceived, there is a function known as selective attention, which enables the mind to notice only particular categories of cues while disregarding others. Thibaut (as cited in Richards) stated that one "inferential set" that influences an individual's selective attention is the "value-maintenance set." From the perceiver's viewpoint the purpose of interaction under value-maintenance is to fulfill one's own personal needs. Therefore, under this set, selective attention is paid to those cues that suggest whether the actor will provide or hinder the perceiver's need for gratification.

This concept of value-maintenance is most likely to explain victim selection techniques by rapists (Richards, 1991). Accordingly, the goal of the rapist's interaction is to fulfill his personal needs and thus he is likely to focus on those cues that will suggest facilitation or complication in the execution of his crime. If perceptual cues indicate the possibility of failure in meeting his needs (e.g. difficult physical accessibility), then the rapist is less likely to victimize that individual. The goal of the rapist is to gain dominance over his victim to gratify his esteem. However, difficulty in obtaining dominance could potentially lead to a loss of esteem, and therefore, the rapist would seek to avoid such circumstances (Richards, 1991).

The concept of perceptual cues in relation to the rapist's perceptions of submissiveness versus assertiveness are also related to the manner in which women clothe and adorn themselves. Body appearance and movement symbolically convey a women's thoughts, beliefs, and ideas in terms of societal values (Richards, 1991). Richards, Rollerson, and Phillips (1991) found that men were able to distinguish between women high and low in passivity and submissiveness based largely on their clothing. Women wearing more body-concealing clothing were perceived to be more passive and submissive and represent more traditional ideas of the dependent woman.

These studies indicate not only the significance of perceived vulnerability as a primary victim selection factor but also reemphasize the interrelationship between various selection criteria. For example, Richards (1991) discussed vulnerability on the basis of perceptual cues determined by the offender; however, she also noted how physical appearance (i.e., an attractiveness feature) contributed to such perceptions. Again, although target selection factors and personal characteristics are categorized to enhance their understanding, such categorizations should not be considered absolute, and mutual influence of the factors should be considered.

Degree of Risk

One final factor related to proneness and vulnerability is the degree of risk a potential victim poses to an offender. When selecting a target, perpetrators have two primary concerns: the chances of success or failure in completing the crime and the risks and dangers of the situation. Therefore, it is seemingly natural that offenders would select those victims that would maximize the potential for criminal success and minimize the risks of failure or apprehension (Fattah, 1991). Fattah identified a number of factors that offenders may use to assess potential degree of risk, including security, surveillability, danger, and sanctions.

SECURITY. Security may involve such measures as alarm systems, security locks, or guard dogs. Although these crime preventive techniques are deterrents for some perpetrators, others offenders are not as easily dissuaded. A variety of research has been performed regarding the effects of various security measures on crimes of burglary and robbery (*see* Fattah, 1991). Although similar studies may seem irrelevant to general rape cases, it is arguable that security factors are an important consideration for particular types of rapists. For example, because the power-reassurance rapist often commits his rapes in the victims' homes, which he often accesses through means of breaking and entering, it is conceivable that factors such as alarms and watch dogs must be taken into account in the planning of the offense.

SURVEILLABILITY. Surveillability essentially refers to the level of visibility or exposure related to a potential target (i.e., the possibility of being seen by neighbors, on-lookers). This factor can be related to the notion of physical accessibility and the elements of layout and location. For example, targets that offer greater seclusion by way of bushes, fences, or distant roadways would decrease the potential level of surveillability and thus increase the potential for victimization. Again, because power serial rapists often rely on breaking and entering and voyeuristic activities in the commission of their offenses, it is likely that surveillability is a potentially key factor in their victim selection.

DANGER. In crimes involving a face-to-face confrontation between the victim and offender, there are potentially three sources of danger for the perpetrator: the victim, others, and the police (Fattah, 1991). Many of the factors that have been discussed thus far, such as manageability, proximity, and vulnerability, are all components that may contribute to an offender's assessment of dangerousness of a targeted victim. Arguably, those victims who appear less of a potential danger through lack of such factors as apparent physical strength, a weapon, or a guardian are most likely to be perceived as more attractive targets. This is relevant to the power serial rapist who may gain access to the victim's home before the assault to assess for others who may be present or any possible weapon(s) that could be at the unsuspecting victim's disposal.

SANCTIONS. Finally, sanctions against particular offenses may serve to increase perceived risk to the offender and thus make the particular crime or targeted victim less appealing.

Fattah (1991) noted that offenders, especially experienced ones, have generally accurate perceptions regarding penalties for certain offenses and for certain groups (e.g., children, elderly, and handicapped). He also postulated that if such considerations were taken into account by offenders during the planning stage, then it was plausible that "socially stigmatized" groups preferred victims because of the relative leniency that followedif the perpetrator was caught.

Although there is no recognized research that has investigated the effect of sanctions on serial rapists, it is interesting to note a comment made by an incarcerated serial rapist named Escobedo. When speaking in regard to one of his last victims, he stated, "I never saw a woman built like her. . . . She was a 'ten'. . . . She was beautiful . . . I told myself, I'll risk a life sentence for this" (Swindle, 1997).

Behavioral Characteristics of Victims

Although the preceding discussion detailed various personal characteristics of the victim, the focus will now turn to examining victims' behavioral characteristics as features of victimization. Fattah (1991) identified three basic categories of behavioral factors: (1) provocation/precipitation; (2) facilitation/participation/cooperation, and (3) temptation/initiation/instigation.

Provocation/Precipitation

The concept of precipitation as it is addressed here is the same as that which was previously discussed in the section regarding the victim-offender relationship (p. 71). As the reader may recall, the notion of the victim playing a role in the crime evolved from early victimologists, such Von Hentig, who focused on the interactional relationship between the victim and offender. However, the term victim-precipitation was not introduced until the work of Wolfgang (1958) in relation to criminal homicide and then again by Amir (1971) in cases of forcible rape. Although the introduction of the concept, especially regarding Amir's work, incited much criticism and debate, purpose of the analysis is not to justify the concept. Rather, the intent of this discussion is to consider the possible implications of such a behavioral aspect on one's risk of victimization.

PROVOCATION. Provocation and precipitation are distinct concepts that serve different purposes and follow separate criteria. The major difference between the terms provocation and precipitation is the nature of the constructs. Provocation is a legal concept that is used in criminal courts to determine criminal responsibility, the issue of guilt, and selection of the criminal sanction. The main criteria for determining provocation is "the state of mind of the accused and the offender's loss of self-control measured against the abstract concept of the *reasonable man*" (italics added) (Fattah, 1991, p. 291). Because provocation is an exculpatory concept, it implies that the individual responsible for the provocation also shares a part in the responsibility and guilt for the act (Fattah, 1991).

PRECIPITATION. The concept of victim-precipitation is a social science construct that is used to explain the etiology of victimization. The only criteria for determining victim-precipitation, regarding victimology, is the behavior of the victim and whether or not that behavior was a direct and positive precipitator of the crime (Fattah, 1991). One of the main criticisms of the term is that it implies guilt or fault on the part of the victim. However, victim-precipitation should not be interpreted as an attribution of blame. Rather the purpose of the concept is to highlight the significance of possible triggering factors and the function that these play in the cause of criminal victimization. Furthermore, it allows researchers to analyze those events or factors that culminate in a person being victimized (Fattah, 1991).

On the basis of the described elements of provocation and precipitation, it should be clear that the terms are not interchangeable. There may be situations that satisfy the criteria of one concept and not the other, or instances in which neither provocation nor precipitation are found. However, one similarity between the two concepts that is important to note is that both provocation and precipitation involve a behavioral *interaction* between the victim and offender. It is for this reason that victim-precipitation is not a relevant focus of this study, which endeavors to understand how personal and behavioral characteristics of the victim relate to *pre*offense elements (i.e., victim selection).

Facilitation/Participation/Cooperation

Unlike victim-precipitation, which emphasizes the victim offender interaction, facilitation focuses on attributes or behaviors of the victim that create special risks for victimization (Sparks, 1982). The terms "facilitation," "participation," and "cooperation," are all used to portray the same basic concept: that the victim has in some manner contributed to his/her victimization either through active, negligent, reckless, or inadvertent behavior (Fattah, 1991). Again, these terms do not imply victim blame but are instead explanatory concepts used by social scientists to show how "temptation/opportunity situations created by the victim" can possibly encourage the commission of a crime (Fattah, 1991, p. 298).

However, Fattah (1991) notes that victim behavior should only be considered a "contributory" factor in cases in which the crime is not premeditated or planned. In other words, crimes in which the offender acts spontaneously to take advantage of a situation that is either deliberately or inadvertently created by the victim. In those cases it is arguable that victimization may not have occurred were it not for the victim's behavior.

Fattah also points out how the unplanned cases must be distinguished from crimes that involve "exchangeable victims," meaning that the victim's behavior does not contribute to the commission of the crime itself but simply influences the selection of the target victim. This differentiation is relevant to understanding victim selection of the serial rapist, because the notion of selecting a target already implies offense planning. Furthermore, serial rape victims *are* exchangeable victims because the rapist intends to fulfill his needs through the commission of the rape act regardless on any one particular victim's behaviors or characteristics. For this type of offender, facilitating factors may influence the selection of one target over another but generally will not impact whether the assault eventually takes place.

Temptation/Initiation/Instigation

Temptation, initiation, and instigation are all victim behaviors that may play a role in the previctimization phase by creating motive(s) for the crime that has yet to be committed. These types of cases are more common with victims who are minors or members of another protected group (e.g., the mentally disabled) who may seek to entice others to violate the laws that are intended to protect them (Fattah, 1991). An example of this type of victim behavior would be a female minor seeking out, or initiating, a consenting sexual relationship with an adult male. Although perhaps consensual, by law this would be considered a sexual offense (i.e., statutory rape); however, it would have been the victim's initiation that caused her "victimization."

However, although temptation, initiation, and instigation may be possible factors in nonviolent and noncoercive sexual offenses, this is not the case in forcible sexual assaults (Fattah, 1991). Therefore, this victim behavior category will not apply to this inquiry, which focuses on cases of forcible rape. Although some of the presented behavioral factors do not apply to the study of victim selection in serial rape, they do provide the reader with a foundation on which to understand micro level behavioral characteristics. It is this understanding that will then allow the reader to comprehend and analyze the features of the conceptual serial rapist victim selection typology.

MACRO-LEVEL EXPLANATIONS

Macro-level theories, such as lifestyle and routine activity, are considered situational models of crime. Situational crime models are founded on the idea that criminal incidents stem "from opportunities and choices made by rational offenders" (Davis et al., 1997, p. 170). Rather than focusing solely on criminal behavior as an individual trait, crime is examined as an interaction between individuals and situations. Much like certain individuals are at a greater risk for victimization based on personal characteristics, others may be at a greater risk because of the choices they make concerning lifestyle, acquaintances, and frequented locations. Essentially, these choices result in potential victims having greater exposure to motivated offenders (Davis et al., 1997).

As implied in the preceding description, the rational-choice perspective (Cornish & Clarke, 1986) is also a situational model of crime. The reader may recall from the introduction that the rational-choice perspective forms a basis for the concept of victim selection and is a predication of this study. Although the rational-choice perspective will not be readdressed in this section, the reader is encouraged to consider its influence on the following theories in relation to victim selection.

Lifestyle Model

Hindelang, Gottfredson, and Garofalo first introduced the lifestyle model in 1978 in their book entitled *Victims of Personal Crime: An Empirical Foundation for a Theory of Personal Victimization.* The book was based on victimization surveys from numerous U.S. cities and was used to explore a variety of crime and victimization issues. However, one of the most notable aspects of the book was the chapter in which they made a "preliminary attempt to develop a theoretical model" using the concept of lifestyle to account for variations in criminal victimization (Garofalo, 1987, p. 24).

The term *lifestyle,* as originally defined, refers to routine daily activities that are either vocational (e.g., work, school, keeping house) or leisure in nature (Hindelang et al., 1978; Garofalo, 1986 & 1987). The purpose of identifying lifestyle patterns is to determine the probability of victimization through the intervening variables of association and exposure. Essentially, lifestyle patterns influence the amount of exposure to and associations with persons, places, and times that are of varying risk to criminal victimization. The basis for the model was empirical data that demonstrated that criminal victimization is *not* randomly distributed across space, time, or the population. Rather there are high-risk locations, time periods, and people (Garofalo, 1986 & 1987).

According to the original model (as diagramed in Hindelang et al., 1978, p. 243), lifestyle patterns are determined by the way in which individuals or groups adapt to role expectations and structural constraints (e.g.,economics, family, education). Although part of what determines role expectations and structural constraints are demographic characteristics (e.g., age, race), these variables are not incorporated into the actual model. However, it is the adaptation and subsequent lifestyle patterns that theoretically determine the associations and exposure that lead to potential victimization (Hindelang et al., 1978; Garofalo, 1986 & 1987).

Lifestyle Model Studies

Several studies have used lifestyle indicators to investigate victimization. For example, Smith (1982) gathered victimization data from a residential community in England and found that various lifestyle indicators (e.g., age and social class) discriminated between victims and nonvictims. However, one of the most powerful discriminating factors between the two groups was their frequency of participation in spare-time activities. In addition, further analysis indicated that the *type* of leisure activity affected victimization rates as well. Structured activities involving mostly friends and family yielded only slight differences between victims and nonvictims. However, relatively large differences were noted between victim and nonvictim groups when the leisure activities were of a less structured nature and involved greater contact with strangers.

Areal studies have also been used to examine the lifestyle model of victimization (Garofalo, 1986). These studies investigate variations in crime patterns within certain spatial areas (e.g., neighborhoods, city blocks). The basis of such studies in regard to the lifestyle model is that certain areas represent the concentration of particular lifestyles. In other words, people choose to occupy certain areas, because those areas are consistent with their lifestyle patterns (Roncek, 1981). These types of studies are also related to the routine activity and social ecology theories of victimization, both of which will be addressed later in this section. However, the brief introduction of areal and spatial research in relation to the lifestyle model should demonstrate to the reader the complex interaction of the various victimization models, both within and between the micro- and macro-level theories.

Roncek (1981) investigated city blocks in Cleveland and San Diego and found an association between crime rates and the aggregate characteristics of the city blocks. In both areas he found that crime rates (both violent and property) were positively associated with the concentration of apartment housing and the number of primary individuals. According to the U.S. Bureau of Census (as cited in Roncek, 1981), primary individuals are defined as household heads who have no relatives living in the household. Roncek's findings demonstrated that individuals who are unmarried or living alone (i.e., primary individuals) tend to concentrate in areas with other such individuals (i.e., they choose areas that fit their lifestyle). Such a concentration of primary individuals minimizes recognition and interaction between neighbors and also results in residencies that are often left unattended, thus increasing chances for criminal victimization (Cohen & Felson, 1979; Roncek, 1981; Garofalo, 1986).

Lifestyle Model and Victim Selection

For purposes of this study, the lifestyle model may be able to provide valuable insight into serial rape victim selection. First, it is possible that serial rape victims share certain lifestyle patterns that make them more susceptible to victimization based on serial rapist victim selection factors. The reader may recall from Hazelwood and Burgess (1989b) that serial rapists reported selecting their victims for their availability and location more than any other reason. Thus, victim lifestyle patterns may be important determinants of availability (e.g., nights out per week or time home alone) or location (e.g., residential area of predominantly primary individual households). Therefore in cases of serial rape, lifestyle patterns may increase a women's risk of victimization by facilitating increased *exposure* to high-risk locations or situations in which the woman is perceived as available (e.g., lack of guardianship).

However, it is also possible that certain lifestyle patterns simply increase women's *association* with potential serial rapists. For example, Hazelwood and Warren (1989a) reported that eighty-five percent of the serial rapists they interviewed were white and between the ages of 21 and 29 years at the time of their rapes. Interestingly enough, most victims were also white and were within a similar age range as the rapists (Hazelwood & Warren, 1989b). In addition, more than half of the serial rapists interviewed reported generally stable employment, at least a high school education, and were of average or above average socioeconomic status (Hazelwood & Warren, 1989a & 1989b). They were also described by study interviewers as well-groomed and articulate individuals who had little difficulty becoming acquainted with people (Hazelwood & Warren, 1989a).

Therefore, it is possible that victims and offenders come into contact, because they share certain characteristics which would influence their lifestyle patterns. In other words, serial rapists may share particular lifestyle patterns with the victims they select (e.g., work, leisure activities, residential area). Thus lifestyle patterns may also increase the risk of serial rape by increasing the *association* factor between serial rapists and potential victims.

A Modified Lifestyle Model

Despite research findings that have proven consistent with the lifestyle model, there have been those who have criticized the usefulness and underlying premises of the model. Although these criticisms are important to the conceptualization of this model, they will not be addressed at this point. Instead, there will be a subsequent section in which each of the presented victimization models will be reexamined and critiqued. However, based on various criticisms and noted limitations, Garofalo (1986 & 1987) modified the original lifestyle model to "provide a more thorough understanding of the risk of victimization" (1987, p. 36).

Garofalo qualified the presentation of his model with three main points. First, the model applies only to "direct-contact predatory violations" as defined by Cohen and Felson (1979). These violations involve "direct physical contact between at least one offender and at least one person or object which that offender attempts to take or damage" (p. 589). This use of *direct-contact predatory violations* allows the modified model to apply to more crime types than the original model, which was based solely on "personal crimes" (Garofalo, 1986, p. 149). Second, the workings of the model may vary depending on the nature of different crime types (e.g., burglary vs. robbery). Third, the model assumes that there are given levels of offender motivation and state protection against crime. These factors produce a certain crime potential, whereas variations in the lifestyle model components allow for the crime potential to be realized to a greater or lesser extent (Garofalo, 1986).

For purposes of the modified lifestyle model, Garofalo (1986 & 1987) maintained the basic principle of the original model. Lifestyles were still perceived as adaptations to role expectations and structural constraints which in turn affected victimization through the variables of association and exposure. However, one modification was that in addition to affecting exposure through lifestyle, structural constraints were also shown as having a direct effect on exposure. Structural constraints, such as the economic system and the housing market, can affect a persons exposure level regardless of their lifestyle choices. For example, an individual who is economically advantaged may be able to select a neighborhood that fits his or her lifestyle. However, someone who is economically disadvantaged may have little or no choice as to the neighborhood or type of housing in which she or he resides. Therefore, based on such structural constraints, the "base level" of risk of victimization is increased for these individuals (Garofalo, 1986, p. 149).

A second modification was the inclusion of a "reaction to crime" factor, which can potentially affect exposure and/or association direct-ly or through lifestyle. Reaction to crime includes behavior modifica-tion based on people's perception of crime (e.g., fear, evaluation of risk), which may evolve from media sources or first-hand experience. Reactions to crime may account for minor behavioral changes (e.g., avoiding dimly lit areas or buying new locks) or may involve signifi-cant lifestyle changes (e.g., moving to the suburbs). These more sub-stantial changes affect association and exposure by way of a new basic lifestyle.

Finally, Garofalo added two additional elements that are unrelated to lifestyle yet have direct effects on potential victimization: target attrac-tiveness and personal idiosyncracies. The concept of target attractive-ness was discussed in the micro-level section and included elements such as accessibility and manageability and could potentially be linked with several other micro-level components. However, for purposes of his model, Garofalo did not wish to include any elements of guardian-ship or proximity within his target attractiveness factor , because he con-sidered those variables to be components of exposure. Rather Garofalo described target attractiveness as "symbolic" or "instrumental" consid-erations that are subjective to the offender and through which he deter-mines a potential victim's "worth" (1986, p. 150). In addition, the per-sonal idiosyncracies factor refers to those variations in risk of victimiza-tion that cannot be accounted for by sociological explanations, includ-ing psychological and biological variables. However, because Garofalo was more focused on incorporating his *reactions to crime* factor, less of an attempt was made to interrelate target attractiveness or personal idio-syncracies with the other factors.

Routine Activities Approach

Routine Activities Approach vs. the Lifestyle Model

During the development of the lifestyle model, Cohen and Felson (1979) were formulating a similar crime rate model known as the "rou-tine activity approach" (p. 588). Much like the lifestyle model, the rou-tine activity approach uses a situational approach in analyzing crime rate trends rather than focusing on offender characteristics. The two models are very similar in substance; however, the apparent differences relate to how the models were explained by their authors. Cohen and

Felson created the routine activity approach to link changes in behavior patterns of the aggregate population to changes in crime rates for both personal and property crimes. However, Hindelang et al. (1978) created the lifestyle model to relate differences in lifestyles of segments of the population to differences in victimization at one point in time.

Elements of the Routine Activities Approach

Routine activities, as originally defined, include "any recurrent and prevalent activities which provide for basic population and individual needs, whatever their biological or cultural origins . . . so long as their prevalence and recurrence makes them a part of everyday life" (e.g., provision of food, shelter, sex, leisure) (Cohen & Felson, 1979, p. 593). Essentially, the approach treats criminal violations as routine activities themselves, which are interdependent on other types of nonillegal routine activities (Cohen & Felson, 1979). The model was created to apply only to *direct contact predatory violations* (as previously defined in the lifestyle model section). For these predatory violations to occur, three minimal elements must converge in time and space: (1) a motivated offender, (2) a suitable target, and (3) the absence of a capable guardian to protect against victimization. The absence of any one of these elements may be sufficient to prevent a predatory violation. However, the basis of the approach is that changes in routine activity patterns affect the convergence of these predatory crime elements in both time and space, thereby, influencing crime rate patterns. Changes in routine activities can also help account for increases in crime rates even when structural conditions normally associated with crime (e.g., unemployment) or the proportion of offenders remains stable or improves.

Theoretical Framework of the Routine Activity Approach

A noted advantage of the routine activity approach is that it helped to integrate previously unconnected criminological theories (Cohen & Felson, 1979). The theoretical framework of the approach consists mainly of micro and macro-level analyses and human ecology. Cohen and Felson stated that "the veracity of the routine activity approach can be assessed by analyses of both micro-level and macro-level interdependencies of human activity" (p. 594). Changes in society's routine activity structure can occur at the micro-level (e.g., increased activity outside of the home) or the macro-level (e.g., technological advances) to heighten the chances of predatory violation through an increase in the convergence of the crime elements (Cohen & Felson, 1979).

As the reader may recall, Cohen and Felson considered criminal acts routine activities that shared attributes of nonillegal activities. It was this interdependence between "the structure of illegal activities and the organization of everyday sustenance" that lead them to consider human ecology (Cohen & Felson, 1979, p. 589). Human ecology can be described as the study of the spatial *and* temporal structure of human activities within a given community (Cohen & Felson, 1979). Although most sociological research of crime had focused mainly on the spatial analyses of illegal activities, Hawley's (1950) classic theory of human ecology also incorporated temporal elements of human activities. Examples of such elements include *rhythm* (i.e., the regular periodicity with which events occur) and *tempo* (i.e., the number of events per unit of time) (Hawley, 1950, p. 289). With the routine activity approach Cohen and Felson hoped to develop an extension of human ecology to explain the change in crime rates over time. Furthermore, they wanted to examine how the spatiotemporal organization of social activities fostered opportunities for individuals to act on their criminal inclinations.

Micro-level Routine Activity Studies

According to the routine activities approach, micro-level analyses may occur (1) at home, (2) at jobs away from home, or (3) at other activities away from home. Although the first category may involve mostly household members, the latter categories are considered to increase contact with nonhousehold members (Cohen and Felson, 1979). It was the contention of Cohen and Felson that, since World War II, American households experienced a significant shift from household routine activities to nonhousehold activities (e.g., jobs and social activities outside of the home), particularly those involving association with nonhousehold members. They considered these changes at the micro-level to have contributed to increased crime rates over several decades (1940's–1970's) despite improved social conditions that would have seemingly indicated a potential decrease in crime.

In testing their routine activity approach, Cohen and Felson (1979) analyzed crime rate trends from 1947–1974 and found a significant positive relationship between their household activity ratio (i.e., dispersion of activities away from home) and crime rates. In other words, as activities increasingly took place outside of the home, crime rates also increased. (To understand the formulation of the household activity ratio, the reader is encouraged to see Cohen and Felson, 1979, p. 600.). In addition, they examined family structure and crime rates in relation to the routine activity approach. In general, the findings showed that single adult households in which the individual worked outside of the home were at a greater risk of predatory violation than larger family households or households in which someone worked within the home, (Cohen & Felson, 1979).

Two notable exceptions were that individuals who were unable to work or who were unemployed had greater victimization rates than other "inactive" individuals (e.g., those keeping house, retired). However, these exceptions were still seen as consistent with the routine activity approach. For example, individuals who are unemployed are also more likely to live in lower income residential areas which places them in greater proximity to potential offenders. Therefore, the risk of victimization is heightened because of the potential increase in the concentration of unguarded targets and motivated offenders, both spatially and temporally (Cohen & Felson, 1979, p. 596).

Kennedy and Forde (1990) stated that micro-level studies had not yielded consistent predictive results based on the routine activity approach. An example of one such study is that of Miethe, Stafford, and Long (1987). Miethe et al. examined U.S. National Crime Survey data to investigate the relationship between crime and both day and nighttime activities in and away from the home. According to the study findings, there was a strong interaction effect between demographic characteristics and routine activities for victims of property crime. In other words, although demographic variables had significant effects on the risk of victimization, the prediction of victimization was substantially improved when the routine activities variables were included.

Yet these same results were not found for victims of personal crime. The inclusion of the activity variables did not change the effects of the demographic variables on personal crime victimization. In fact, the odds of violent victimization remained fairly stable whether the activities variables were included or not. Miethe et al. had concluded that because violent crime is more often spontaneous in nature, it defies the assumptions of the routine activity approach, thus making the approach less predictive of violent crimes. However, Kennedy and Forde (1990) performed their own study examining the relationship between demographic variables and both day and nighttime activities outside of the home using data from the Canadian Urban Victimization Study. Instead of having a general measure of nighttime activity, they used several specific measures (e.g., times per month spent at sporting events, bars, movies) to determine any differential crime effects between the activities. Kennedy and Forde's findings were quite different from those of Miethe et al. and were more consistent with the routine activities model. Although the demographic variables alone (e.g., sex, age, marital status) were significant predictors of personal victimization, the addition of the routine activities variables improved the fit to the data. It was found that young, unmarried, men who spent time outside of the home at bars, the movies, working, or walking/driving around were the most vulnerable to violent crimes such as assault and robbery.

In a more recent study, Felson (1997) used the routine activity approach to investigate the effects of an active "nightlife," or nighttime recreational activities, on the involvement in interpersonal violence either as an actor, witness, or target. A representative sample of 245 persons between the ages of eighteen and sixty-five years was collected, with an equal number of men and female respondents. According to the study results, there was a clear relationship between an active nightlife and interpersonal violence factors for men. Those men who went out at night were more likely to witness, experience, or engage in violence with someone outside of their family. However, this same effect was not found for the women. Felson (1997) postulated that this gender difference may be because women primarily experience violence *within* the family (i.e., domestic violence). Yet, it is interesting to note that those men who did report an active nightlife (i.e., greater likelihood of interpersonal violence) were no more likely to engage in domestic violence in their homes.

Felson believed that this strengthened the study's reliance on the routine activity approach. If those men who were involved in or witnessing the interpersonal violence during their nights out were more violent by nature of their character, it would then be expected that they would also demonstrate more violence within the home.

However, because the relationship between nightlife and domestic violence was insignificant (and in fact negative), these findings indicated that the relationship between the nights out and interpersonal violence were more consistent with the routine activities approach versus personality characteristics (Felson, 1997).

Macro-level Routine Activity Studies

According to Kennedy and Forde (1990), most of the research related to the routine activity approach had incorporated macro-level analyses (e.g., urban structure, community size, and density), which yielded good predictive capability for crime patterns in urban environments. In a study examining the link between micro- and macro-level factors of criminal victimization, Sampson and Wooldredge (1987) used data from the British Crime Survey to examine the differences in victimization associated with demographics, routine activities/lifestyle, and community structure. Their overall findings indicated that demographic characteristics *and* structural variables had the largest impact on victimization. Furthermore, routine activity variables that were not related to these characteristics were less important in predicting victimization (Sampson & Wooldredge, 1987).

In their analysis of the routine activities approach, Kennedy and Forde (1990) also investigated the effects of urban structure on personal and property victimization by including the use of *group level* variables (e.g., unemployment, percentage of single person households). The study results were consistent with those of Sampson and Wooldredge (1987) and indicated that urban structure had a significant impact on both property and personal crime. Nevertheless, demographic variables seemed to be the most important predictors for most forms of victimization. Because of the effects of both demographic and structural variables, Kennedy and Forde (1990) noted the importance of incorporating both micro- and macro-level variables into the development of the routine activity approach.

Although the macro-level studies related to the routine activity approach are of equal importance as are the micro-level studies, there will be no further review of the macro-level research at this point. Because many of the macro-level factors (e.g., neighborhood structure, community density) will be discussed in detail under *social ecology*, it would be repetitious to discuss such studies at length in both sections.

Routine Activities and Victim Selection

Miethe et al. (1987) suggested that violent crime was spontaneous and, therefore, defied the assumptions of the routine activity approach. However, the current study of victim selection assumes that not all violent crimes are in fact spontaneous, an assumption based on the previously discussed rational-choice perspective of offending. For example, cases of anger rape are generally unplanned and impulsive acts of violence that would seem to follow the assumption put forth by Miethe and colleagues (1987). In contrast, cases of power rape seem to indicate a higher level of planning. This is evidenced by serial rape research data regarding preoffense behaviors that are consistent with the power rapist (e.g., voyeurism or breaking and entering a victim's residence prior to the attack).

According to Felson (1986), "routine activity patterns provide choices to individuals, including criminals, and set the stage for subsequent events. . ." (p. 120). Therefore, based on this rational-choice perspective, the analysis of routine activities may offer useful information for understanding victim selection techniques of the power serial rapist. A premise of the routine activity approach is that increased activity outside of the home heightens an individual's risk of criminal victimization. However, this assumption may not be consistent with both types of power rape.

The reader may recall that power rapists use both the "con" and "surprise" techniques (as described by Hazelwood, 1995) in approaching their victims. The power-assertive rapist is commonly associated with the "con" approach, in which the offender openly interacts with the victim and then suddenly becomes aggressive once she is under his control. This type of approach is typical in settings such as bars or public streets in which the offender can easily approach a potential victim. With this style of attack, routine activities may be extremely useful in predicting victimization. For example, women who spend more time alone outside of the home (i.e., shopping) or who frequently take part in nightlife activities (i.e., bars or nightclubs) may be at a greater risk of victimization by this type of offender.

However, the power-reassurance rapist tends to use the "surprise" approach in which he commonly enters the victim's home while she is sleeping. This is significant because according to study findings by Hazelwood & Warren (1989b), fifty percent of serial rapes took place in the victim's home. Therefore, this style of attack does not support the basic premise of the routine activities approach, because the amount of time the victim spends outside of the home would potentially *decrease* her risk of victimization by the power-reassurance rapist. The exception would be instances in which a woman comes in contact with a would-be perpetrator while engaged in activities outside of the home and, on interacting with him, becomes a potential target for him to seek out later. For instance, Gilbert Escobedo, a convicted power serial rapist who worked for some time as a cashier, would look at the address on potential victim's checks so that he could perpetrate the rape in the victim's home at a later time or date (Swindle, 1996). Hence, although the routine activities approach may be useful in understanding power rape victimization, the type of rapist must be considered when attempting to identify those routine activity variables that would best predict possible rape victimization.

Opportunity Theory

Several years after the emergence of both the lifestyle model and the routine activity approach, Cohen, Kluegel, & Land (1981) integrated both approaches into a newly proposed opportunity theory. The theory was based on the *opportunity model of predatory victimization* perspective which underlies the lifestyle model and the routine activity approach. The opportunity theory was based on the premise that criminal victimization was highly dependent on both "the lifestyle and routine activities of persons that bring them and/or their property into direct contact with potential offenders in the absence of capable guardians" (Cohen, Kluegel, & Land, 1981, p. 507). In addition, the model considered the time and space relationships in which the potential for victimization was the highest. However, opportunity theory sought to explain variations in the risk of predatory victimization among certain dimensions of social stratification, including age, race, and income. To understand the relationship between age, race, and income on the likelihood of victimization, Cohen and colleagues (1981) also focused on what they considered to be five mediating risk factors: (1) exposure, (2) guardianship, (3) proximity to potential offenders, (4) attractiveness of potential targets, and (5) definitional properties of specific crimes.

Definitions and Assumptions of the Five Factors

According to Cohen and colleagues (1981), the five mediating risk factors were defined in the following manner and incorporated the following assumptions:

1. *Exposure* is the physical visibility and accessibility of a target person or object to a potential offender at any given time or place. The assumption of the exposure factor is that with all else being equal, increased exposure leads to an increased risk of victimization.

2. *Proximity* is the physical distance between areas in which potential targets reside and those areas with a relatively high proportion of potential offenders. The assumption of proximity is that with all else being equal, the closer the residential proximity of potential targets to high concentrations of potential offenders, the greater the risk of victimization.

3. *Guardianship* is the effectiveness of persons (e.g., neighbors, security personnel) or objects (e.g., alarms, locks) in preventing victimization either through mere presence or by direct or indirect action. The assumption underlying the guardianship factor is that with all else being equal, offenders prefer those targets that are less well guarded. Hence, the greater the guardianship, the lower the risk of victimization.

4. *Target attractiveness* refers to the desirability, either symbolic or material, of persons or property, as well as the perceived ability of the target to resist the illegal act (e.g., ability of a victim to resist an attack or the inability to remove property due to weight, size). Target attractiveness also differentiates between illegal acts in which the motivation is instrumental (i.e., the illegal act is performed to acquire something else which is desired) or expressive (i.e., the illegal act is performed simply for the reward of performing the act itself). The assumption of the attractiveness feature is that with all else being equal, if the motivation for the criminal act is primarily instrumental, those targets of greater attractiveness will be at a greater risk for victimization.

5. *Definitional properties of specific crimes* refers to features of specific offenses that constrain strictly instrumental acts by potential offenders. Cohen et al. (1981) used the crime of burglary as an example for definitional properties of a specific crime. Burglary is a more difficult crime to commit and requires more knowledge of victim routine activities than the crime of larceny. Therefore, these constraints related to burglary limit the ability of an offender to consistently select targets that would increase their economic gain and, thus, requires them to often select less attractive targets. The assumption of this factor is that the effects of exposure, guardianship, and proximity are largely dependent on the degree of constraint a crime has on strictly instrumental acts. Therefore, the greater the degree of constraint, the stronger the effects of exposure, guardianship, and proximity, relative to the effects of attractiveness. However, Cohen et al. (1981) noted that this assumption underlying the *properties of crime* factor did not apply to the crime of assault. It was their contention that assault tends to be a crime largely motivated by expressive, rather than instrumental, means. Nevertheless, for purposes of this discussion, the assumption underlying the *properties of crime* factor will be considered in regard to assault, specifically attacks of the power serial rapist.

Inclusion of Power Rape as an Instrumental Action

On the basis of the literature, power rape can be considered an act that is the result of instrumental motives. The assault itself is not the motivating factor for the power rapist, instead the assault serves as a means by which to attain something of greater desire. For the power-reassurance rapist, his assault is an attempt to overcome doubts regarding his virility and adequacy. Therefore, by controlling his victim to the point that she cannot reject him, he is able to bolster his sense of self-worth (Groth et al., 1977). For the power-assertive rapist, the rape represents a sense of entitlement regarding women, and the assault is viewed as an expression of masculinity and dominance. However, regardless of his seeming confidence, his rapes are actually an indication of feelings of inadequacy (Groth et al., 1977). Therefore, in both cases of power rape the assault is not performed simply for the satisfaction of assaulting the victim, as would be the case in assaults with expressive motivation. The assault of the power rapist actually serves as a means by which to gain control, increase self-worth, overcome feelings of inadequacy, and so on.

In addition to motivation, the terms instrumental and expressive can also refer to types of aggression. The reader may recall that Prentky et al. (1985) defined these types of aggression in cases of sexual assault. Instrumental aggression was defined as a degree of force that does not exceed that which is needed to gain the victim's compliance, whereas expressive aggression is more uncontrolled and may appear seemingly frenzied. On the basis of these descriptions, the power rapist would most often be associated with instrumental aggression, because the level of aggression rarely exceeds that which is necessary to overcome the victim. In contrast, the anger rapist would be associated with expressive aggression since the amount of force used is often excessive, brutal, and may even lead to the unintentional death of the victim. In summary, with power rape considered an instrumental act, the effects of exposure, guardianship, and proximity will be considered in relation to target attractiveness based on the assumption set forth in the *properties of crime* factor.

Opportunity Theory Studies

In testing opportunity theory, Cohen et al. (1981) developed nine propositions pertaining to the distribution of various types of victimization across age, race, and income. The propositions included both *bivariate* (two-way) and *multivariate or partial* (three way) interactions. For example, proposition 1 advanced that the bivariate distribution of assault would be negative by income. In other words, as income increased the risk of assault would decrease. However, proposition 9 asserted that, with all other factors held constant, race and age would not have a direct effect on burglary or larceny victimization (Cohen et al., 1981). These propositions were based not only on the definitions and assumptions of the five risk factors, but also on existing principles regarding the links between victimization and social inequality. These principles included that of *homogamy* (i.e., degree to which potential victims and offenders share similar characteristics), *dependence of guardianship, and residential segregation.* (Although a thorough overview of the propositions and principles is beyond the scope of this discussion, the reader is encouraged to see Cohen et al., 1981, pp. 509–513).

The study sample consisted of victimization data obtained from the National Crime Survey from 1974–1977. The three types of crimes investigated were burglary, assault, and personal larceny. The types of victim information recorded included demographic characteristics (i.e., age, race, and income) and index measures of risk factors (i.e., exposure, guardianship, and proximity). The factors of exposure and guardianship were indexed by a proxy measure, referred to as *lifestyle*, which incorporated information regarding household composition and labor force involvement. The proximity variable was measured using neighborhood median income and geographic features of the residential areas.

The overall research findings indicated that the relationship between the variables of income, race, and age, and the risk of predatory victimization was much more complex than many criminologists had presumed (Cohen et al., 1981). The results were quite detailed because of the bivariate and multivariate interactions of the various social and risk factor variables. However, the findings provided empirical evidence for all five risk factor assumptions and strongly supported propositions 1–6, with mixed results for propositions 7–9. Some of the more noted bivariate findings concluded that age and lifestyle have the most consistent effects on victimization for all three crimes investigated, whereas race has little direct effect. Although income shows a direct effect for all three crimes, the effect is stronger for larceny than for either assault or burglary. Finally, the effect of proximity is less than each of the effects for lifestyle, income, or age.

The results of the three-way interactions show that the effect of age is conditioned by both lifestyle and income. For example, age is a stronger predictor of victimization for those who are unmarried *and* either employed or out of the work force. In addition, the effect of age on victimization differs by income, with the stronger effects observed among the poor for each of the three types of crime. Finally, the effect of age is also conditional on race for the crimes of larceny and assault, with the risk of victimization decreasing faster by age for whites than nonwhites. Although the results provided are not an exhaustive account of Cohen et al.'s (1981) findings, they provide a brief overview of the type of information the study provided. In conclusion, Cohen et al. noted that their efforts were "encouraging and indicate that we are moving in the proper direction in our effort to predict criminal victimization patterns in the United States" (p. 523).

Sampson (1987) not only tested the opportunity model of criminal victimization but also attempted to extend the model to crimes of personal violence by strangers. Sampson contended that previous personal victimization research had neglected crimes perpetrated by strangers and, for the most part, had merely lumped together both stranger and nonstranger offenses. Furthermore, those studies that did differentiate between stranger versus nonstranger crimes typically focused only on individual (or micro-level) factors and ignored the larger community context (Sampson, 1987).

Research aimed specifically at understanding stranger assaults has important implications for the opportunity model, as well as the routine activity and lifestyle theories. Sampson (1987) noted that constructs used in such theories (e.g., routine activities, target attractiveness, guardianship, and lifestyle) specify certain hypotheses regarding victimization by strangers. For example, according to the various theories, an increase in activities outside of the home would decrease potential guardianship, increase potential contact with strangers, and therefore, increase the risk of stranger victimization. However, Sampson noted that most empirical tests of the various theories failed to differentiate between stranger and nonstranger crimes. Sampson's study is not only pertinent to the current discussion of the opportunity model but is also significant to the present victim selection study, which is focused specifically on serial rape victimization perpetrated by strangers.

The study data were collected from the 1982 British Crime Survey (BCS). The use of the BCS was very advantageous to the study because: (1) the survey was stratified resulting in an oversampling of inner-city respondents, which is relevant because urbanization is a strong predictor of victimization, (2) the BCS included a great deal of personal and lifestyle information, and (3) the survey incorporated geographical information for each household sampled, which allowed for the inclusion of neighborhood context as a victimization variable.

The study analyzed individual-level social and demographic characteristics, lifestyle, community context, and urbanization factors. The social/demographic characteristics included age, sex, marital status, and education. The lifestyle variable was measured by the number of nights per week the respondent spent outside of their home. Community context consisted of four separate measures, including guardianship (percentage of primary or single adult households), mobility (percentage of persons residing at their residence for less than one year), family (percentage of female households with children); and racial heterogeneity (distribution of whites versus non-whites). Finally, urbanization was ascertained through the determination of inner-city residency *and* housing density (i.e., percentage of apartments).

In general, the study results showed that age, gender, and marital status all had direct effects on the risk of stranger violence, with age being the strongest determinant of victimization. Furthermore, it was also found that the risk of stranger violence increased with the number of nights spent outside of the home as determined by the lifestyle variable. Overall, younger persons, men, single individuals (including those divorced and separated), and those with more nights out per week were at a higher risk for violent victimization by a stranger. In regard to the community context variables, the findings indicated that those areas characterized by primary households, residential mobility, and family disruption were at a greater risk for stranger violence. Interestingly, however, once community context and demographic variables were controlled, the lifestyle factor no longer showed an effect on stranger violence (Sampson, 1987).

Because of the extensive nature of Sampson's (1987) study findings, only the initial results related to stranger violence were presented earlier. Nevertheless, these initial results were described as generally consistent with the opportunity model (Sampson, 1987). Despite the usefulness of demographic and lifestyle/routine activity variables (all of which are components of the opportunity model) in predicting victimization, Sampson emphasized the need to incorporate more measures of community context into future predictive models. Furthermore, he encouraged future crime rate and victimization studies to make attempts to differentiate between stranger versus nonstranger crimes.

Opportunity Theory and Victim Selection

Throughout the previous sections attempts have been made to relate specific models to the concept of victim selection with the power serial rapist. However, because opportunity theory includes several elements of the previously discussed models (e.g., guardianship, proximity, target attractiveness), commentary regarding victim selection based on those same elements would be fairly repetitious. Nevertheless, a unique feature of opportunity theory that should be recognized in relation to victim selection is the concept of *definitional properties of specific crimes*. This factor is relevant, because it attempts to identify elements of specific instrumental acts that will constrain the effects of exposure, guardianship, and proximity in relation to target attractiveness.

Although Cohen et al. (1981) did not apply this factor to crimes of assault, arguments were made based on the serial rape literature as to why the crime of power rape should be considered an instrumental act for purposes of the present study. Essentially, the underlying motives for the crime of power rape are for the offender to increase his feelings of self-worth and adequacy; a motive that can be considered instrumental in nature. Therefore, on the basis of such motives the power rapist would most likely avoid those situations that would risk his feelings of self-worth, such as situations in which he could not maintain control of a victim or incidents, which would place him at an increased risk for apprehension.

For example, a power rapist may identify a victim who is easily visible *(exposure)*, physically appealing and small in body size, which allows for easy physical control *(target attractiveness)*, and who has few evening activities outside of the home *(routine activities)*. With all of these factors, the potential victim may seem to be an attractive target. However, the presence of security personnel, security cameras, alarms, and motion lights *(guardianship)* may limit the ease of accessibility and increase the risk of apprehension. Because of constraints related to the act of power rape (e.g., the need to enter the victim's home), the effect of the guardianship factor would be quite strong. Therefore, although the target may be very attractive in some aspects, certain constraints related specifically to the crime of power rape may limit the rapist's ability to act on such a target.

The Social Ecology of Crime

Sampson (1987) noted that "students of criminal victimization place too much emphasis on lifestyle in explaining victimization risk. . . . Too little time has been spent examining how criminal opportunity structures are rooted in ecological and community context" (p. 355). Therefore, the final portion of the macro-level section will focus on the risk of victimization related to social ecological factors. The social ecology literature incorporates a broad array of studies and research areas that, although founded upon the same notion, results in an expansive amount of material. According to Georges-Abeyie and Harries (1980) in writing about the social ecological approach, ". . . its legacy has not only remained but grown and can be directly credited with the birth of numerous theoretical and research orientations. . ." (p. 1).

Because of the expansive nature of the topic it is difficult to pinpoint a solid definition for the social ecological approach. Unlike the previous macro-level theories for which the original formulations could be traced, the concept of social ecology has developed over the decades with contributions from numerous researchers. Nevertheless, in an attempt to simplify the topic for purposes of this discussion, the notion of social ecology will be described here as the study of crime within specific spatial areas and social structures (*see* Byrne & Sampson, 1986).

The Shaw and McKay Tradition

The social ecology of crime can be traced back as far as nineteenth century Europe to the works of Quetelet and Guerry in France, and Rawson and Mayhew in England (Dunn, 1980; Georges-Abeyie & Harries, 1980). However, the contemporary theory is founded on the work of Shaw and McKay conducted at the University of Chicago during the 1920's and 1930's (Dunn, 1980; Byrne & Sampson, 1986). In 1929, Shaw introduced his book *Delinquency Areas* and was noted as one of the first American sociological researchers to evidence the considerable variations of delinquency rates within a major city (Shaw, 1929). Specifically he noted that delinquency rates decreased as distance from the center of the city increased (Dunn, 1980; Byrne & Sampson, 1986). A few years later Shaw and McKay (1931) demonstrated that the highest rates of delinquency in Chicago were found in areas characterized by deterioration and industrialization. These areas were specifically noted for their low economic status, heterogeneity, and mobility. Overall, they concluded that delinquency was related to the growth processes of the city (Byrne & Sampson, 1986).

Subsequently, Shaw and McKay (1942) investigated the relationship between neighborhood social systems and city growth processes. Specifically, they sought to account for persistently high rates of delinquency in certain areas over many years, aside from usual population turnover. Shaw and McKay argued that delinquent and criminal patterns that persisted in certain areas were due to the *social* transmission of delinquent subcultures that arose because of social disorganization (Byrne & Sampson, 1986). It was this argument that led the way for research investigating the social structure of particular areas, otherwise known as social area analysis. The concept of social area analysis played a prominent role in changing the focus of social ecology. It emphasized the notion that social structure can affect criminal behavior in ways that transcended mere geographical and spatial analyses (1986).

Neighborhood and City-level Research

Because of the extensive nature of the Shaw and McKay framework of social ecology, a thorough review of their work is beyond the scope of this study. However, it is important to note that the work of Shaw and McKay provided a basis for the outgrowth of numerous related studies. For example, Byrne and Sampson (1986) noted that many of the ecological studies that followed the work of Shaw and McKay focused on the variable of economic status as a determinant of variations in delinquency rates. In addition to economic status, neighborhood-level research demonstrated a positive relationship between delinquency and various community factors, including percentage of nonwhite residents, proportion of young men, crowded housing, structural density, and mobility (1986).

City-level research, which utilizes a broader unit of analysis, has also documented a link between delinquency and physical characteristics and/or aggregate characteristics of resident populations. Examples of physical characteristics include density, city size, overcrowding, and division of labor. Aggregate characteristics refer to such factors as ethnicity, age, occupation, and family composition. Nevertheless, assessment of the degree of the relationship between delinquency and the preceding factors has been difficult with much of the city-level research. This has been due to variations between studies along such dimensions as different data sources (i.e., Uniform Crime Report victimization surveys), sample sizes, units of analysis (i.e., city urbanized area), and so on (Byrne & Sampson, 1986). Therefore, these variations have made it difficult to generalize the results of city-level research.

Social Ecological Studies

As previously noted, decades of social ecological research have been spent analyzing various social and structural factors at both the neighborhood and city level. For example, Sampson (1985) investigated the effects of various neighborhood characteristics on the rates of personal crime, including rape, robbery, larceny, and assault. The specific factors examined included unemployment, income inequality, racial composition, structural density, family structure, and residential mobility. The study was based on data from the National Crime Survey between the years 1973 and 1975 and resulted in a sample of approximately 400,000 residents.

The study factors were operationally defined (e.g., racial composition was defined as the percentage of African-Americans in the neighborhood) and then trichotomized into categories of low, medium, or high. The overall study results showed that the social integration factors (family structure and mobility) and the opportunity factor (structural density) had the strongest effects on personal victimizations. Specifically, female-headed households and density demonstrated the strongest effects for theft, whereas mobility had the strongest effect on the violent crimes. Although both racial composition and income inequality were also statistically significant, these effects were decreased when the social integration and opportunity factors were held constant.

Crutchfield, Geerken, and Gove (1982) also investigated the effect of mobility on both property and violent crimes. The basis of their research was that areas with high rates of mobility result in weak social integration (i.e., less informal social control), thus increasing the potential for crime. Their study sample consisted of sixty-five Standard Metropolitan Statistical Areas (SMSAs) from the 1970 census. Crime rates and other variable information for those areas were gathered using the Uniform Crime Reports (UCR) and reports from the U.S. Bureau of the Census.

According to their results, Crutchfield et al. found that lack of social integration (i.e., high mobility) was a greater predictor for some crimes than other factors that they had associated with opportunity structure (e.g., poverty, race, age, etc.). Although the lack of social integration was a notably poor predictor for such crimes as murder and assault, it was a moderately strong predictor for rape and burglary. This pattern was explained as a result of the greater rationality often associated with some violent crimes (e.g., rape), which is not found in other types of violent offenses (e.g., homicide or aggravated assault) (Crutchfield et al., 1982).

Roncek (1981) also conducted neighborhood-level research investigating how the characteristics of residents and housing environments of various city blocks affected the occurrence of crime. Specifically, he hoped to identify those conditions most associated with criminal incidents. The units of analysis were city blocks in Cleveland, Ohio, and San Diego, California, during the year 1970. City blocks were selected as the unit of analysis, because "blocks are relatively homogeneous socioeconomically and in housing conditions" (Roncek, 1981, p. 79). Furthermore, Taeuber and Taeuber (as cited by Roncek) noted that city blocks were the smallest identifiable areas for which reliable data could be recorded.

The study was designed to test three major hypotheses: (1) the higher the concentration of primary individuals in an area, the greater the occurrence of crime; (2) the size of the resident population, the concentration of the surrounding population, and the types of housing will all affect the frequency of crime; and (3) crimes rates will be highest in those areas in which the characteristics of the residents and the environment heighten the opportunities for crime (Roncek, 1981). The study investigated both property crimes (i.e., burglary, grand theft, and auto theft) and violent crimes (i.e., murder, rape, assault, and robbery).

The study results indicated that for both property and violent crime, the concentration of primary individuals *(hypothesis 1)*, the block population, and the concentration of apartment housing *(hypothesis 2)* all had strong effects on the occurrence of crime. However, it did seem as though environmental effects were more important determinants of property crime than violent crime. Roncek explained this difference by noting the importance of interpersonal relationships in many violent offenses. Because most rapes, murders, and assaults occur among individuals who know one another, environmental factors tend to have less influence on these types of crime.

Roncek noted that his study findings were consistent with the association between residential areas and anonymity in explaining high-crime rate neighborhoods. All of the study variables that were found to have strong effects were also related to the amount and type of contact in the residential area. Much like the concepts explained in the lifestyle and routine activities models, areas which are high density and/or have a high percentage of primary individuals often offer less guardianship. Hence, with less guardianship, there is greater anonymity, which allows for increased criminal opportunity. The three major conclusions of Roncek's study were: (1) conditions that produce anonymity (e.g., greater concentration of primary households) are significant for understanding crime occurrence; (2) environmental features are important for explaining where crimes occur; and (3) because crime patterns are complex, both characteristics of the environment *and* the residents need to be considered (Roncek, 1981).

Although Roncek demonstrated a strong effect between population density and crime occurrence, Sampson (1983) noted that there had been much conflicting evidence in regard to the assumed relationship between density and crime. One problem with density-crime studies was that there were inconsistencies in the way in which density was defined (e.g., population density versus building density). Nevertheless, Sampson chose to examine a somewhat neglected area of density research: structural density of the physical environment. Using data from the National Crime Survey for the period of 1973–1978 Sampson investigation the relationship between structural density and criminal victimization. For purposes of the study, the concept of structural density was defined as "the proportion of units in structures of five or more units to the total number of units in a neighborhood" (p. 280).

The theoretical framework for Sampson's study consisted of the previously discussed lifestyle and opportunity models, as well as the defensible space theory as defined by Newman (1972). According to Newman, neighborhoods that have high levels of structural density (e.g., multiple dwellings) are more conducive to criminal behavior, because they lack the open space needed for surveillance by residents. In other words, as the number of dwellings in a given area increases, residents are less able to recognize their neighbors and, therefore, are less likely to serve as guardians. Therefore, by linking the defensible space theory with the opportunity model, it becomes apparent how structural elements of the physical environment can increase the opportunity of predatory victimization (e.g., through decreased guardianship, increased exposure) (Sampson, 1983).

The study findings revealed that there was a positive relationship between structural density and criminal victimization for both robbery and assault, with the strongest effect being for robbery. The relationship between these variables persisted even when controls were made for such factors as age, race, and sex of the victim, urbanization, and other neighborhood features (Sampson, 1983). Sampson concluded that the study results, along with conflicting findings of past research, indicated that the effect of density on crime can vary considerably, depending on such factors as type of density, type of crime, unit of analysis, and extent of urbanization.

However, Sampson further noted how the strength of the study findings in relation to the crime of robbery supported the opportunity/defensible space framework. Sampson argued that because robbery can be described as a more instrumental (versus expressive) crime, it is likely that robbers give greater consideration to such factors as exposure and guardianship when planning their crimes. However, expressive crimes (e.g., assault) are assumed to be more impulsive and thus imply less planning. Therefore, Sampson logically assumed that structural density had a stronger effect on instrumental acts than expressive ones.

The reader may recall that despite most violent crimes being described as expressive, an argument was made for deeming power rape as an instrumental crime. Therefore, on the basis of Sampson's conclusions, if power rape is considered an instrumental act, then it is plausible to assume that power rapists also consider such factors as structural density. This notion would be consistent with much of the serial rape literature, because it has been shown that many power serial rapists partake in acts that would either be hindered or enhanced by the degree of structural density (e.g., voyeuristic acts and/or breaking and entering).

Spatial Approach: The Geography of Crime

The spatial approach in the study of crime emerged from the Chicago School's social ecology perspective and developed into an analysis commonly referred to as the geography of crime. The *geography of crime* examines situational factors in what the Chicago School defined as the "criminal area, i.e., the area of crime occurrence and the area of criminal/delinquent residence, which may or may not coincide" (Georges-Abeyie & Harries, 1980, p. 1). In addition, the geography of crime incorporates both macro-level analyses of geographic units as well as micro-level data regarding specific crime sites (Georges-Abeyie & Harries, 1980).

Rengert (1980) stated that for most crimes that are not spontaneous in nature, there exists a two-stage planning process. The first stage of the planning process involves the decision to commit the criminal act. Once the criminal act has been decided, the second phase is the determination of how and *where* to commit the crime. Nichols (1980) referred to the subconscious search for the crime location as a "mental map" that includes "action space" (i.e., potential locations for the actual offense) (p. 156). However, the ideal location for the criminal act depends both on the spatial structure of the environment and elements of the specific crime (Rengert, 1980). According to Rengert, when criminals are selecting the crime location they are:

> rationally attempting to approximate a set of criteria which they have established in the planning process . . . there are different underlying objectives associated with different types of crime, and these underlying objectives occasion different types of spatial behavior on the part of the criminal. (p. 50)

Based on the geography of crime premise, Rossmo (1997) explored the use of geographic profiling for the investigation of serial murders and serial rapes. As defined by Rossmo, geographic profiling "focuses on the probable spatial behaviour of the offender within the context of the locations of, and the spatial relationships between, the various crime sites" (Rossmo, p.161). The selected location for a given crime is a function of both victim selection and characteristics of the area in which the victim is encountered. However, site selection also implies information about the offender such as organization and mobility (Rossmo, 1997).

Predatory offenders will often use a particular "hunting" style in an effort to obtain their victims (Rossmo, p. 166). Therefore, based on the geography of crime theory and existing serial crime data, Rossmo created a serial offender hunting typology. The typology consists of four subtypes: (1) hunter—an offender who specifically searches for his victim using his city of residence as the base of the search; (2) poacher—

an offender who specifically searches for his victim outside of his home city or from an activity site other than his residence; (3) troller—an offender who encounters a victim opportunistically; and (4) trapper—an offender type who maintains a given position that enables him to encounter the victim in a location under his control.

Using Rossmo's hunting typology, it is possible to argue that the power-reassurance rapist could be described as either a *hunter* or a *poacher*. The reader should recall that the power-reassurance rapist often identifies his victims through voyeurism and also tends to attack in the victim's home. Therefore, this would indicate that this type of rapist is an active hunter. In other words, unlike the *troller* or *trapper* subtypes which essentially allow their victims to come to them, the hunter and the poacher seek out their victims. However, the question still remains as to whether or not he is more likely to seek victims within or outside of his area of residence. Nevertheless, it is interesting to note that according to FBI data, fifty-one percent of seventy-six serial rapists who were active within the United States lived outside of the circle in which they were committing their offenses (Warren, Reboussin, & Hazelwood, 1995).

Although the hunter and poacher categories may also apply to the power-assertive rapist, it is likely that this type of offender could also be included in the trapper subtype. In previous sections, the power-assertive rapist was described as an offender who would approach his victim in a open setting, so that the potential victim would initially feel comfortable with the offender (e.g., asking directions on the street or casual conversation at a bar). However, once the offender has the victim under his control, he then becomes aggressive. Therefore, it is possible that this type of offender frequents certain areas in which he presumes potential victims will be readily available to him (e.g., busy streets, nightclubs, bars).

The area of social ecological research is expansive, and it is therefore difficult to summarize the approach in a succinct, yet coherent, fashion. Nevertheless, social ecology is an important component of the present victim selection typology. As illustrated throughout the victimology section, many of the micro- and macro-level theories of victimization overlap and are mutually influential. For example, to fully understand the opportunity model of predatory victimization, one must also understand the underlying concepts of routine activities and lifestyle models. However, intertwined within each of these macro-level approaches are also elements of micro-level theories as well. Therefore, the inclusion of social ecology helps to bring the victimology discussion full circle: Having begun with the examination of the individual, micro-level factors, and ending with an introduction to the larger social and structural elements involved in crime.

SUMMARY OF VICTIMIZATION MODELS

The initial section discussed the typological approach, describing it essentially as a system of classification based on a set of particular criteria. Elements of past victim typologies were briefly introduced and compared with present efforts to create more inclusive victim typologies. Finally, the review then moved to the creation of early victim typologies based on the foundational ideas of the field of victimology. The typologies of Von Hentig, Mendelsohn, and Fattah were introduced, including an abridged description of the various typology categories.

The discussion of micro-level factors introduced the reader to both personal and behavioral characteristics of the victim that may contribute to his or her victimization. The section began with a discussion of demographic factors (e.g., age and race) and then proceeded to a categorization of personal characteristics (e.g., attractiveness and proximity). Each category and the relevant subsections were first described in general terms and, when appropriate, related to specific information regarding the serial rapist or victim selection techniques. Emphasis was also placed on conceptualizing these terms as mutually overlapping and influencing factors.

The review then moved to behavioral characteristics of victims in relation to victimization. The three broad categories (precipitation, facilitation, and instigation) were described in terms of their usage (i.e., legal versus social science purposes) and their respective criteria. Furthermore, it was noted that although many of the behavioral categories are not applicable to this study, their discussion will facilitate a greater understanding of the proposed victim selection model.

The final section introduced the reader to four macro-level approaches to victimization, including the lifestyle model, the routine activities approach, opportunity theory, and the social ecological approach. Each perspective was first described in terms of its original formulation, with particular emphasis on those concepts defining the uniqueness of the models. This notwithstanding, special effort was made throughout the section to stress the interrelatedness among the various approaches. Relevant research findings were presented to substantiate the application of each model and, where applicable, attempts were made to relate the various approaches to the act of power serial rape.

Chapter 4

THE METHOD OF CRITIQUE AND INQUIRY

OVERVIEW

We begin by introducing the reader to the analytical process of critiquing the existing victimization approaches. We initiate this material by substantiating the need for such an analysis. This is followed by a presentation of the various victimization approaches as critiqued by past scholars. Reviewing the existing critiques helps identify notable strengths and weaknesses of previously developed typologies and models. In addition, however, this review helps justify the inclusion of other criteria that may prove useful in analyzing the victimization approaches for purposes of establishing our own typology. We conclude this section by explaining the bases for our critique (i.e., the selection criteria) as they relate to the existing victimization approaches.

The second section of this chapter engages in a critique of the existing victimization typologies and/or models. This assessment is based on past investigations along these lines and any new or additional factors identified in the process. Having chosen specific criteria and/or factors for purposes of performing the critique, we then apply our strategy to several notable victimization approaches. The typologies and/or models critiqued include (1) the victim typologies of Von Hentig, Mendelsohn, and Fattah; (2) the general concept of micro-level factors; (3) the four macro-level theories presented earlier (i.e., lifestyle model, routine activities approach, opportunity theory, and social ecology); and (4) the power rapist typology presented by Groth et al. (1977).

The third section of this chapter presents our own method of inquiring about and conceiving a victim selection typology. We begin this portion of the chapter by defining and explaining the heuristic approach and why it was chosen as the basis for conceptualizing our power serial rapist victim selection scheme. We then compare and contrast the heuristic model with other research methods, assessing the overall usefulness of the approach selected. We conclude by commenting on the limitations of using a heuristic method for social science investigations

THE METHOD OF CRITIQUE: ASSESSING EXISTING TYPOLOGIES AND MODELS

The Purpose of the Critiques

The purpose of critiquing the existing approaches to victimization is to gain a more thorough understanding of the typologies and models that currently exist and to understand the elements used in their creation. Using established criteria for the critique, it will be possible to identify both strengths and weaknesses of existing victimization approaches. In addition, the selected power rapist typology will also be critiqued to acknowledge the value and limitations of using that particular rapist subtype. Overall, the use of the critique process will be used to substantiate the need for a more current and comprehensive victimization approach. By identifying strengths associated with the current victimization approaches, a solid foundation can be created on which to base the formulation of the power rape victim selection typology. Specific factors of any approach that have proven to be important determinants of criminal victimization should remain essential features in the conceptualization of the present victim selection typology. However, by also examining the weaknesses of the existing victimization approaches, it becomes possible to determine any previously neglected elements that need to be incorporated into the conceptualization process.

Two particular areas have been notably neglected in many victimization approaches, and both of them have been identified at various points throughout the first few chapters. First, there is a lack of typologies or models that combine both criminological and victimological elements (*see* Fattah, 1991). In general, most approaches are either victim or offender specific. Although the integration of both crime and victim theories may be difficult, it is an inclusive process in the study of victim selection. The development of more interactionist models would not only help to advance the field of victimology but would also provide a more comprehensive view of various offender types.

The second issue is the lack of crime-specific victim approaches, which is a matter also related to the need for more interactionist models. As evident in Chapter 3, most of the victim typologies and victimization models were not specified by type of crime. Many of the validation tests performed for the various victimization models did assess the suitability of the model to the determination of a specific type of criminal victimization. However, most of the approaches were not conceptualized given the elements of a particular crime or type of offender. One exception to this issue is the concept of *definitional properties of specific crimes* as it relates to the opportunity model of predatory victimization. However, although this factor takes into account specific crime elements when determining the probability of victimization, the reader may recall that this factor only relates to crimes that have *instrumental* motive (Cohen et al., 1981)

Examples of Past Critiques

Silverman (1974) critiqued three of the early victim typologies, including that of Von Hentig, Mendelsohn, and Fattah (as previously described in Chapter 3). For purposes of his critique, Silverman used the following criteria, which he identified as essential elements of any typology: (1) categories that are "exhaustive of the variable under consideration" (e.g., a victim typology should include all possible types of victim); (2) categories that are mutually exclusive; and (3) a typology that proves useful in empirical research. Through the application of these criteria, Silverman was able to identify particular weaknesses of each victim typology. For example, Von Hentig's typology was noted as having neither exhaustive nor mutually exclusive categories. The reader may recall that Von Hentig classified victims into general classes (e.g., the young, women) and into psychological types (e.g., the mentally defective, the depressed) (Hentig, 1948; Silverman, 1974). Using Silverman's criteria, it becomes quite evident that Von Hentig's typology does in fact lack the necessary degree of delineation needed to accurately classify distinct victim types.

Fattah based his victim typology on behavioral characteristics of victims (e.g., nonparticipating, provocative) from both a sociological and psychological perspective (Fattah, 1967; Silverman, 1974). Although Fattah's work did include mutually exclusive categories, Silverman believed that the classifications were still not exhaustive. To fulfill the exhaustiveness criteria, Fattah would have needed to continue beyond his five major categories to include additional classifications that would account for all possible victim behavior characteristics. Finally, Mendelsohn created his typology based on the amount of victim guilt regarding the victimizing event. Despite the fact that Mendelsohn's typology seems to offer mutually exclusive categories, Silverman claimed that Mendelsohn had failed to define the concept of guilt well enough for research purposes. Furthermore, Mendelsohn had only included personal victims, which cannot be considered exhaustive of all victim types. Overall, Silverman indicated that none of the three typologies fit all of the required elements.

Although Silverman's specified criteria are arguably beneficial in creating a sound typology, not all of the three aspects are applicable to this study. First, this study is attempting to create a conceptual typological model that will basically be a twofold process. Essentially this means that, through the use of various rape and victimology theories and approaches, an overall model of components related to power serial rape victimization will be created. However, once the essential components of the model have been diagramed (e.g., relation of routine activities to structural density), the most significant elements related to the crime of power serial rape will be drawn out to create the power serial rape victim selection typology. Therefore, because we are looking at numerous theories and approaches versus discrete typological subtypes, the idea of mutually exclusive categories is not applicable.

The reader should recall that in the presentation of the selected victimization approaches (Chapter 3) , it was repeatedly noted that the various models and theories shared a great deal of overlap and were not to be considered mutually exclusive concepts. In addition, because this study is focused only on victims of the power serial rapist, the concept of exhaustiveness is not an issue. Specific use of the power serial rape victim for purposes of this study has been justified, thus there is no need to address whether the conceptual model will be exhaustive of all rape victim types. However, in regard to the third criteria, attempts will be made to create the conceptual typological model in such a way as to prove beneficial to empirical research. Indeed, one goal of the this study is to present a model that can be empirically validated.

Knight, Rosenberg, and Schneider (1985) assessed the process of creating classification systems with particular focus on the analysis of sex offender typologies. Among the factors considered to be most problematic in the development and testing of reliable and valid sex offender classifications were (1) absence of operational definitions of typological constructs; (2) limited specification and testing regarding the relationship between given constructs and also resulting subtypes (e.g., possible overlap); and (3) unsystematic methods of classifying empirical cases (1985). According to Knight et al., any attempt to create a taxonomy must be based within some conceptual framework. Furthermore, they stated that:

> . . . both the descriptive and clinical literatures, in spite of their manifold methodological failings, are important sources of discovering those behaviors, traits, and symptoms that are relevant to any typological investigation. . . . To the degree that we are successful in selecting the crucial discriminating variables and rejecting irrelevant ones, we increase the probability that our typological schemes will be useful. (p. 224)

It is important to note that Knight et al. identified both rational and empirical (i.e., theoretically based) strategies as key elements in the derivation of classification schemes. Although both approaches have their own strengths and weaknesses, they serve as complimentary methods when used concurrently. In addition, they emphasized the importance of incorporating both victim and offense characteristics into the delineation of an offender typology. Groth et al.'s (1977) typology was noted as a partial example of this concept, because offense styles were incorporated into the typology. However, the reader may also recall that Groth et al.'s clinical rape typology was based on accounts from both victims and offenders.

When applied to the objective of this study, the commentary of Knight et al. seems to validate the approach being used in the conceptualization of the power serial rapist typology. Because such a typology is not known to currently exist, the conceptualization of the model must rely on existing empirical knowledge related to both rape and victimology. However, it is also necessary to approach the study from a perspective that is based largely on rationale. Because this study uses a heuristic approach, it can be considered the initial phase in the creation of an empirically testable theory of power serial rape victimization. Nevertheless, given the fact that this typology will be a "first of its kind," and because it involves the unification of a mixture of philosophies and theories, the concurrent use of empirical and rational strategies is a necessary approach. Furthermore, the use of both criminological and victimological theories has also been validated by Knight et al.'s statement regarding the necessary importance of including both victim and offender perspectives.

Fattah (1991) summarized limitations of the lifestyle, routine activity, and opportunity models as presented by various researchers. Five main limitations noted with the lifestyle/routine activity/opportunity models included (1) lack of direct measures of key lifestyle variables in Hindelang et al.'s (1978) original formulation of the model; (2) ignoring the possible link between delinquent activities and victimization; (3) inadequate performance in explaining violent victimization; (4) ignoring the possible association between community structure and victimization; and (5) an oversimplified view of the association between demographic variables and victimization. Although these limitations have been summarized to increase brevity, each issue has been argued on the basis of a substantial amount of research. Nevertheless, in relation to this study, it is arguable that the conceptual victim selection typological model will address many of the presented issues.

For example, the argument of the third limitation is that the aforementioned victimization models have not adequately explained violent victimization. In fact, Miethe et al. (1987) argued that perhaps the models were appropriate only for explaining property crime victimization. In addition to this argument, it was noted that perhaps the inability of the models to explain violent victimization is because most violent crimes are expressive, violative acts and, therefore, do not follow the rationale of the routine activity/lifestyle approaches (Fattah, 1991). However, throughout the previous chapters it has been argued why power serial rape should not necessarily be classified as an unplanned act of expressive motivation. Rather, justification has been made as to why power rape may be considered a planned and instrumental act. Therefore, although in most cases the lifestyle/routine activity/opportunity models may not apply to most violent crimes, it may be possible that being more crime specific in focus will allow the various models to be applied more effectively.

In addition, the fourth and fifth limitations are also being addressed within this study. The power serial rape victim selection typology is being based on both micro- and macro-level theories of victimization. Therefore, the interaction between variables, such as demographics and community context as they relate to victimization, will not only be explored, but the variables as they relate to one another will also be addressed. For example, instead of merely focusing on the effects of personal demographic characteristics in relation to criminal victimization, this study will also explore how such individual characteristics relate to lifestyle choices, mobility, structural density, and so on. Therefore, this study will not only attempt to provide a higher degree of integration among various victimization models but will also base these models on a more crime specific focus than most studies have done thus far.

Given the length and detail of Fattah's review, only a very brief portion of the limitations was presented in this section. However, it is important to note that this study is attempting to address some of these limitations by nature of the study's victim/offender interactionist approach and the specificity of the proposed model. Nevertheless, the following chapter will involve a more thorough discussion of weaknesses of the various victimization models as they apply to purposes of the current study.

What will be the Basis of the Critiques.

Based largely on the noted limitations of victimization and victim selection studies presented in the existing literature, there will be two main criteria used for purposes of the critiques. First, each typology and/or model will be assessed on the basis of their inclusion of offender and victim factors. The purpose of this criterion is to compare how either victim only or offender only models are limited in their applicability to understanding victimization, particularly victimization by a specific offender type. Furthermore, by establishing the weaknesses of the existing models based on this criterion, we will demonstrate how a more integrated victim/offender model is more efficient in explaining criminal victimization than a strictly victimological or criminological approach. This criterion will be applied to all of the previously discussed victimization models, in addition to Groth et al.'s (1977) power rape category.

Second, each typology and/or model will be assessed based on its inclusion of micro- and macro-level factors. As has been argued throughout the previous chapters, most of the existing victimization approaches are either micro- or macro-level focused. However, as noted, the degree of overlap and mutual influence between these factors is too great to obtain a clear understanding of victimology based solely on one approach or the other. Therefore, by incorporating both levels of analyses, the current efforts will result in a more encompassing model than most of those that currently exist. As Sampson (1987) stated, "Future studies should look to more definitive linkages of micro and macro-level opportunity models in the examination of victimization by strangers." Overall, the purpose of using these criteria is to integrate the recommendations put forth by past researchers in regard to existing typologies and models and also to further substantiate how the present victim selection model will represent a more comprehensive and integrated approach.

What are the Procedures that will be Followed for the Critiques?

For purposes of critiquing the existing models, the following procedures will be used. First, the underlying criminological or victimological basis of each model will be examined either by: (1) referring to the theoretical framework of the original formulations for each model to assess the use of victim and/or offender theories and characteristics; or (2) determine the use of criminological and victimological perspectives based on reference to such factors in the actual models. Once the basis of a typology or model has been determined, the categories or concepts of each approach will be assessed to see whether the established focus (i.e., victim only, offender only, or combined) has been followed.

Second, the basis of micro-level, macro-level, or combined approaches will be established by: (1) referring to the original formulation of each model to assess if the researchers stated or implied a specific level of focus for the constructed typology or model; or (2) determine the use of micro- and/or macro-level factors based on reference to such concepts in the actual models. Once a basis has been established, the categories or concepts of each approach will be examined to determine whether elements of the typology or model do in fact follow the established formulation. In addition, each approach will be assessed on the basis of excluded micro- or macro-level factors. For example, if an approach is determined to be primarily macro-level orientated, the model will then be examined to ascertain how micro-level factors may be influencing the larger macro-level structure.

This portion of the chapter informed the reader about the process of the critiques that are to follow in the subsequent section. In the previous discussion, the reader was first introduced to various critiques and analyses as they have been presented by past researchers. Furthermore, the elements of these assessments were then related to the (likely) conceptualization of our own victim selection typology where applicable. Next, the bases of the criteria to be used for the critiques were established and the procedures for the analysis were outlined. In the following section, the outlined criteria are systematically applied to the selected typologies and models to determine the strengths and weaknesses of each. We argue that in doing so, the advantages and limits uncovered through this process of inquiry will facilitate the creation of our own victim selection typology.

CRITIQUES: THE APPLICATION PROCESS

Von Hentig's Typology (1948)

1. The reader may recall that Von Hentig's typology consisted of eleven categories based on biopsychosocial factors. Examples of his categories include *the young, the female, the mentally defective, and the lonesome.* Although Von Hentig advocated the importance of victim-offender relationships, he made no distinctions between the "doer" and "sufferer" in the creation of his typology. Based on his categories, which are not crime specific and are focused solely on characteristics and actions of the victim, it is determined that Von Hentig's typology has a victimological basis. By reviewing each of his elleven categories, it is apparent that his victim-only approach was maintained throughout the typology.

   The victim-only focus is limited in that it does not incorporate factors specific to a particular crime or offender type. The problem with this approach is that most anyone can be placed into one of the categories at some point and time in their lives. Overall, the lack of specificity does not allow for the determination of individuals who are at the *greatest* risk or those individuals who need to be most cautious in regard to particular types of criminal victimization. By including offender factors into a victim typology, there is greater specificity and thus increased application of the categories.

2. Although not expressly stated, it is apparent that Von Hentig's typology is based on micro-level factors. His categories are divided either by inherent human traits (e.g., age, sex, mental status) or personal behaviors (e.g., sexual behavior, family interactions). By excluding macro-level factors, elements that extend beyond the individual person are not taken into account. These factors (e.g., environmental, structural, social, etc.), in combination with micro-level factors, may subsequently increase or decrease a person's risk of criminal victimization. By limiting the focus of the typology to only one perspective (i.e., micro or macro), the applicability and accuracy of the typology are reduced.

Mendelsohn's Typology (1956)

1. Mendelsohn formulated a six-part typology based on the amount of guilt attributed to a victim. Examples of his categories include *the completely innocent victim* and *the victim as guilty as the offender*. As an early victimologist, Mendelsohn objected to the victim being studied subsequent to the offender and believed victimology should have been a distinct area of science. It is evident from his categories that, much like Von Hentig, Mendelsohn also relied on a victimological perspective in the creation of his typology. Although some of his categories imply the necessary relationship between the offender and victim (e.g., *victim more guilty than the offender*), Mendelsohn did not rely on the use of offender-related elements. For example, some of Mendelsohn's categories do not actually involve an offender (e.g., victim as guilty as the offender such as in cases of suicide). Rather, he used a victim-only approach that he maintained throughout his six categories. As previously dis-

cussed, the exclusion of offender-related factors results in a
typology that lacks delineation and results in less than optimal
use.

2. It seems that Mendelsohn relied most heavily on the use of
   micro-level factors in developing his categories. His typology
   is focused primarily on behavioral characteristics of victims,
   and his attribution of *victim guilt* is related to the perceived level
   of victim involvement in the commission of the criminal act.
   Although Mendelsohn did not directly address any macro-level
   factors (e.g., neighborhood structure, social environment,
   lifestyle constraints), these elements can have considerable
   influence on a person's behavior. Therefore, the exclusion of
   macro level components limits the use of Mendelsohn's typology.

Fattah's Typology (1967)

1. Fattah's five-part typology was based on sociological and psychological characteristics of victims. As previously noted,
   Fattah emphasizes the need to combine both criminological
   and victimological theories and factors in the attempt to understand victimization. Compared with Mendelsohn, Fattah
   places greater emphasis on the offender/victim relationship.
   Although he alludes to what can be perceived as different
   offender types, he does not explicitly address how specific
   crime and offender-related factors influence the likelihood of
   criminal victimization. Therefore, although Fattah's typology
   seems to incorporate both a victimological and criminological
   approach, the criminological aspects are less prevalent.
   Nevertheless, it seems that Fattah maintained this *loosely* combined approach throughout his five categories.

2. Similar to Mendelsohn's approach, Fattah was focused primarily on the behavioral aspects of individuals. However, one
   particular category (i.e., *the latent or predisposed victim*) is also
   based on inherent character traits that may increase one's
   chances of victimization. Much like his proposal for increasing
   the use of both criminological and victimological theories,
   Fattah also stressed the need to incorporate both micro- and
   macro-level factors in the attempt to understand victimization.

On the basis of his five categories, it seems that Fattah created his typology in such a way as to encourage consideration of both micro- and macro-level factors. For example, the *latent or predisposed victim* category alludes to more personal, micro-level factors, whereas the *provocative* and *participating victim* categories imply more macro-level elements (e.g., creating a situation likely to lead to crime). Therefore, based on his inclusion of both criminological/victimological elements and micro/macro-level factors, Fattah's typology seems most analogous to the proposed goals of this study. Nevertheless, Fattah's typology lacks specificity, in regard to crime/offender type, which the current research will emphasize.

What is notable about all three of the presented typologies is that they each include a level of victim participation. The various victim types range from the completely unsuspecting and unwilling victim to the victim who seemingly encourages or provokes the criminal act. To the credit of those who developed the early victim typologies, attempting to include all factors that could be relevant to a person's risk of victimization is a seemingly exhaustive, if not impossible, task. Furthermore, to create a typology that is too expansive yields either unreliable or meaningless categories. It is for these reasons that the current typology is crime specific. By narrowing the scope of the focus in an attempt to understand victimization, the task of investigating pertinent risk factors becomes a less futile effort.

Lifestyle Model: Hindelang, Gottfredson, and Garofalo (1978)

1. Hindelang, Gottfredson, and Garofalo sought to identify lifestyle patterns to determine the likelihood of personal victimization through the intervening variables of association and exposure. The lifestyle model, developed from victimization survey data and other crime sources, was based on a victimological approach to understanding criminal victimization. The primary focus of the model was to determine those characteristics or behaviors that were commonly found among crime victims; however, the model did not address a specific type of offense or offender. In reviewing the components of the lifestyle model, it is evident that the model maintained a victim-

only approach. Overall, the lifestyle model provided a vague understanding of criminal victimization, but its ambiguous nature made it difficult to verify or falsify its effectiveness. Although it may be useful in determining whether or not a person is predisposed to victimization, it provides no description as to the type of victimization to which a person is prone. However, the creation of a crime specific model will allow for verification of its usefulness through the application of real-life cases.

2. Although not explicitly stated, the lifestyle model integrates both micro- and macro-level factors. Examples of such factors in the lifestyle model include demographic characteristics (micro) and economic constraints or subcultural influence (macro). However, as previously discussed, there is not always a clear line between micro- and macro-level elements. The two categories are neither exhaustive nor mutually exclusive. Therefore, there are components of the lifestyle model that could essentially be related to both levels. For example, leisure activities may have as much to do with one's personal preference as with the availability of various activities as dictated by one's area of residence. Nevertheless, despite the lack of clarity, it is evident that both micro- and macro-level factors played a role in the creation of the lifestyle model.

Routine Activity Approach: Cohen and Felson (1979)

1. The basis of the routine activity approach is that changes in routine activity patterns affect the convergence of predatory crime elements in both time and space and, thus, influence crime rate patterns. The characteristics that Cohen and Felson were most interested in were the activity patterns of both criminals and victims that influence criminal opportunity. Because the routine activity approach incorporates both victim and offender elements, it can be viewed as both victimological and criminological in nature. Although the approach did not focus on a specific offender type, it did focus on a specific category of offenses: predatory violations. In this sense, the routine activity approach is similar to the goal of this study. However, instead of focusing on the general category of *predatory viola-*

tions, this study is focused specifically on the power serial rapist.

2. The routine activity approach is a prime example of an attempt to explain criminal victimization through the combination of both micro- and macro-level elements. Cohen and Felson noted one advantage of the routine activity approach was that it combined previously unrelated criminological theories (e.g, micro- and macro-level approaches and social ecology). Throughout the introduction of their approach, Cohen and Felson consistently relied on micro- and macro-level data and research. They made evident the unequivocal relationship between micro- and macro-level factors. Overall, the routine activity approach was the result of careful consideration and combination of elements of victimization as they relate to both victims and offenders and micro- and macro-level factors. Thus, the routine activity approach is similarly related to the end goal of the proposed victim selection model: to illustrate the necessary relationship between both criminological and victimological theories and micro- and macro-level approaches in the understanding of criminal victimization.

Opportunity Theory: Cohen, Kluegel, and Land (1981)

1. As the reader may recall, opportunity theory integrated elements of both the lifestyle model and the routine activity approach. Each of these approaches to understanding criminal victimization was based on a perspective referred to as the *opportunity model of predatory victimization.* This perspective considers time-space relationships and lifestyle/routine activities that increase the likelihood of criminal victimization. Opportunity theory was intended to explain variations in the risk of predatory victimization among certain dimensions of social stratification (i.e., age, race, and income). In addition, the theory was based on five risk factors: exposure, guardianship, proximity to potential offenders, attractiveness of potential targets, and definitional properties of specific crimes themselves. Because most of these factors focus specifically on victim characteristics and/or behaviors, the use of these risk factors implies a victimological approach. However, because Cohen, et al. used crime data and general offender information,

there is also a criminological aspect to the theory. Therefore, the theory can be viewed as combining criminological and victimological approaches throughout.

2. As previously noted, opportunity theory specifically sought to explain criminal victimization across specific dimensions of social stratification. Investigating personal victimization at a greater social level implies a macro-level approach. The use of a macro-level approach in the creation of opportunity theory is evident, not only through the examination of crime data across social stratifications (i.e., age, race, and income), but also crime data that varies across residential areas (e.g., central city versus rural areas). Yet, there is also explicit use of a micro-level approach as indicated by inclusion of the risk factors (e.g., such as exposure, proximity, and attractiveness). The reader may recall that several of these risk factors were previously described by Fattah (1991) in the section regarding micro-level victim selection factors. The definitions provided by Fattah may differ somewhat from those provided by Cohen et al.; however, the underlying micro-level premise of the factors remains the same. Therefore, opportunity theory also consistently relies on both micro- and macro-level approaches. Interestingly, the theory also considered specific elements of particular offense or offender types as demonstrated by their inclusion of the *definitional properties of specific crimes* factor. The reader may recall that this factor related only to those crimes motivated by an instrumental purpose and excluded crimes of assault. However, we argued that power serial rape can in fact be considered a crime of instrumental motivation. Overall, Cohen et al.'s focus on the influence of specific crime factors is most similar to the purpose of the current victim selection model, which is based solely on characteristics and behaviors of the power serial rapist.

Social Ecology

1. Unlike the previous approaches, social ecology is an approach that has developed through years of contribution by numerous researchers and theorists. Social ecology is not a specific model but rather a collective approach to understanding crime.

Therefore, because there is no one original study or theory, the idea of critiquing the approach seems rather unwieldy given the mass of social ecology literature that currently exists. Yet the history of social ecology research is grounded in criminology, and much of contemporary criminological theory can be traced back to the early social ecology studies (Byrne & Sampson, 1986). Although social ecologists make use of victimization data and may investigate issues concerning victimization, the foundation of social ecology research is grounded in criminological theory. However, to truly understand the act of crime it is necessary to study the two most significant elements: the offender *and* the victim.

2. Although there is not a single definition of social ecology, the approach was described by Byrne and Sampson (1986) as the study of crime within specific spatial areas and social structures. Therefore, social ecology is by definition a macro-level approach. Social ecology studies investigate specific geographical areas, social structures, social composition, and so on. These are studies of the larger macro-environment that is both social and physical in nature. Therefore, although micro- and macro-level factors undoubtedly contribute to and influence one another, the focis of social ecology research are the effects of the greater macro-level environment on crime. Social ecology research has proven to be a great contributor to the study of criminology and will prove useful for purposes of this study. However, the current victim selection study seeks to provide a level of detail and specificity not found in social ecology research, thus allowing for application of the study to specific criminal cases.

Clinical Rape Typology: Groth, Burgess, and Holstrom (1977)

1. A unique element of Groth et al.'s rapist typology, compared with other such typologies, is that Groth and his colleagues relied on both victim and offender data in their research. By relying on the self-report of a combined total of 279 rapists and rape victims, the researchers were able to devise a typology that integrates two very distinct views of the same offense. The use of both victim and offender data offers a more holistic view

of the phenomenon of rape, because victims and offenders alike may not be fully aware of all the elements that contribute to the occurrence of a rape. For example, during the course of a rape an offender may not be fully aware of the nature of the language he is using or the level of life-threatening fear that he is instilling in his victim. However, having such information may provide a key to understanding the motivation of the offender. Overall, on the basis of the combined use of victim and offender data, the typology may be viewed as incorporating both a victimological and criminological approach.

2. In reviewing Groth et al.'s clinical rape typology, the description of the rape categories seemed to be influenced primarily by micro-level factors. Such factors included motivations and personal characteristics of the offender and particular offense behaviors. The researchers also included brief descriptions of real-life rape accounts, which include some reference as to where victims were attacked, details of the particular assault, and so on. However, there is no reference as to whether larger macro-level factors (e.g., neighborhood structure) may have played a role in influencing the offender's choice of victim or location of the assault. It is possible that most offenders are not consciously aware as to how macro-level factors influence their choice of victim and/or assault location. Moreover, it is likely that most individuals do not consider how larger macro-level factors influence their risk of becoming crime victims. However, the purpose of the current research is to investigate those macro-level factors, in addition to micro-level factors, that may sway victim selection of rape offenders, particularly the power serial rapist.

SUMMARY OF CRITIQUES

The preceding section offered critiques of past victim typologies and victimization theories in terms of whether they were based on (1) victimological and/or criminological theory; and (2) micro- and/or macro-level factors. The purpose of these critiques was to provide a basis of comparison for the current victim selection research that endeavors to offer a more comprehensive typology than those that presently exist. This will be accomplished by offering an offender-specific typology based on both victimological/criminological theory and micro-/macro-level factors.

OUR METHOD OF INQUIRY: DEFINING A HEURISTIC APPROACH

The conceptualization of the power serial rapist victim selection typology is based on a heuristic approach. As briefly described in the introduction, heuristics is an analytical process of examining existing knowledge to uncover new information. McGuire (1997) discusses the use of the heuristic approach as a hypothesis generating tool. He divides heuristics into five categories and fourteen subcategories to elicit a total of forty-nine possible heuristics. On the basis of McGuire's categorizations, this study can be described under category IV *Heuristics demanding reinterpretations of past research,* and subcategory L *Discovery by integrating multiple past studies.* Category IV includes the researcher "working creatively with the area's research literature" (p. 21) and subcategory L explains:

> Reviewing the literature or writing a theoretical integration requires one to organize and integrate a heterogeneous set of studies, interpreting them creatively so that the whole set is more meaningful than the sum of the individual studies, as patterns emerge and new integrating and bridging hypotheses suggest themselves. (p. 25)

Why Heuristics?

As the reader may recall, the hypotheses underlying the current research are that serial rapists use selection techniques or criteria when seeking victims and that there are general and/or specific factors that compose the selection processes. Although there is research that addresses rapist victim selection techniques (*see* Terry & Doerge, 1979; Richards, 1991; Stevens, 1994), the literature lacks any indication of a *typology* of rape victim selection, particularly for the serial rapist. Therefore, this study will attempt to uncover those factors involved in the postulated selection process through an analysis of the existing literature.

However, based on the paucity of rape victim selection material and because this study endeavors to incorporate both criminological and victimological theory and research, this analytical process will consist of integrating and organizing the existing knowledge (as described in subcategory L) into a singular body. It is for these reasons that a heuristic approach is considered the most appropriate method for purposes of this investigation.

Why Not Other Methods?

To further substantiate the use of heuristics, it is important to note why other methods of study are less applicable to the present inquiry. Because it would be excessive to analyze all existing methods, only four specific methods that could arguably be used in this investigation will be discussed: (1) quantitative analysis; (2) content analysis; (3) grounded theory; and (4) case study.

Quantitative Analysis

Babbie (1992) defines quantitative analysis as a "numerical representation and manipulation of observations" to describe and explain a given phenomenon. This method of study has been predominant in traditional psychological research, which emphasizes natural scientific methods and positivist theory, such that only observable and quantifiable data are given significance (Giorgi, 1992).

However, to perform quantitative research, the investigator must be able to specify those concepts that he or she intends to study.

As previously mentioned, although there are some studies that focus on victim selection in rape, there are no studies that investigate this phenomena in the power serial rapist. Also, most victimization studies tend to focus on only micro- or macro-level factors and neglect the mutual influence of both. Therefore, the specific concepts that may contribute to the serial rape victim selection phenomenon have essentially yet to be identified and thus cannot currently be measured. However, it is hoped that this inquiry will provide a foundation upon which future quantitative research can be performed.

Content Analysis

Content analysis is a social science research method in which answers to research questions are sought through the examination of written documents. This method is particularly well suited to forms of communication (e.g., books, laws, and speeches), and sampling may occur at any level from words and phrases to paragraphs or entire chapters. A disadvantage of content analysis is that only *recorded* information can be examined (Babbie, 1992). Nevertheless, if a sufficient amount of accessible documentation existed on serial rape cases, this method of study could be potentially useful.

For example, there are existing biographies that account the lives and crimes of serial rapists. Although rather extensive victim information is incorporated into some of these accounts, it should be kept in mind that these narratives are essentially interpretations of the writer and not always direct depictions from the offender himself. Thus, the units of analysis (i.e., the biographical stories) may not accurately reflect those selection techniques applied by the rapist.

An interesting study would be to perform content analysis on police records of serial rape cases that includes accounts of the assault from both the victim and perpetrator. This method could potentially provide valuable data of victim selection from a more micro-level perspective. However, to account for possible macro-level factors, additional information such as the geographical locale of the crime, the community structure of the area, etc., would also need to be addressed. Therefore, because of such factors, in addition to the accessibility of such information, time, and expenses, this type of study was not pursued. .

Grounded Theory

Grounded theory is a methodology used to develop theory that is grounded in systematically collected and analyzed data (Strauss & Corbin, 1998). The "centerpiece" of the approach is that the developed theory is closely related to the context of the phenomenon being studied (Creswell, 1998). This method may be used to generate entirely new theory or to elaborate on and modify existing theory (Denzin & Lincoln, 1998). The method consists of collecting interview data, making field visits, creating and interrelating categories from the information, and writing theoretical propositions or hypotheses (Creswell, 1998). Analysis of the data takes place concurrently with the collection of the information, such that Creswell describes it as a "zigzag" process (1998, p. 57). Ideally, the researcher should move back and forth from the field to analyzing the data.

As previously noted on a variety of occasions, the creation of the serial rapist victim selection typology is a conceptual approach. Essentially this means that the results of this study will serve only as an initial and *analytical* understanding of victim selection techniques; however, it will not serve as theory. Rather, it becomes a basis from which future efforts to create and test related theories can evolve.

The reason for not selecting the grounded theory approach through which to create an introductory victim selection theory is based on an underlying assumption of the current investigation. Although this study rests on the contention that serial rapists make rational choices in the selection of their victims, it is also speculated that several of the factors that contribute to victimization are not overtly recognized by either the victim or offender. For example, a rapist may describe selecting a particular victim on the basis of her accessibility, which stemmed from her daily lifestyle activities. However, these same lifestyle activities may have led the woman to select a particular residential area which in turn may have increased her risk of victimization because of the neighborhood's structure or guardianship.

Grounded theory uses interviews as the primary data source. However, because there are factors that may contribute to a rapist's victim selection of which he is not ultimately aware, such factors may not be elicited in an interview. Therefore, a conceptual approach based on an integration of the existing literature was concluded as a more fitting method.

Case Study

Case study is not necessarily "a methodological choice, but a choice of object to be studied" (Stake, 1998, p. 86). It involves exploring either a single or multiple cases over time through the use of detailed and in-depth data collection involving a variety of sources. These sources may consist of interviews, observations, documents, archival records, and so on (Creswell, 1998). A case study may take different forms. For example, it can be an instrumental case study in which the particular case is chosen only to provide insight on an issue or to refine theory. However, the case is only of secondary interest. For purposes of this study, performing a case study on a known serial rapist would not necessarily be to understand that rapist in particular but rather to shed light on the issue of victim selection.

A second type of case study is a collective case study in which more than one case is studied at a time to gain a greater understanding of a particular phenomenon. Again, for this study this would perhaps involve studying several serial rapists at one time to gain a collective sense of victim-targeting techniques. However, as discussed in regard to the grounded theory method, it is conceivable that there are factors involved in an offender's victim selection process of which he is ultimately not aware and thus would not communicate in the context of an interview.

Furthermore, one of the possible future implications of the typological model is that it will be used for law enforcement purposes in the apprehension of offenders and in preventive measures for potential victims. However, if the information is based solely on one case, or even a select few, then the generalizability and applicability of the typology is arguably limited.

Limitations of a Heuristic Approach

Probably the greatest limitation of a heuristic approach is that because it is a strictly analytical process, the findings are not tested. However, on the basis of the purposes of this study, this is not seen as a limitation but rather a starting point in the process of understanding and explaining the given phenomenon. There is a paucity of research regarding victim selection techniques, particularly for serial rapists. Therefore, the current study is seen as an opportunity to develop a useful typology based on a systematic and analytical approach to the existing serial rape, general victim selection, and victimization literature.

As previously mentioned, the creation of this conceptual model will allow for future empirical studies to test the reliability and validity of the typology. It will provide a basis on which to expand or necessarily modify the understanding of victim selection. Furthermore, if empirical data validate the typological model, then they can serve as a foundation for the creation of actual theory. Therefore, although heuristics include certain methodological weaknesses, and although there may be other research approaches that could provide useful findings, the heuristic approach was chosen on the basis of its function as a hypothesis and, ultimately, theory-generating tool.

The following chapter describes the creation of the typological model, graphically depicted in Appendix A (see p. 147). The typological model consists primarily of four components (1, 2, 3a, and 3b) that we believe contribute to the manner in which power serial rapists select their victims. The four components will be described independently and as they relate to one another. These interconnected elements constitute the victim selection model. The model itself demonstrates the features of power serial rapist victim selection and the order or process this offender follows in his sex crime. However, the individual factors within each component also offer a typology of power serial rape victims as they describe those characteristics and/or behaviors seemingly common among such victim types.

We note that because the research supporting the creation of the typological model was explained in detail in previous chapters, it will not be elaborated on in the subsequent chapter. However, references to prior research will be used to remind the reader of the data that were used in determining the components of and connections among the model. In Chapter 5, the words "rape" and "rapist" will be used frequently. The reader should note that these words are being used in place of "power serial rape" and "power serial rapist" for purposes of brevity, unless otherwise indicated. The following statements represent postulates based on our conceptualization of the power serial rapists' victim selection techniques. Accordingly, the typological model signifies a notion and has not been tested theoretically.

Chapter 5

THE POWER SERIAL RAPIST: A VICTIM SELECTION TYPOLOGICAL MODEL

OVERVIEW

This chapter conceptually presents our victim selection typological model. Along these lines, we systematically describe each of the model's components. In brief, these include the following: (1) geographic location; (2) personal characteristics/ microl-level factors; (3a) routine activities/lifestyle patterns; (3b) residential location. Throughout this presentation, we situate our observations within the criminological literature on rape and victimological literature on victims. For purposes of clarity and simplification, Appendix A is included at the end of this Chapter, visually depicting the manner in which our typological model functions.

GEOGRAPHIC LOCATION

The model begins with *geographical location* or Component 1. This refers to the rapist's area of residence or any other area in which he may spend a great deal of time (e.g., area of work). In general, geographical location refers to the location from which the rapist seeks his victims and initiates the rape offenses. This component appears first as it represents the foundation of the power serial rapist's victim selection process. In most cases, before he considers any personal victim characteristics or situational factors relevant to target selection, he has established his search within a given geographical space. LeBeau (1987a) reported that serial rapists tend to restrict their rapes to a small

127

geographic location and specifically noted a distance of one half mile between rape locations. In Swindle's (1997) description of the rapes committed by power serial rapist Gilbert Escobedo (the case to which the typological model will be applied), Swindle noted that Escobedo's rapes occurred approximately within a two-mile radius of one another.

The purpose of noting these findings is to demonstrate how serial rapists tend to limit their victim selection, and subsequent rapes, to rather small geographical areas. An understanding of the geographical patterns of serial rapists may be useful in several ways. First, it illustrates something about this offender type's personality or pattern of thinking. It seems that power serial rapists find comfort or satisfaction in committing their crimes close to home or within any other area with which they are highly familiar. Recall that the power-reassurance rapist is in general a person who lacks a sense of competence in his abilities (e.g., personal, sexual). Although such an offender may exude a sense of confidence and self-assurance on a superficial level, internally his feelings about himself are much different. The power-reassurance rapist is uncertain of his capabilities and of his masculinity. Thus, by remaining in an area with which he is well acquainted, the rapist is afforded an increased sense of fitness in his ability to successfully commit the rape act. His familiarity with the area is likely to provide him with a sense of comfort and security as he goes about committing his offenses.

For the power-assertive rapist, the motivation for the rape is control and dominance. Unlike the power-reassurance rapist, the power-assertive rapist typically has less doubts about his manhood (although it can be argued that this offender's confidence is based on a false sense of self). Rather, he tends to view women as objects to be taken and used at his convenience. As such, the power-assertive rapist may limit the geographic range of his attacks to remain within his "domain." In essence, he may feel a secondary sense of power not only in being able to commit the rape act but also being able to do so on his own terms and in his own dominion. Another reason to include a geographical factor in the typological model is that an understanding of the spatial patterns of the power serial rapist may assist law enforcement officials in tracking and apprehending the offender. Law enforcement officials can also use such information to notify individuals within communities or areas that may be at risk to be targeted by an at-large offender.

Component 1 does not offer a specific number of miles within which victims may be targeted or rapes may be committed. However, the purpose of this component is to make evident that the rapist is often in close proximity to his victims, and he often uses his own familiar geographical location (e.g., residential area, local community) to seek out and approach victims. By seeking victims within his own geographical location, the rapist has increased exposure to and possible association with potential victims. With increased contact, the rapist has greater opportunity to study personalities, behaviors, and vulnerabilities of potential victims. In addition, such contact may offer more detailed information, including where a victim lives, her daily routines, and when she is most often alone. This knowledge affords the rapist the opportunity to decide the best time and location for the rape, or if a woman is even a suitable victim. By remaining in his own geographical location, the rapist also has a "home court advantage," such that he becomes more familiar with the quickest travel routes, patrolling routines of local law enforcement, and potential escape plans should he come close to being apprehended. In general, the rapist has greater proximity to and thus more repeated exposure and contact with potential victims when he seeks his victims within his own geographical locale.

PERSON CHARACTERISTICS AND MICRO-LEVEL FACTORS

Component 2 includes *personal characteristics* and *micro-level factors*. This component follows the geographical location component, because it is the next factor that the rapist considers in the selection of his victim. The logic of placing this component second is based on the idea that even though a victim may be in the offender's target area and although various situational factors may contribute to a woman being a prime target, she may not fit his personal preference. Again, it is likely that offenders have a particular type of victim in mind during their target search. This does not have to include physical factors of the victim (e.g., height, weight, hair color); however, it may include broader factors such as age, race, or marital status.

For example, consider two victims who are both equally easily accessible to the rapist. Assume one victim is young and single and the other is older and married. It is likely that the rapist would select the younger, unmarried victim. For one, the offender may consider the younger women to be more physically ideal based on her youth. Because the power serial rapist is seeking to regain his masculinity, he may seek out victims that fit social standards of femininity and beauty to further attest to his manhood and virility. He may also consider younger women more naive, more trusting, or more passive, thus making them generally more vulnerable. In addition, the fact that she is unmarried decreases the likelihood of someone being present in the home or possibly turning up in the process of the rape act. Overall, despite situational factors that may contribute to a rape, it is assumed that the rapist first considers personal characteristics and micro-level factors related to a potential victim.

Personal characteristics may or may not include physical features of the victim. Although some rapists may have a physical preference or look for features of a woman that relate to their rape fantasies, others may consider physical characteristics less significant in the selection of a victim. However, Component 2 also includes such demographic factors as age and race. The reader is reminded that the typological model applies only to female victims, therefore, the inclusion of gender as a factor in this component seemed unnecessary. Power serial rapists target female victims almost exclusively because the motivation for his offense is to possess and sexually conquer his victim. Although some other rapes (such as many prison rapes) (*see* Groth & Birnbaum, 1979; Hodge & Carnter, 1998) are also committed to display a man's power and dominance, the power serial rapist specifically wants to confirm his sexual adequacy. The power-reassurance rapist fantasizes about sexually pleasing his victim and may even ask about his performance during the assault. In addition, as if he were attempting to maintain some sort of relationship with them, he may at times contact his victims after the assault to inquire about them or express the satisfaction he gained from the assault. With the power-assertive rapist, the assault is more about fulfilling feelings of entitlement, because this rapist type considers women objects to be conquered. He may be more aggressive and more demeaning during the assault than his counterpart, which in a sense reestablishes traditionally defined roles of women being inferior to men.

The component includes an 18–40 age range. This age range is rather a loose interpretation of the literature. The age range begins at

18 years, because the typological model is meant to apply to adult victims. In addition, according to Hazelwood & Warren (1989b), serial rape victims were typically between the ages of 18 and 33 years. Although it is impossible to impose an exact age range, the range in Component 2 was extended roughly to 40 years. This is because by age 40 it is assumed that most women will have been married, had children, and become established in their homes and occupation. The connection between age, marriage, and a more established lifestyle will be explained in detail momentarily when the concept of mobility is discussed. However, in general, women who are older, married, and have children are seen as less attractive victims and are less likely to be considered prime targets. Overall, the 18–40 age range is not rigidly defined but rather provides a flexible guideline by which to determine potential victims.

Race is another primary factor, and it is likely that most of the selected victims will be white. This is based on Hazelwood and Warren's (1989b) serial rape study which they found that eighty-eight to ninety-five percent of the serial rape victims were white. In addition, of the serial rapists interviewed, eighty-five percent were white. The race of the rapist becomes an important factor, because Hazelwood and Warren also noted that although white rapists did not cross the racial line, black rapists tended to rape both black and white women. Therefore, logic dictates that based on the fact that most serial rapists are white, and that they tend to rape women of their own race, most serial rape victims would also be white. However, consideration for victims of other races can be made in the typological model if it is determined that an offender is nonwhite.

The reader may remember that according to Hazelwood and Warren's (1989b) serial rapist study, most rapists attacked women who were of similar age and race as the rapists themselves. The factors of age and race could certainly be related to the concepts of exposure and association discussed in Component 1, such that potential offenders may simply have more daily contact with women who are demographically similar to the rapists. However, given the power rapist's psychological makeup, it also seems likely that he would target women who fit his concept of a dating partner. Many power rapists are involved in relationships before or at the time of their assaults. According to Hazelwood & Burgess (1987), seventy-one percent of serial rapists had been married at least once. Thus, although the power rapist may be able to refrain from acting on negative emotions (e.g., feelings of sexual inadequacy) and impulsive behaviors (e.g., feelings of need for control) while with his partner (e.g., girlfriend, fiancé, wife), he may let out the pent-up frustration and aggression on women who represent his mate or women from his past.

The next factor included in the component is marital status. Although married individuals can also be selected as victims, non-married women often seem to be more vulnerable and attractive victims. As will be addressed with the subsequent components, unmarried or single women tend to have lifestyles and live in residential areas that increase their vulnerability. In addition, they are more apt to live alone or with female roommates, which allows for easier access and greater manageability of the victim during the rape offense. Again, although the status of unmarried or single is not a necessary factor, it is more likely that the rapist would target such a victim.

The factors of age and marital status can also be associated with the factor of high mobility. High mobility essentially refers to people who are less settled in their lives and, thus, have a tendency to move more often or live in less-established neighborhoods. A prime example would be a female student who lives in apartment housing. The general assumption is that younger, single women are more likely to be more mobile. The relevance of this factor will be further explained in Component 3b, the *residential location* component. However, the importance of this feature within Component 2 is that high mobility may influence other lifestyle factors, which may increase a woman's chances of being victimized.

The final factor of Component 2 is structural proneness as described by Fattah (1991). The reader may recall that structural proneness refers to social elements that may increase a person's chances of victimization, such as being young, female, or a minority. For the power serial rapist, both the structural factors of being young and female are key elements increasing the likelihood of victimization by this offender type. However, because age has already been addressed, the term structural factor within this component refers only to those social elements related to being female. The reader may recall that Fattah (1991) discussed socially derived power differences between men and women as a result of historical, cultural, economic, and political factors that make women more attractive, legitimate, and vulnerable targets.

Fattah addressed four main factors that contribute to women's proneness, including (1) women being perceived as less powerful than men, (2) economic dependency, (3) gender inequality, and (4) system inequality. Nevertheless, only factors 1 and 3 will be included in the component. Economic dependency is excluded, because it refers to the institution of marriage and women being financially dependent on men. In terms of victim selection, this factor has little direct relevance. Financial dependence may lead some women to marry and, thus, based on their marital status, they may be more or less apt to be victimized. However, because marital status is an already included factor in the component, economic dependence does not need to be addressed separately. System inequality refers to the way in which the criminal justice system perpetuates injustice toward women. Although this factor may be relevant to how rape victims are treated within the criminal justice system after the offense, it has little to do with how victims are selected before the offense. Although how rape victims are treated after an assault may continue to legitimize them as victims within society, this issue offers little beyond the first factor of women being perceived as less powerful than men in societal terms.

Recall that for the power rapist, the goal of the rape is to achieve a sense of self-satisfaction. The power-reassurance rapist has doubts and insecurities about himself that motivate him to commit the rape offense in order to boost his sense of masculinity and virility. The power-assertive rapist, on the other hand, feels the need to dominate women as part of his masculinity. He perceives women as objects to be used at his discretion, although it is likely that he also has deep-seated insecurities that perpetuate this view of women. Regardless, the fact that women are perceived as less powerful (most obviously in the physical sense) allows them to be viewed as more easily intimidated and controlled. Thus, women are seen as natural victims by men who are seeking to increase their feelings of self-worth by being able to conquer and dominate another human being. Remember that the sexual component of rape is only a means to an end, thus women are not necessarily chosen simply for sexual reasons.

In addition, gender inequality is another important structural factor for the power rapist. Recall that gender inequality refers to socially established gender roles that place women in an "inferior role in the hierarchy of power and reinforces the values of a male sexist culture" (Fattah, 1991, p. 271). Again, based on the motivations of the power

rapist it is not unlikely that he would choose a victim seen as inferior–
a woman. When considering both of the aforementioned structural
factors, it could be argued that the power-reassurance rapist would be
more associated with the concept of women being less powerful.
Because this rapist type doubts his virility, he wants to select a victim
that he will be easily able to control to renew his sense of self-worth.
However, the power-assertive rapist would arguably be more associated with the concept of women as inferior to men in a male-dominated
society. Because this rapist type feels it is his privilege to "have" a
woman whenever he pleases, he would rely on the view of women as
socially inferior to achieve his goal of feeling highly masculine.

ROUTINE ACTIVITIES/LIFE STYLE PATTERNS AND RESIDENTIAL LOCATION: AN OVERVIEW

Component 2 has two arrows leading to the final two components:
The *routine activities and lifestyle patterns* component, 3a, and the *residential location* component, 3b. Labeling the Components 3a and 3b
signifies that either of the two components could follow Component 2
in the typological model. Neither component is necessarily more
influential than the other in the victim selection process, but rather
they are interchangeable, often depending on the rapist type. The
interchangeability of the components based on rapist type will be
explained in concordance with the respective components. In addition, both components may play an equally important role in the
selection of a victim.

These two components have been placed last in the typological
model, because we believe that they are the final two components
used in the victim selection process. Their placement is not to indicate in any way that they are less important components in the typological model. But rather, these components include factors that "tip
the scale" so to speak. Recall that first the rapist begins his search
within a small geographical region. Seeking victims in his own region
may provide him a sense of security or a sense of entitlement. For
practical reasons, it also may provide him with greater knowledge of
residential or community layouts, travel routes, escape routes, and so
on. Nevertheless, after beginning the search within the given area, he
then seeks out victims that fit his ideal.

The power rapist fantasizes about the right victim (Groth et al., 1977; Groth & Birnbaum, 1979; Groth & Hobson, 1983), and his depiction of this victim may include physical features, personality characteristics, and basic demographic factors (e.g., age, race). However, it is likely that the offender has a preconceived notion of the type of woman he is seeking. Yet, after identifying a woman who may fit his notion of the ideal victim, there are additional factors to be considered. The rapist may also fantasize about the location or means by which he approaches his target. For example, the power-reassurance rapist may fantasize about violating the victim in her own home while she sleeps. Thus, in this case, additional factors such as ability to access the victim's home, presence of others that may prevent the assault from occurring, and so forth must be considered by the offender. Recall that Fattah (1991) described "exchangeable victims" in relation to the concept of facilitation. According to Fattah, the concept of exchangeable victims implies that a victim's behavior does not contribute to the commission of the crime, but rather merely influences the selection of the target. Yet, it can also be argued that the concept of the exchangeable victim relates to factors other than victim behavior, including factors outside of the victim's control (e.g., neighborhood density, placement of trees and shrubs). Thus, although an offender may have found a victim within his search area that meets his expectations of a suitable victim, whether or not the victim is targeted may depend on additional macro-level factors (i.e., routine activities, lifestyle choices, and residential setting).

The subscripts *a* and *b* are used for purposes of simplification in referencing the components. The arrows leading from Component 2 to Components 3a and 3b signify that personal characteristics and micro-level factors may influence an individual's routine activities, lifestyle choices, and selection of residential location. In addition, the reader will note there is an arrow between both Components 3a and 3b, which indicates that the features of these two components may be mutually influential as well. For example, an individual's lifestyle may determine where a person decides to live. Conversely, where an individual lives may influence her routine activities and lifestyle choices.

The reader may notice that several features within Components 3a and 3b are highly interrelated. For example, the factors of accessibility and guardianship are considered to be negatively correlated for purposes of the typological model. In other words, the lower the degree of guardianship, the greater the degree of accessibility. An argument could be made that these two factors essentially explain the same concept; however, they are presented separately, because they are also addressed separately in the literature. It is difficult to discern how much any one feature actually contributes to the victim selection process. Although there may be nuances between the features, it is important to address them individually to ensure that multiple facets of the victim selection process are considered.

ROUTINE ACTIVITIES/LIFE STYLE PATTERNS

Component 3a includes factors related to *routine activities and lifestyle patterns.* The routine activities approach and the lifestyle model were detailed in Chapter 3. Although Component 3a is based on several features related to these theories of victimization, the component is loosely structured around those concepts and includes factors from other sources as well (e.g., opportunity theory and social ecology literature). In general, Component 3a refers to a person's regular daily activities and routines, places frequented, regular travel routes, and so on. The component was not created to identify specific high risk activities or locations. Rather, it incorporates those factors that, when present, increase a woman's attractiveness as a potential rape target. However, activities considered in the component may include places of employment and work schedules, regular shopping locations, repeated travel patterns, leisure time activities, and less regular events, such as appointments with doctors and beauty salons. This list is by no means exhaustive, but is intended to give the reader an idea of the types of activities that should be considered when trying to determine a woman's risk of rape or times and places where an at-large power serial rapist may seek victims.

In Component 3a, the reader will notice reference to power-assertive rapist definitional crime properties. Recall that Cohen, Kluegel, and Land (1981) discussed definitional properties of specific crimes as part of opportunity theory (also discussed in detail in Chapter 3). They defined the concept as features of a specific crime that constrain instrumental acts by possible offenders. (The reader is also reminded that, for purposes of this study, the crime of power rape has been argued to be an instrumental act.) Based on the definitional crime properties factor, it was postulated by Cohen et al. (1981) that the greater the degree of constraint, the more significant the effects of exposure, guardianship, and proximity, relative to the effects of attractiveness. For example, in the case of the power serial rapist, the offender may see a particularly alluring woman. This allure may be based on a woman's physical features, seductive behavior, social standing, or any number of factors. Perhaps it is a woman that the rapist perceives as a "prize" or a "conquest." The ability to complete the rape act with such a woman would offer great satisfaction to the rapist who perceives himself as lacking self-worth or the rapist who views women as things to be dominated and used at will. However, regardless of the great instrumental gains that may be achieved with such a victim, if exposure and proximity to such a woman are low and if guardianship is high, the woman becomes a less-attractive target.

As previously discussed, the power-assertive rapist often uses the con technique in approaching his victims. This means that he uses an open approach in more public areas (e.g., making conversation in a bar or asking for directions on a public street) in which to approach his victim. However, once he has gained control of the victim, he quickly turns aggressive and overcomes the victim. The power-assertive rapist was included in Component 3a because this component incorporates routine activities and lifestyle patterns, both of which are elements that increase the potential for use of the con approach. Recall that proximity and exposure, both associated with the definitional crime properties factor, are already elements of Component 1. However, they are again included in Component 3a because they are essential parts of the victim selection process for the power-assertive rapist.

An analogy can be made to a spider sitting and waiting on a web. The spider may not actively move to seek victims, but rather it remains relatively still until prey is within its reach. Although the power-assertive rapist may not merely sit and wait for a victim, it is likely that he routinely visits the same locations and waits for the right victim to appear. Nevertheless, it is important to recognize that regardless of identified patterns, not all power-assertive or power-reassurance rapists will rely on similar methods of selecting victims. Therefore, although the power-assertive rapist is included in Component 3a and the power-reassurance rapist in component 3b, it does not exclude either rapist type from using alternate methods or criteria for seeking out and selecting their victims. The power-assertive rapist is also included in Component 3a because this offender type is likely to feel more comfortable approaching potential victims openly than the power-reassurance rapist. The power-assertive rapist tends to view himself as particularly masculine and thus may feel rather confident in his abilities to attract or approach a potential victim. He may even get a sense of excitement and pleasure from being able to lure and then attack his victims. Therefore, the power-assertive rapist is included in Component 3a because psychologically he is more apt to get satisfaction and fulfillment from his assault if he is able to find and approach his victims in the course of daily activities.

The first feature of Component 3a, high exposure and possibly increased association, has already been addressed in discussing the definitional crime properties of the power-assertive rapist. Essentially, if a woman spends more time engaging in activities outside of the home, it is likely to put her in greater contact with potential rapists who use public or common areas to seek their victims. The second feature of the component is high accessibility. The reader may recall that there are several types of accessibility, including physical and temporal. In Component 3a, the term refers to whether the victim is "in the right place at the right time" so to speak, thus making her attainable for the rapist. Although temporal accessibility is important in both Components 3a and 3b, physical accessibility, as described by Fattah (1991), is most relevant to Component 3b. This issue will be addressed when Component 3b is presented; however, accessibility in Component 3a refers to a more general ability of the rapist to actually be able to make contact with the potential victim.

The next feature is related to guardianship, which refers to whether or not a potential target is being overseen by another person. Guardianship may include the mother who oversees her child while he plays on the playground or the person who casually takes notice of strangers in the neighborhood or unusual activities at a neighbor's home. Low guardianship is a factor within Component 3a, because the rapist seeks victims who are less likely to be overseen by others. Essentially, the rapist wants a victim that he can approach without being easily noticed or without raising the suspicion of others. This does not necessarily mean that the potential victim needs to be alone, but rather that, if she is in the company of others, she is not under direct or constant watch by someone else. The degree of guardianship may not be obvious to the rapist, because persons unknown to each other can also provide a source of protection whether it is intended or not. For example, a bartender may casually observe the interaction between a male and female patron in the bar. Although the bartender's observations may be nothing more than a way to pass the time, on some level he is providing a degree of guardianship for the man and woman.

Another feature of Component 3a is manageability, which refers to the rapist's ability to control his victim. Manageability may refer to a number of factors, including the victim's physical size and strength, her likelihood of resistance, ease of intimidation, and potential use of a weapon, among others. As repeatedly noted, the goal of the power rapist is to fulfill a personal or internal need. The rape is not about the physical act of sex but rather about the sense of virility, self-worth, power, and dominance the rapist achieves as a result of the offense. If a potential victim demonstrates behaviors or characteristics that make her seem more difficult to manage, then the rapist is putting himself at a higher risk of failure. Such failure would ultimately serve to reinforce the negative personal perceptions of the power-reassurance rapist and defeat the power-assertive rapist in his need to dominate and control. Thus, the instrumental motive of the rape offense is not achieved. Therefore, to avoid the possibility of not successfully completing the rape act, the rapist seeks a victim who seems highly manageable, thus ensuring his success.

The next feature of Component 3a is vulnerability. Reiss (as cited by Fattah, 1991) described victim vulnerability as an offender-based phenomenon, such that vulnerability is determined by factors related to the offender rather than the victim. These factors may include offender characteristics and behaviors, personal networks, and relationships to potential victims. For example, with the power-assertive rapist, his routine activities, social circles, and lifestyle choices may make a woman with similar interests and social connections highly vulnerable. Although such vulnerability has nothing specifically to do with characteristics of the victim, the offender's behaviors and choices increase the likelihood of victimization for some individuals. Thus, vulnerability does not necessarily need to be a characteristic of the potential victim.

However, Stevens (1994) noted that in his study of serial rapists' victim selection techniques, vulnerability (or easy prey) was noted to be the most important selection factor. The rapists in Steven's study determined vulnerability based on a number of factors, including a woman's physical size and strength, her social status, and social roles. For example, according to the study, women of middle-class standing were considered to be more vulnerable. These women were more often perceived as polite and accommodating when approached casually by the rapists who would initiate contact with potential victims by asking for directions or perhaps accidentally bumping into them while shopping. Again, for the power-assertive rapist, such actions may be perceived as a game of cat and mouse. The rapist may feel a sense of power in just being able to openly approach the unsuspecting victim and, although he may not initiate the assault immediately, he has likely already made a determination of if and when the rape will occur.

The reader may recall that vulnerability is actually a feature of proneness. Specifically, the perception of vulnerability may be related to structural proneness, such that women are perceived more vulnerable based on social expectations, social roles, and so forth. This also relates to the power-assertive rapist who tends to view women as inferior objects to be used at his disposal. Therefore, vulnerability may be construed in many ways by the rapist. It may be based primarily on the rapist's easy access to the potential victim if she is often exposed to the offender or in situations in which she often interacts with him. However, the rapist may also perceive a victim as vulnerable based on very personal characteristics of the woman, including both physical and behavioral characteristics. As indicated, the feature of vulnerability can be related to several other factors already addressed. The reader is reminded that the features within Components 3a and 3b overlap and should not be construed as mutually exclusive. The components also do not include an exhaustive list of possible factors that may contribute to victim selection; however, based on both victimological and criminological research, the described factors seem to be most prominent in the understanding of victimization by the power serial rapist.

The final factor in Component 3a is facilitation, which describes behaviors on the part of the victim that potentially increase her likelihood of victimization. The concept of facilitation may refer to any number of behaviors, including a potential victim's manner of dress, speech, and interpersonal interactions, to name only a few. Although other types of facilitation will be discussed in Component 3b, facilitation under Component 3a refers to a potential victim's behavior while in the course of her daily routines, particularly outside of the home. For example, a woman who goes to a bar and becomes highly intoxicated may facilitate her victimization. A highly intoxicated state would make a potential victim more vulnerable, and possibly more manageable, because her physical and mental abilities would be compromised. Depending on her behavior while intoxicated, an otherwise quiet or reserved woman may also make herself more noticeable by being less inhibited. Thus, by her own behavior a victim may potentially contribute to her victimization. Nevertheless, as discussed in Chapter 1, although the attempt to understand victim selection necessitates study of the victim, it does not place blame on the victim.

RESIDENTIAL LOCATION

The final component of the typological model is Component 3b, which involves the victim's *residential location.* Much like Component 3a references definitional crime properties of the power-assertive rapist, Component 3b includes definitional crime properties of the power-reassurance rapist. As discussed in previous chapters, the power-reassurance rapist typically uses the surprise technique in approaching his victim, which means that he attacks his victim while she's asleep in her home. In addition, this rapist type often relies on the use of voyeurism to select his victims, indicating that his determination of an attractive target most likely includes factors related to the residential setting. Because the power-reassurance rapist has feelings of self-doubt and inadequacy, it is likely that he is intimidated by approaching a victim openly. He may fear rejection from the victim and to experience such rejection would only further legitimize his negative sense of self. Thus, by approaching the victim while she sleeps, the rapist has increased potential for successfully dominating her. It is for these reasons that the power-reassurance rapist is included in the residential location component, because he is more apt to seek his victims while they are asleep or in the confinement of their homes.

Again, although the power-reassurance rapist is included in Component 3b, this does not preclude the power-assertive rapist from using the surprise technique and approaching his victims within their homes as well. For example, Hazelwood and Warren (1990) noted that fifty-four percent of serial rapists used the surprise approach in the victim's home for their first rape. However, because the use of the victim's home as the rape location is seemingly more common among the power-reassurance rapist, the definitional properties of this rapist type is included in this final component. Despite the fact that exposure, proximity, and guardianship are all factors related to definitional crime properties, all of these factors are not specifically noted in Component 3b. Proximity is included in Component 1, and although exposure and guardianship are included in Component 3a, only guardianship is included in 3b. As previously explained, proximity is included in Component 1 and thus it was decided that the factor did not need to be reiterated in Components 3a and 3b. Exposure is included in Component 3a because this factor is crucial for the rapist to be able to sight potential rapists. Recall the analogy of the spider waiting in the web. However, the power-reassurance rapist may seek victims in "ideal" residential locations, thus the victim may not necessarily need to have previous exposure to the rapist.

The first component of 3b is low surveillance. Surveillance refers to the ability of neighbors or other onlookers to visually see what is occurring in the area around them. Low surveillance suggests that there is limited visibility or observation by others that may be due to physical structures (e.g., number of dwellings in a neighborhood and division walls) or natural features (e.g., trees and bushes). The low surveillance feature enables the rapist to move about more freely and to partake in victim selection techniques, such as voyeurism, without notice. Low surveillance also means that the rapist is less likely to be noticed in his attempt to flee the rape scene. Those features that contribute to low surveillance (e.g., busy streets, crowded sidewalks, thick woods, and structurally dense areas) may also aid in the rapist's ability to quickly allude detection and apprehension.

The second factor of Component 3b is low security, which refers to the lack or limited use of crime deterrents such as alarms, flood lights, guard dogs, security personnel, and so forth. Some neighborhoods and dwellings have protective features built in (e.g., security gates, secured entrances); however, in some cases the rapist may need to explore the presence of such devices or measures before the offense. Although security measures may decrease the attractiveness of a target, the rapist may have enough knowledge and skill to follow through with the rape and still avoid detection. Again, the rapist often relies on preoffense behaviors such as scouting, voyeurism, and entering potential victims' homes to gain an understanding of the obstacles he needs to overcome to determine the most attractive target and to ensure success of the rape act. The features of low surveillance and low security are also seemingly important factors related to the act of voyeurism. Recall that the power-reassurance rapist frequently engages in voyeuristic activities in the selection of his victims. Again, as he lacks comfort in openly approaching potential victims, he stalks them and watches from afar. This allows him to gain knowledge of his victims, to enhance his anticipation of the offense, and to fuel his fantasies.

The next factor of Component 3b is high accessibility, which was described in Component 3a and is relatively the same in this component. In general, it refers to the rapist's ability to make contact with his potential victim. However, physical accessibility is particularly important in Component 3b. The reader may recall that physical accessibility refers to elements of location or layout of a potential crime area, which increase or decrease the successful commission of the crime. For example, doors and windows of lower level, or first-floor, apartments are easier to access than those of upper-level apartments. The presence of parked cars, multiple buildings, fences, hedges, and so forth, make access for the rapist easier because he is less likely to be noticed. In addition, windows and doors carelessly left unlocked contribute to the attractiveness of a victim because physical accessibility becomes easier. There are multiple examples of increased physical accessibility; however, an exhaustive list of this factor is not necessary in the explanation of the typological model. Rather, individuals who may make use of the typological model are encouraged to consider any possible factors that may contribute to the rapist's ease of physical access in approaching his victims.

Low guardianship, as discussed in Component 3a, is also included in Component 3b. The concept remains the same in this component and it is increasingly evident how the previously addressed factors (low surveillance, low security, and high accessibility) correlate with guardianship. Again, the reader is reminded that several factors overlap and are interrelated; however, they are addressed separately to emphasize the importance and mutual influence of the numerous factors within victim selection. The next factor, high mobility, was previously discussed in Component 2. Again, high mobility refers to individuals who, because of personal factors and lifestyles, are less socially integrated. This lack of social integration is primarily related to guardianship, because neighbors are less likely to oversee those people with whom they have little or no contact. Individuals who are highly mobile (e.g., younger, single, less settled with career and family) are more likely to live in residential areas that are potentially lower in cost, more crowded, and less socially coherent. A prime example of such a setting is an apartment complex.

More mobile individuals may also be more likely to engage in activities outside of the home, thus increasing their potential exposure to rapists outside of the residential area. Although mobility could conceivably be included in Component 3a based on the preceeding notion, mobility refers to more of a geographical or social ecology issue and thus is included in the residential location component. The inclusion of the high mobility factor is not to imply that all, or even most, rape victims live in apartments or similar type housing. Rather, it is to demonstrate how factors relating to the larger macro structure (e.g., social ecology factors) affect victim selection.

Related to the factors of high mobility and low guardianship is high anonymity. Although anonymity is included as a unique factor, it is highly interrelated with the concepts of mobility and guardianship. As previously discussed, highly mobile individuals may be afforded less guardianship than those who are more settled and stable within a given community. This lack of guardianship is likely based on the fact that highly mobile persons are often more anonymous within their neighborhoods, such that neighbors either do not recognize or feel a sense of community with such people. Anonymity may be attributed to short length of time within a given community, more socialization on the part of the individual outside of the community rather than within, or simply an overall lifestyle that is less conducive to community bonding.

High manageability, included and explained in Component 3a, is also encompassed in Component 3b. This factor is defined the same in this component as in the previous one. It involves the rapist's ability to manage the victim in the course of the rape act. This may refer to the rapist being able to physically over power the victim, to overcome the use of possible weapons, and to control her while others may be present in the home (e.g., roommates or children). This is likely to be an important factor for the power-reassurance rapist because failure to manage the victim, and thus to complete the rape act, would confirm his feelings of self-doubt and rejection. Although the victim may fight or express fear and disdain for the offender during the assault, the power-reassurance rapist is not likely to regard these acts as rejection if he is still able to complete the rape act. For this offender type, he fantasizes that he has sexually satisfied his victim and possibly believes that she has positive feelings for him regardless of how she may have resisted the assault.

High vulnerability, as discussed in Component 3a, is in addition an element of this component. Again, vulnerability may refer to offender-based factors that increase a victim's likelihood for victimization or it may refer to actual characteristics of the victim herself. For example, with the power-reassurance rapist, his selection of prime residential locations for seeking victims makes those women who live within those residential areas increasingly vulnerable; however, this is based on the rapist's choices and behaviors and not those of the victim. Finally, in relation to vulnerability, there are certain victim behaviors that may increase her chances of being victimized. In the case of the power-reassurance rapist, women who leave doors and windows unlocked or leave blinds or curtains open such that individuals outside may readily see in may facilitate increased likelihood of victimization. For the power-reassurance rapist, such acts make the selection, and subsequent access, of the victim much easier.

The final element of the model is the rapist's selection of the most attractive target, given all the interrelated factors discussed in Components 1 through 3b. As previously stated, although the model does not provide an exhaustive list of victim selection factors, it highlights the most pertinent factors from various fields and types of research. It incorporates both victimological and criminological aspects of victim selection and victimization, and it incorporates both micro-level and macro-level factors. The reader should recall that both of these issues were goals for the creation of the model. Many of the factors discussed are intricately interwoven, and it is difficult to determine which factors are essentially the most crucial to the rapist in the selection of his victim(s). However, the model is meant to serve as a stepping stone for future research and as a basic guideline for use in clinical and law enforcement applications.

SUMMARY OF THE POWER SERIAL RAPIST VICTIM
SELECTION TYPOLOGICAL MODEL

This chapter introduced the reader to the Power Serial Rapist Typological Model. Figure 1 visually depicted the typology and the body of the chapter described the operation of the model. The components of the scheme were explained separately and as they related to one another. In addition, the specific factors of each component were carefully delineated. Although the model addressed victim selection of the power serial rapist in general, where possible an attempt was made to reference the power-assertive and power-reassurance rapist.

Figure 1

POWER SERIAL RAPIST
VICTIM SELECTION TYPOLOGICAL MODEL

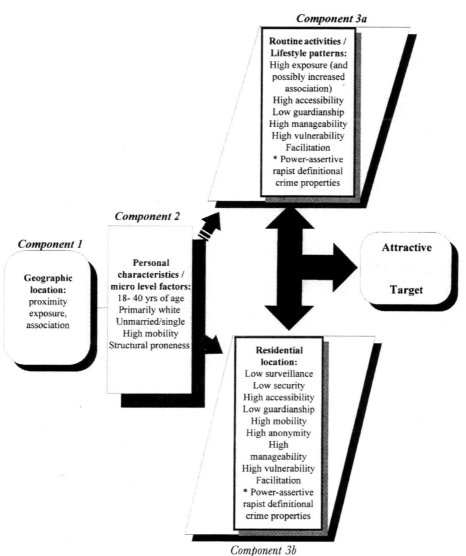

Component 3a

Routine activities /
Lifestyle patterns:
High exposure (and
possibly increased
association)
High accessibility
Low guardianship
High manageability
High vulnerability
Facilitation
* Power-assertive
rapist definitional
crime properties

Component 2

Personal
characteristics /
micro level factors:
18- 40 yrs of age
Primarily white
Unmarried/single
High mobility
Structural proneness

Component 1

Geographic
location:
proximity
exposure,
association

Attractive

Target

Residential
location:
Low surveillance
Low security
High accessibility
Low guardianship
High mobility
High anonymity
High
manageability
High vulnerability
Facilitation
* Power-assertive
rapist definitional
crime properties

Component 3b

Chapter 6

THE APPLICATION PROCESS: THE CASE OF GILBERT ESCOBEDO

OVERVIEW

This chapter addresses the explanatory and predictive capabilities of our victim selection typological model in relation to those victimization theories or approaches previously outlined in Chapter 3. This is accomplished by presenting a true case of a serial rapist and by assessing what the respective victimization typologies and models tell us about the sexual offender's process of victim selection. Accordingly, we begin by providing background material on the case of Gilbert Escobedo, a power-reassurance rapist. Information about Escobedo's victims will be outlined and then applied to the victimization theories and approaches in the order in which they were discussed in Chapter 3. The victim data will then be applied to the Power Serial Rapist Typological Model and a comparison between past approaches and our model will be delineated. The goal of this chapter is to demonstrate where and how the model we propose is a more comprehensive and encompassing approach by which to understand victimization, particularly the victim selection process for the power serial rapist.

Preliminarily we note that the information on serial rapist, Gilbert Escobedo, and his victims was obtained from the book entitled *Trespasses: Portrait of a Serial Rapist* (Swindle, 1997). The book offers a thorough account of the life and crimes of Escobedo and detailed information about his victims. The data in the text were collected in cooperation with law enforcement officials, actual victims, and friends and family of the offender. Although the book is considered a popular media rather than an academic source, it was selected for its thorough and thoughtful account of the crimes of a power serial rapist. *Tresspasses* offers information about the offender and, more importantly, the victims, which could not have been obtained by the researchers without direct access to police files or personal interviews. Given the nature of the topic, access to such records and interview cooperation would have been difficult, if not altogether impossible. In addition, the book approaches the case from psychological and law enforcement perspectives, both of which are highly relevant to this study and its future implications.

There are additional reasons for relying on Swindle's work as the basis for our own investigation on the victim selection process of power serial rapists and for developing a typology for the same. These reasons are briefly documented below. In addition, we comment on the use of a single case as the focus of our inquiry. Here, too, several justifications are delineated in the pages that follow.

JUSTIFYING OUR DATA SELECTION AND USING A SINGLE CASE FOR INVESTIGATORY PURPOSES

There are several reasons that the Escobedo case was deemed most appropriate for purposes of this study. First, as will be described, Escobedo was a notorious serial rapist who committed dozens of rapes over a five-year period. The sheer number of sexual assaults he committed makes his case particularly useful because it offers a great deal of rich, detailed data for application purposes. Recall that, for purposes of this research, a serial rapist is defined as someone with two or more different victims. According to Holmes (1991), most rapists typically sexually offended approximately 14 times before being apprehended. However, Escobedo admitted to forty-eight sexual assaults and is believed to have committed more than double that number. Therefore, the case of Escobedo offers a greater sample of victims than most serial cases might otherwise provide.

Second, because Escobedo committed his rapes over a five-year period, there is an extensive amount of information available regarding his offense behavior (e.g., modus operandi, geographical offense patterns, temporal patterns, preferred method of entry). Again, if a serial rapist has fewer victims or commits his offenses in a shorter time frame, it is more difficult to determine his behavioral patterns or any commonalities among his sexual assaults. This behavioral and victim selection information is useful because it helps to differentiate between sporadic or uncommon offense characteristics of this offender type versus more stable and typical characteristics. In addition, because Escobedo was able to avoid apprehension for a long period of time, he was a practiced and proficient sexual criminal. Thus, we maintain that examining the case of Escobedo allows for a more sophisticated understanding of the power serial rapist, given his demonstrated prowess with his type of sexual crime.

Third, the source used to obtain information on Gilbert Escobedo offers a considerable amount of detail on both the offender and his victims. As previously mentioned, the information was obtained from the book, *Trespasses: Portrait of a Serial Rapist* by Howard Swindle (1997). Swindle not only has experience with investigative reporting, but he is also an accalimed journalist having won various literary awards. His text offers a thorough and thoughtful account of the life and crimes of power serial rapist Gilbert Escobedo and includes detailed facts regarding his victims. The data in the book were collected in cooperation with law enforcement officials, actual victims, the offender, and numerous other individuals. Moreover, the inclusion of various professional and personal accounts of Escobedo's crimes gives the text depth and connectedness.

Although it may seem unsound to rely on a single case in presenting our typological model, there are two principal justifications for why this has been done. First, as previously noted, there are few biographical accounts of serial rapists, particularly power serial rapists. However, the case of power serial rapist, Ronnie Shelton, was also considered for potential application to our typological model. Shelton's offense history is vividly described by James Neff (1995) in his work, *Unfinished Murder: The Capture of a Serial Rapist.* This book is also a popular media source. We note, however, that the presentation of the offender and victim data here did not lend itself to easy identification or interpretation. Rather, Neff's book provided more of a narrative account. Relatedly, although Neff also relied on various personal interviews and historical data, he did not use the same degree of law enforcement data or rape research that Swindle incorporated into his writing.

Second, as previously stated, the purpose of the case application is to demonstrate how the typological model can be used and why it may be useful. Although reviewing additional cases may have resulted in a stronger demonstration of the typological model's explanatory and predictive capability, the use of more than one case is unwarranted and unnecessary. The nature of our investigation is grounded in a heuristic method. Accordingly, the usefulness of our method depends on its ability to extend theory to real-life applications and not to prove the absolute value of our conceptualizations. The case of Gilbert Escobedo more than adequately accomplishes this objective.

GILBERT ESCOBEDO: THE MAN BEHIND THE MASK

Gilbert Escobedo, dubbed the Ski Mask Rapist, was a prolific serial rapist in the Dallas, Texas, area from 1985 to 1990. Although he admitted to only forty-eight assaults on his arrest in April of 1990, law enforcement officials estimate that the actual number of sexual assaults committed by Escobedo may have ranged from seventy-five to more than 100. Escobedo was approximately thirty-three years old when he began his "career" as the Ski Mask Rapist. Although it was unknown how many rapes he had potentially committed before that time, Escobedo had a lengthy criminal history. As a teenager he was arrested for automobile theft and burglary and spent some time in juvenile detention. As an adult, he had several arrests and convictions for residential burglary and disorderly conduct (i.e., indecent exposure), as well as a conviction for evading arrest. He also had a history of voyeurism. Overall, the number of legal infractions committed by Escobedo ranged in the twenties. Although he was sentenced to a total of eighteen years in the Texas Department of Corrections, he served only a fraction of that time based on reductions for "good time." Despite the fact that he was a recidivist criminal, he often seemed to receive lesser sentences, because his lengthy criminal history was often overlooked. Unfortunately, such freedom only enabled Escobedo to craft his skill as a serial rapist.

Escobedo had been divorced twice and had two teenage daughters before beginning his spree as the Ski Mask Rapist. Over the five-year course of his rapes, he was engaged to a woman thirteen years his junior. After that relationship ended, he began another long-term serious relationship with a woman whom, unbeknownst to her, had been one of his victims. Escobedo came from a large, tight-knit family and often attended family gatherings, bringing his significant other along. He also had many friends with whom he engaged in social activities. He was perceived as quiet, yet affable, and a generally good-natured person. He was described as handsome, with a muscular build, "perfect teeth," and an overall "immaculate" appearance. He had a successful business in which he bought, restored, and sold old cars. He wore expensive clothes and jewelry and was so meticulous in his appearance that he often matched the color of the lenses in his sunglasses to his outfits. His meticulous attention to detail also carried over into the way he kept his home. He drove high-priced cars and lavished his girlfriends with costly gifts and dates. Overall, he presented himself as a gentleman and a romantic. After his arrest, a girlfriend reported "I was totally shocked. . . . He was successful in his business, was a very sharp dresser, had nice things, and all of this [the arrest] seemed completely contrary to his character."

Gilbert Escobedo was identified within Swindle's (1997) book as a power-reassurance rapist. According to Swindle, it was the detectives who worked the case of the Ski Mask Rapist who identified Escobedo as such. However, in discussing characteristics of the power-reassurance rapist, Swindle refers to *Men Who Rape: The Psychology of the Offender* (Groth & Birnbaum, 1979). As the reader may recall, Groth's work has been referenced throughout previous chapters of this study, and it is also Groth's rapist typology that informed the creation of the present victim selection typological model. Based on descriptions by Groth et al. (i.e., Groth & Birnbaum, 1979; Groth, Burgess, & Holstrom, 1977; Groth & Hobson, 1983) and Hazelwood (1995), Gilbert Escobedo fits the rape typology of the power-reassurance rapist.

Escobedo used voyeurism and techniques associated with the acts of burglary and breaking and entering to identify and access his victims. He also repeatedly stole expensive items (e.g., jewelry) directly from his victims after the assault or as he was in the process of fleeing the victim's home. Although he often threatened the use of force with his victims by stating that he had a gun, he only used force when necessary (i.e., when victims fought back or were uncooperative). In fact, despite his use of threats, it is not known whether Escobedo actually carried a weapon in all of his offenses. However, according to the data provided by Swindle (1997), none of Escobedo's victims appeared to have been severely physically injured as a result of the rape. One victim even described him as "calm and gentle." He would repeatedly ask victims if they were enjoying themselves, if he was sexually adequate, and other personal questions during and after the assault. On a few occasions, he even made phone contact with victims within days after they were raped. During those calls he would ask the women if they were alright or he would tell them how much he enjoyed them.

VICTIMS OF THE SKI MASK RAPIST

At the end of this chapter Figure 2 introduces the reader to the *Victim Rape Chart: Victims of Power-Reassurance Rapist Gilbert Escobedo*, which provides a description of thirty of Escobedo's victims. The chart was not intended to include all of his victims, because there is no certainty of the exact number. Overall, the data in the chart are meant to serve only as an illustration of how the Power Serial Rapist Typological Model compares and contrasts with other existing victimization theories and approaches. The chart offers important victim-related information on those victims for which such data were available. In total, there are seven categories of victim information included in the chart.

These seven categories consist of: (1) victim's age = victim's age at the time of the assault; (2) type of residence and residence description = type of dwelling in which the victim resided and any descriptive factors concerning the residence; (3) method of entry = manner in which the rapist entered the victim's residence;(4) time and duration of assault = time of day during which the assault occurred and the duration of time the rapist spent with the victim; (5) personal characteristics of victim = any descriptors of the victim, including physical features, marital status, occupation, and number of children; (6) others in residence at time of assault = any individuals (roommates, spouses, children, etc.) who were in the home at the time of the assault; and (7) miscellaneous = any other pertinent victim related information. The term *unknown* is used for categories in which the needed information was not specified within the book. In addition, under the category of *victim's age*, the reader may notice that some listed ages are preceded with an asterisk. The asterisk signifies that the listed victim was not sexually assaulted. However, these women were still victims of crimes committed by the Ski Mask Rapist including breaking and entering, burglary, voyeurism, and attempted rape. They are included in the victim chart, because the use of victim selection techniques is still applicable to such victims and because in most cases these other crimes were only the result of botched rape attempts.

The following information regarding each category is provided to simplify or generalize the data for purposes of the case application. Again, some categories are lacking information, because some data were unknown or unspecified. However, it is helpful to identify patterns that emerged within each category. Under the *victim's age* category, the majority of victims (seventeen of thirty) fell within the 20–30 year age range. Only one victim was under the age of eighteen, and only two victims were older than forty. In addition, six victims were between the ages of 31 and 40. Under the *type of residence and residence description* category, nine victims lived in apartments, seven were in houses, four were in condominiums, and one lived in a townhouse. For nine of the victims, their type of residence was not identified. However, Swindle (1997) made reference to the fact that most of the Ski Mask Rapist's victims lived in apartment complexes. Under the *method of entry* category, Escobedo accessed eleven victims' homes with no forced entry, which was most often through an unlocked door or window. On three occasions, Escobedo broke into victims' homes with force, and for sixteen of the assaults, the method of entry was unidentified.

Under the *time and duration of assault* category, most of the rapes (eleven of thirty) occurred between the early morning hours of 12:00 AM and 6:00 AM. In three of the cases, the rapes occurred between the hours of 12:00 PM and 6:00 PM, and four rapes occurred between 6:00 PM and 12:00 AM. The time for the remaining cases was unspecified. As for duration of the assaults, the shortest assault lasted seven minutes, whereas the longest lasted two hours. However, it seems that most of his rapes, particularly those committed during early morning hours, were rather long in duration. Under the *personal characteristics of victim* category, five of the victims were married or had live-in boyfriends at the time of the assault, whereas six were single, divorced, or separated. The marital status of the remaining victims was unspecified. In addition, seven of the women were mothers with children living in the home at the time of the assault. Under the *category of others in residence at time of assault,* seven rapes occurred with children in the home, two occurred with roommates in the home, and two happened with other individuals in the home (i.e., a victim's husband and a victim's maid). In fourteen cases, there was no one else in the home besides the victim at the time of the rape.

CASE APPLICATION: COMPARING AND CONTRASTING

This section will compare and contrast existing victimization theories and models with the Power Serial Rapist Victim Selection Typological Model. The case of power serial rapist Gilbert Escobedo will first be applied to the victimization theories and models previously described in Chapter 3. For each theory or model, data from the victim chart will be used to determine whether the theory or model adequately explains victim selection of the Ski Mask Rapist. As the case is applied to each individual theory or model, there will be discussion as to which victim selection factors are accounted for and which are essentially overlooked. Although additional data besides those that are included in the victim chart may be used in demonstrating the usefulness of the model (e.g., data regarding distance between rapes), the information included in the victim chart will be the primary reference for illustrating the applicability of each model. Although the case of Escobedo offers additional data beyond those that are in the victim's chart, the victim chart provides some of the most basic and essential information in investigating victim selection of the power serial rapist. The point of the following section is to highlight the ineffectiveness of the preexisting models in explaining the victim selection techniques of power serial rapists. Therefore, primarily the data in the victim chart will be discussed along with the main factors of each theory or approach in order to reduce repetition.

The preexisting victimization theories and models will also be compared with the Power Serial Rapist Victim Selection Typology throughout the section. Finally, the case of power serial rapist Gilbert Escobedo will then be applied to the Power Serial Rapist Victim Selection Typological Model. Again, a discussion will ensue that describes which victim selection factors are and are not accounted for. However, an attempt will also be made to demonstrate why the present victim selection model is more encompassing and comprehensive than already existing victimization theories or models. The reader should recall that the theories and models that are to follow are not crime specific, rather they are generalized to include all victim types. Therefore, some of the categories of the victim chart will not be applicable to each theory or model to be addressed. Also, for purposes of brevity, the Power Serial Rapist Victim Selection Typological Model will be referred to as the victim selection model for the remainder of this section.

THE TYPOLOGIES: VON HENTIG, MENDELSOHN, AND FATTAH

As discussed previously, Von Hentig's (1948) typology consisted of eleven categories based on biopsychosocial factors. In applying the case of Escobedo, essentially the first factor to be considered is gender, because the victim chart refers only to female victims. Although Von Hentig included women as a group more susceptible to victimization, he did not attempt to address why this is so. He referred to the female gender as being recognized by law as the weaker sex, yet this does little to explain a female's increased risk for victimization. The victim selection model discusses how personal characteristics (e.g., age and marital status) and structural proneness (e.g., physical weakness and social inequality) contribute to a woman being more susceptible to victimization. Relating the female gender to other factors arguably helps promote greater understanding of why female victimization occurs.

The next factor on the victim chart to be considered is *victim's age*. Von Hentig included the category of the young and noted that younger individuals are most likely to be victims. First, he did not operationally define "young," which makes it difficult to ascertain whether he was referring to a particular age range or rather speaking in comparative terms. In addition, because the typology was not created to be crime specific, it is difficult to determine to which types of crime younger persons are more vulnerable. Finally, and most importantly, Von Hentig did not address which characteristics of a young person make him or her more likely to be victimized. Again, the victim selection model relates the factor of age to other personal characteristics (e.g., marital status) and to larger macro-level factors (e.g., selection of residential location) in determining how younger age relates to increased victimization.

The next victim chart category that is applicable to Von Hentig's typology is personal characteristics. Essentially, all of Von Hentig's categories refer to personal characteristics of an individual (i.e., age, gender, mental status, or behavior). Again, although it may be true that the individual types referred to are truly at increased risk for victimization, there was no explanation why this was true. Although victims may exhibit the characteristics Von Hentig described, such characteristics do not exist in a vacuum but rather influence and are influenced by other features of the person. In addition, although the use of such general categories allows for greater applicability of the typology, it offers very little usefulness. The remainder of the victim chart categories are not applicable to Von Hentig's typology, nor do any of Von Hentig's remaining categories help to explain the victim selection of Escobedo. Overall, although Von Hentig's typology acknowledged some surface level victimization issues (i.e., age and gender), it did not provide sufficient justification for the selection of Escobedo's victim types nor would it be particularly helpful in explaining victimization by any other specific offender type.

Mendelsohn's six-part typology was based on the amount of guilt attributed to the victim. Except for one victim type, Mendelsohn's typology does not contribute to the understanding of Escobedo's victim selection. Mendelsohn referred to the *victim with minor guilt or victim because of his ignorance*, which refers to individuals who may have in some way furthered their victimization. This category may be equivalent to the facilitation factor described in the victim selection model (e.g., victims leaving doors and windows unlocked). However, Mendelsohn's other categories offer no help in understanding the victim selection of a power serial rapist. Although his typology may be useful in looking at the role of the victim across various types of offenses, it was certainly not designed to be crime specific. In addition, although he described ways in which victims may contribute to their own victimization, he did not address what other factors may have contributed to a particular victim being targeted.

Fattah's (1967) typology consists of five categories based on sociological and psychological characteristics of victims. Again, not all of the categories within the victim chart can be applied to Fattah's typology. However, some of his victim categories are applicable to the case of Escobedo. First, Fattah described the *nonparticipating victims* as those individuals who are repulsed by the offender and have in no way contributed to the cause of the offense. On the basis of personal descriptions, it seems that this category would fit most of Escobedo's victims, because it is highly doubtful that any of them were not repulsed by the rape act nor did any of them intentionally cause the offense to occur. However, although this category may accurately depict Escobedo's victims, it does not offer any understanding as to *why* the women were selected. If a woman contributes to her own victimization in some way, then it is easier to assume that her own behavior caused her to be selected as a victim. However, if a woman in no way contributed to her victimization (as Fattah describes), then understanding why that particular woman was selected as a victim becomes even more enigmatic.

Fattah's second category includes *latent or predisposed victims*, individuals who are more likely to be victimized on the basis of predisposed traits. This category could include the *victim's age* and *personal characteristics* categories of the victim chart.

Included in the underlying basis of the victim selection model is the idea that certain individual traits (e.g., age, gender, race) increase a woman's potential to be victimized by a power serial rapist. However, the model further describes why these factors contribute to increased victimization by detailing how other personal, environmental, and situational factors are interdependent and interrelated. Again, Fattah, like Von Hentig and Mendelsohn, did not offer an explanation as to why predisposed traits would contribute to a person being victimized.

Fattah's next category includes *provocative victims* or those individuals who in some manner provoke an offense by either instigating the offender or creating a situation that leads to the crime. This category could include the *method of entry* category in the victim chart. Recall that many victims were targeted, because they inadvertently left windows and doors unlocked. Although these victims would not be seen as instigating the rape, they may have created a situation (i.e., easy access) that increased the odds that they would be targeted.

Fattah also described the category of *participating victims* or those persons who play a role in the commission of the crime by being passive, making the crime easier to commit, or by actually assisting the criminal. Although this category may not seem to relate directly to Escobedo's victims, it could be argued that some victims did play a passive role or make the crime easier to commit. For example, those victims who had children in the home at the time of the assault may have been less willing to put up a fight during the rape simply to protect their children. Yet, although this may explain the behavior of some victims during the actual rape, it does not help explain why the victims were chosen in the first place.

The preceding typologies represent attempts by early researchers to understand the phenomenon of victimization. Although these typologies have served as important stepping stones in the field of victimology, they are more theoretical than practical. For the most part, they offer nominal categories that provide little explanatory value. In addition, these typologies are based mainly on victimological theory and incorporate little, if any, criminological theory or offender information. Although it is crucial to determine the role of the victim in an offense, it is the relationship between the victim and offender that provides the greatest understanding of the crime itself. Therefore, the exclusion of offender information further limits the usefulness of the typologies. Although it may be ideal for victim typologies to be crime specific, it is certainly not necessary. However, criminological theory and offender information should be incorporated if victimization is to be truly understood. Finally, the typologies were mainly focused on personal or micro-level characteristics of victims and did not include relevant macro-level factors. Again, although certain personal characteristics may predispose a person to victimization, these characteristics are not isolated. Rather, it is an individual's personal characteristics in combination with other social and environment factors that ultimately determine his or her risk of victimization. Overall, the preceding typologies offer little in the way of understanding the victim selection process of Escobedo.

THE LIFESTYLE MODEL

Hindelang, Gottfredson, and Garofalo (1978) created the lifestyle model to demonstrate how routine daily activities and lifestyle patterns determine the likelihood of victimization through the variables of association and exposure. According to Hindelang et al., lifestyle patterns are influenced by the way people adapt to role expectations and structural constraints (e.g.,economics, family, education). In addition, role expectations and structural constraints are partially determined by demographic characteristics (e.g., age, gender); however, these factors were not included in the actual lifestyle model.

Nevertheless, Hindelang et. al. postulated that adaptation and subsequent lifestyle patterns theoretically determine the associations and exposure that lead to potential victimization.

Again, although demographic characteristics were not included in the actual lifestyle model, Hindelang et al. recognized the effects of such characteristics on lifestyle patterns. Included in their definition of demographic characteristics were the factors of age, gender, race, income, marital status, education, and occupation. Several of these factors are incorporated in the victim chart. First, the chart includes only female victims and the ages of the victims are identified under the *victim's age* category. In addition, the *personal characteristics* category includes such information as the victims' marital status and occupation. Finally, income is alluded to under the *type of residence* category, through the use of such descriptors as "upper-class," "affluent," and 'luxury." Overall, there are several factors in the victim chart that are included in the determination of lifestyle patterns according to Hindelang et al.'s model. However, the next step is to ascertain how these factors influenced the rape victims's lifestyle choices and, ultimately, their victimization.

According to the lifestyle model, the next components of the model are role expectations and structural constraints (including economic, familial, educational, and legal). These factors are interrelated and combine to influence the individual's adaptations (i.e., individual and subculture adaptations). Yet, on the basis of the information provided regarding Escobedo's victims, it is impossible to determine how the factors of role expectations and structural constraints subsequently affected the women's means of adaptation. Nevertheless, without such information, the essential feature of the lifestyle model (i.e., the person's lifestyle choices) can still be used to aid in the understanding of Escobedo's victim selection. Recall that lifestyle refers to vocational activities, daily routine activities, and leisure activities. Although there was little information offered regarding the victims' daily routines or how they spent their leisure time, assumptions regarding their lifestyle may be made on the basis of their choice of residence or occupation. For example, the thirty-six year-old victim who lived in an upper-class neighborhood and whose maid was cleaning the home during the assault is likely to have somewhat different lifestyle patterns from the twenty-one-year-old victim who was a student and lived in an apartment. Yet such assumptions allow only for conjecture as to when and how the victims were associated with or exposed to Escobedo.

However, for at least one victim, Escobedo commented that he saw her at work and followed her home. The case of this particular victim illustrates how the association and exposure elements of the lifestyle model work. Essentially, the victim's vocational choice increased her association with and exposure to a power serial rapist, thus leading to her victimization. The lifestyle model takes into account micro-level factors such as personal characteristics and addresses how these factors relate to lifestyle patterns and routine daily activities. Furthermore, it uses the features of association and exposure to identify why certain individuals are targeted. In the case of one of Escobedo's victims, the lifestyle model seems to explain a great deal of why the woman was targeted as a rape victim.

Yet, in the cases of several other victims, the connection is not necessarily as clear. For example, Escobedo found most of his victims in apartment complexes. The choice to live in an apartment complex is essentially a lifestyle choice (and based on Hindelang et. al., the choice is more than likely an adaptation to role expectations and structural constraints). If it is then argued that power serial rapists seek victims in areas such as apartment complexes, then it would naturally seem that the choice to live in an apartment increases one's association and exposure to, and thus potential victimization by, a power serial rapist. However, the purpose of investigating victim selection is to ascertain *why* certain individuals are selected as victims. Even if the lifestyle model can determine that women who live in apartment complexes are at an increased risk for victimization by a power serial rapist, it fails to explain why this is the case. Arguably, based on previously addressed research, there are inherent factors associated with apartment complexes (e.g., guardianship, accessibility, and anonymity) that make them more alluring to this offender type. Nevertheless, the lifestyle model does not reference these factors and assumes that the factors of association and exposure alone are enough. Yet, even if a woman associates with or is exposed to a power serial rapist, there may be other personal, environmental, or social factors that make her an undesirable victim.

Much like the previously discussed typologies, the lifestyle model is not crime specific, and it does not include offender information or criminological theory. Without the inclusion of offender factors, simply understanding a victim's lifestyle patterns is not enough. Different

lifestyle patterns may be associated with different types of victimization. Therefore, to discuss lifestyle choices as they relate to general
criminal victimization seems to offer little usefulness.   Overall,
although the lifestyle model provides some answers in explaining the
victim selection techniques of Gilbert Escobedo, it does not provide a
full account of his victim selection processes. Specifically, it does not
address those factors that increase or decrease the potential for victimization when the factors of association and exposure are held constant.

THE ROUTINE ACTIVITIES APPROACH

Cohen and Felson (1979) defined routine activities as recurrent and
prevalent activities that provide for an individuals' basic needs (e.g.,
food, shelter, leisure) The approach included criminal offenses as routine activities that are reliant on other nonillegal routine activities. It
also applied only to direct-contact predatory violations in which three
elements converged in time and space: (1) a motivated offender; (2) a
suitable target; and (3) the absence of a capable guardian to protect
against victimization. Overall, the basis of the approach was that
changes in routine activity patterns affect the junction of predatory
crime elements in time and space, thus influencing crime rate patterns.
These changes in routine activity structure could occur at the micro-
level or the macro-level to increase the chances of predatory violation.

The application of the Escobedo case to the routine activity
approach will in some ways be similar to its application to the lifestyle
model. Essentially, the victims' routine or daily activities are again
being considered as prime factors leading to the rape victimization.
As previously discussed, daily routine activities of the victims were not
explicitly stated in the victim accounts provided by Swindle (1997);
however, certain other factors may allude to potential victim activities.
Essentially, all the categories of the victim chart can provide possible
information as to a victim's daily routines. When a victim's age, her
type of residence, and other personal characteristics (e.g., marital status, occupation) are taken into account, it is possible to make assumptions as to the type of activities in which the victim may have engaged.
For example, the twenty-five-year-old victim who lived in a condo-
minium community of mostly young, white collar workers along with

her two female roommates, likely to have different routine activities from the thirty-eight-year-old victim who was divorced, worked as an interior decorator, and lived with her two children in an affluent community. Yet, the key to understanding their victimization is knowing how these routine activities affected the convergence of the predatory crime elements (i.e., the motivated offender, suitable target, and absence of a capable guardian) in time and space.

For purposes of the Escobedo case, we know that all of the victims included in the victim chart were attacked while in their residences. Thus, regardless of their other daily routine activities, those activities that they performed while at home were the activities that increased their potential for victimization by this offender. For many of the victims, the routine activity simply involved them sleeping, and based on the time that Escobedo most often sought out his victims (i.e., between 12:00 AM and 6:00 AM), it appears that his expectation was that his targeted victims would be asleep at those hours. However, there are other indications that Escobedo watched for other types of routine activities when seeking out his victims. In the case of one victim, Escobedo waited until after the woman's husband went out for his early morning jog, leaving the house alarm off and the door unlocked, before he then attacked. With two other victims, he approached in mid-afternoon while one victim was babysitting and another victim was alone in her apartment. In addition, a third victim was watching television in her living room at 9:20 PM when the rapist boldly entered her living room window. The fact that Escobedo knew that these women would be home and alone at these times indicates that he studied his victims' routine activities and identified repeated patterns.

In the case of Escobedo, the convergence of the motivated offender and suitable target always took place within the victim's home; however, the remaining key element was the issue of guardianship. The reader should recall that in eleven of the thirty cases, at least one other individual was present in the home at the time of the rape. Although it would be assumed that the presence of another individual in the home would be a deterrent in most cases of rape, it did not deter Escobedo. However, this may relate to Cohen and Felson's (1979) description of a *capable guardian*. Of the eleven cases in which someone was in the home, seven of the individuals were children and three of the remaining four were women. Thus, perhaps Escobedo did not consider children or other women as capable guardians. Interestingly, in the one case in which a man was present in the home, Escobedo fled after being discovered peering through the window, thus no assault occurred.

The routine activities approach incorporates both micro- and macro-level factors and also includes criminological theory. It recognizes the role of daily routine activities and how such activities affect the convergence of the offender and the victim in time and space. Furthermore, it acknowledges the influence of a guardian on the likelihood of criminal victimization. Overall, some of the data in the victim chart (i.e., method of entry, time and duration of assault, and others in residence) relates to routine activities by the victims and attests to the fact that Escobedo studied his victims' behaviors. Thus, the logic of the routine activity approach seems to fit with several of Escobedo's rapes. However, unlike the lifestyle model, the routine activity approach does not address specifically how personal characteristics of the victims influence their routine activities. It also does not account for why, although all the rapes occurred within a residential setting, most occurred in apartment housing. Therefore, although the routine activities approach answers some questions regarding the victim-selection techniques of Gilbert Escobedo, the approach is not comprehensive enough to include all the many facets of victim selection used by the power serial rapist.

OPPORTUNITY THEORY

Cohen, Kluegel, and Land (1981) integrated the lifestyle model and the routine activities approaches into opportunity theory. The theory, like its predecessors, was based on the opportunity model of predatory victimization and the ideas that (1) lifestyle and routine activities bring people into direct contact with potential offenders in the absence of capable guardians; and (2) there are time and space relationships in which the potential for victimization is the highest. However, opportunity theory also attempted to explain differences in the risk of predatory victimization among dimensions of social stratification (e.g., age, race, and income). To determine the influence of such factors, Cohen et al. (1981) also focused on five mediating risk factors: (1) exposure, (2) guardianship, (3) proximity to potential offenders, (4) attractiveness of potential targets, and (5) definitional properties of specific crimes.

The case of Escobedo has already been applied to both the lifestyle model and the routine activities approach, thus, it is not necessary to recount these issues in the application of the case to opportunity theory. In summary, it was discovered that for several of Escobedo's victims, their personal characteristics, subsequent lifestyle choices, and daily activities often increased their association with and exposure to the rapist. Also, because the offender and victim converged in space and time, it seems that on some level, Escobedo considered the issue of guardianship in determining whether a victim was suitable. Again, both the lifestyle model and routine activities approach provided some understanding of the victim selection of Escobedo; however, neither approach provided a comprehensive explanation. Therefore, the case will now be applied to the remaining elements of opportunity theory to elicit what the theory has to offer above and beyond what has already been identified in the previously discussed lifestyle model and routine activities approach.

Again, in determining the risk of predatory victimization across dimensions of social stratification, five mediating risk factors were considered by Cohen et al. (1981). Two of these factors included *exposure* and *guardianship*, but will not be readdressed here, because they were discussed in previous sections. However, opportunity theory also considered the factors of *proximity, target attractiveness,* and *definitional properties of specific crimes.* In the case of Escobedo, proximity is not directly discussed in the victim chart. However, Swindle (1997) noted that Escobedo's offenses occurred primarily within a two-mile radius. This proximity between Escobedo and his victims most likely allowed him increased opportunity to study his victims. This may have included him learning his victims' daily activities, travel routes, elements of their residential setting, presence of others in the home, and so on. Essentially, by being closer to potential victims, Escobedo could have obtained information regarding all of the categories in the victim chart (e.g., his victim's estimated age, her type of residence, time when she was most likely to be alone). In addition, by living in close proximity to his victims, Escobedo was most likely very aware of easy access roads, quick escape routes, law enforcement presence, and so on.

The next factor included in opportunity theory is *target attractiveness.* This factor refers to the desirability (i.e., symbolic or material) of the potential victim, as well as the perceived ability of the targeted victim to resist the offense. Therefore, once the offender sees an appealing target, he then determines whether the victim is manageable enough to successfully commit the offense. In the case of Escobedo, several victims were described as physically attractive under the *personal characteristics* category. Therefore, it could be argued that Escobedo selected attractive victims to symbolize his virility and ability to "have" such women. It is also likely that his physical preferences for his victims were continually redefined in his fantasies.

Physical features of the victim were not incorporated in the victim selection model, because it would be impossible to determine what physical characteristics any one offender finds appealing. However, target attractiveness serves as a useful factor as it is presented within opportunity theory. This is particularly true in attempts to understand the power serial rapist. Yet, target attractiveness also differentiates between illegal acts that are motivated by instrumental versus expressive means. Essentially, the assumption is that if a crime is primarily instrumental, targets of greater attractiveness will be at a greater risk for victimization. The reader may recall that for purposes of the present research, the act of power rape was argued to be an instrumentally motivated offense. Power rapists are motivated to rape by feelings of inadequacy and low self-worth, thus it seems only fitting that such offenders would select victims who fit socially accepted standards of attractiveness and beauty to assist them in overcoming their feelings of self-doubt.

The final factor of opportunity theory is the definitional properties of crime factor. The idea underlying this factor is that the effects of exposure, guardianship, and proximity largely depend on the degree of constraint a crime has on strictly instrumental acts. Essentially, the greater the degree of constraint, the stronger the effects of exposure, guardianship, and proximity relative to the effects of attractiveness. In the case of Escobedo, he primarily used the "surprise" approach with his victims. Therefore, such an approach required him to have increased knowledge of his victims' routine activities, the layout and composition of their residential areas, the presence of others in their homes, and so forth.

Ultimately, these constraints limited Escobedo's ability to select targets based solely on a given factor, such as a victim's physical appearance or her social standing in the community. Without exposure and proximity to a victim or when there is high guardianship, there is the potential for the successful commission of the rape act to be compromised. Therefore, at times Escobedo was required to select targets that were less attractive in terms of one particular factor (e.g., physical appearance), but ultimately the victim would be seen as more attractive because there would be a greater likelihood that the rape could be completed successfully.

Overall, opportunity theory seems to offer the best explanation thus far as to the power serial rapists victim selection, as it incorporates personal characteristics, along with lifestyle patterns and routine activities. It addresses differences in victimization across various social groups, and it relates such differences to factors such as exposure, proximity, guardianship, target attractiveness, and specific properties of the crime. Overall, opportunity theory seems to be based on both victimological and criminological theory, and it references both micro- and macro-level factors. However, opportunity theory is a theoretical approach to understanding victimization and, therefore, practical application of the information to specific cases is rather difficult. It can be said that most of the factors in the victim chart are discussed at some point in opportunity theory, and the theory does seem to be relevant to cases of power serial rape. However, the theory does not readily allow for the practical application of specific offense cases. In other words, although many relevant factors are present within the theory, it is difficult to ascertain how these factors flow together in determining victimization.

SOCIAL ECOLOGY

The concept of social ecology has been described as the study of crime within specific spatial areas and social structures (*see* Byrne & Sampson, 1986). Although many researchers have contributed to the study of social ecology, the field essentially studies the occurrence of crime in relation to greater social, geographical, and spatial factors. Examples of such factors include urbanization, mobility, and the ratio of primary households within a given community. Because social ecology focuses on macro-level factors, most information contained in the victim chart is not applicable to the approach. For example, those categories detailing personal characteristics of the victims (e.g., age, marital status, occupation) cannot be explained by social ecology.

However, social ecology may help explain the small geographical range in which Escobedo committed his rapes and his selection of particular residential areas as sources of potential victims.

The reader may recall that Escobedo committed his offenses within an approximate two-mile radius of his home. As discussed earlier, it is possible that he relied on the factors of exposure and association to guide his victim selection, because he may have just targeted those victims with whom he came into regular contact. However, it is also possible that his knowledge of and comfort with his own home area allowed him to stalk, assault, and flee with greater ease than if he had sought out victims in an area less familiar to him. Yet, did Escobedo target particular residential areas simply because they were close to him, or were there specific features of those residential areas that afforded opportunities for assaults by this offender type? According to Rossmo (1997), the selection of a location for a given crime is based on both victim selection and characteristics of the area in which the victim is encountered. Based on this idea, although Escobedo may have relied on particular victim selection techniques in identifying potential victims (e.g., age, physical attractiveness, easy access), it is also likely that there were features of his surrounding neighborhoods that made them prime victim locations.

For example, according to Swindle's (1997) account, Dallas was a "burgeoning city whose population was growing hourly." In addition, there were "two million people packed into 880 square miles." Therefore, in terms of social ecological factors, Dallas was a prime area for criminal victimization. With increased urbanization and density, there is often a decrease in guardianship or familiarity with neighbors and, subsequently, an increase in anonymity. In addition, the more people there are within a relatively small geographical area, the greater the likelihood that potential offenders will be exposed to potential victims.

For Escobedo, Dallas served as fertile soil on which to seek out his targets. Not only did he live in an area that provided increased exposure to victims, but the type of area itself generated residential communities that fit the victim selection patterns of power serial rapists. In fast-growing areas, it is not uncommon for large-scale residential communities (e.g., apartment complexes) to be built rapidly to accommodate for the influx of people. Based on Escobedo's victims, apartment complexes seemed to offer an increased possibility of finding a suitable victim because such residential settings are commonly dense structures filled with single persons or small groups who are often unfamiliar to one another, because they are less likely to remain in the residence for an extended period of time.

Because social ecology is focused solely on macro-level factors, it offers only minimal understanding of the victim selection techniques of Escobedo. Although social factors are undoubtedly important in understanding victimization, personal or micro-level factors must also be considered to fully inform the victimization and victim selection process. On the basis of descriptions by Swindle (1997), it seems that Escobedo lived in a prime area in which to act out his rape fantasies. Specifically, Swindle noted that in the 1980's, the number of rapes that occurred in the Dallas area were three times the national average, and the rape statistics in Dallas exceeded those in New York or Philadelphia. Such statistics as these attest to the significance of social ecology in understanding victim selection, particularly for rapists. However, the field of social ecology alone is not encompassing enough as to address all of the relevant factors related to victim selection.

POWER SERIAL RAPIST VICTIM SELECTION TYPOLOGICAL MODEL

The case of Gilbert Escobedo will now be applied to the Power Serial Rapist Victim Selection Typological Model. It is our contention that the present model will provide a more thorough explanation of the case of Escobedo compared with other victimization theories or models. Again, this assumption rests on the fact that the current model was created based on victimological and criminological theory, and it incorporates both micro- and macro-level factors. In addition, the model was designed specifically to investigate the victim selection techniques of the power serial rapist. Thus, it is argued that the current model offers more explanatory and predictive usefulness in understanding cases of power serial rape.

The first component of the model is *geographical location*, which includes proximity, exposure, and association. In the case of Escobedo, all of the rapes noted in the victim chart occurred within a two-mile radius of the offender's home. By seeking out victims close to his own area of residence, it is believed that Escobedo had increased opportunity to interact and study his victims. This is evidenced by the knowledge Escobedo had of many of his victims before the assaults. For example, in one case he knew exactly where the victim's bedroom was directly on entering the home. In another he described her in detail. This type of information alludes to the fact that Escobedo had exposure to and, on some level, association with his victims before the assaults. In addition, as described by Swindle (1997), Escobedo often went on late-night searches for victims and at times would be within only blocks of his home. On one occasion, Escobedo's fiancé found him lurking between their apartments buildings looking up at windows. Finally, Escobedo also committed his rapes within close proximity to one another, such that some of his victims lived only blocks from one another. Overall, all of this information indicates that Escobedo stayed rather close to home in seeking out his victims.

The next component of the model includes *personal characteristics of victims.* The assumption of this component is that, after the rapist's selection of a prime geographical location in which to find victims, he then focuses on potential victims' physical characteristics in making his target selection. As justified in the creation of the model, serial rape literature indicates that serial rapists tend to target younger women, particularly those in their early twenties to mid-thirties. In reviewing the victim chart, it seems that Escobedo primarily selected victims within this age range. As previously noted, in seventeen of the thirty rapes the victims were between the ages of twenty and thirty. The idea of selecting rather young victims seems to have numerous advantages. For one, the power serial rapist is looking to restore his feelings of adequacy and desirability to women through the rape act. In hopes of regaining his sense of self-worth, it is logical that the rapist would seek women who are socially attractive, sexually capable, and who in some sense represent those types of females that he may seek to become involved with in his personal life. Recall from previous research that most serial rapists are also rather young and, therefore, it seems that on some level they select victims who are similar to them in age or other personal characteristics. In addition, as previously indicated, younger victims are less likely to be married or have children, which increases the ease with which the offender can access the victim. Also, it is assumed that a younger woman may engage in more activities that expose her to a potential offender or even allow her to associate with offender types. Overall, although age is an important factor, how age interrelates to other micro- and macro-level factors is what makes it most significant.

The next factor under *personal characteristics* is race, which in the model is delineated as primarily white. Again, this relates to rapists selecting victims who are personally similar to them. Because most serial rapists are white, so are their victims. In the case of Escobedo, all of his victims were white. The next factor involves marital status and within the model, it is unmarried or single women who are assumed to be at higher risk. As described earlier, single women are often younger, easier to access, and they may have increased exposure to potential offenders. In addition, because single women are presumed to be more mobile in their lifestyles, they may also be more likely to select residential areas that offer decreased guardianship and higher anonymity (e.g., apartment complexes). In the victim chart under the *personal characteristics* category, it may be noted that six victims were identified as single, divorced, or separated. The marital status of nineteen victims was not specified. However, given additional information (e.g., age of the victim, presence of roommates in the home, alone late at night), it may be assumed that several of the nineteen victims were in fact single or did not have a live-in significant other.

The next factor of Component 2 is high mobility. Again, high mobility refers to an individual who is less established in his or her occupation, residence, and so forth. Again, the importance of the factor is that those women who are more mobile (and again are probably younger and single) are more likely to have daily activities that increase their contact with potential offenders and who are less likely to be afforded guardianship by neighbors. In the victim chart under *type of residence*, nine of the victims were identified as living within apartments. Although in nine victim's cases the type of residence was unspecified, Swindle (1997) noted that most of Escobedo's victims lived within apartment complexes. Again, apartments are often associated with individuals who are going to live in an area for a relatively short period of time, who tend to make less money, and who are less likely to have a spouse and children. Essentially, all of these characteristics indicate that an individual has more mobility in his or her life. Of the rape victims who lived within apartments, none of them were specified as being married and only one of them was identified as having children.

The final factor of the component is structural proneness. For purposes of the victim selection model, structural proneness refers to a woman's lack of physical power and her social inequality. Although this factor does not necessarily relate directly to characteristics of the victims, it informs the mind set of the power rapist, such that he construes women as weaker or lesser creatures to be dominated, used, and controlled. However, in the case of Escobedo, it is interesting to note that at least one of his victims was described as having a physically strong physique. Her physical strength could have potentially been a deterrent to Escobedo, because he may have viewed her as being to difficult to physically manage. Yet, on the other hand, a physically strong woman may also be quite alluring to a power rapist, because sexually conquering such a woman would only increase the offender's feelings of dominance and power.

Although Escobedo seems to have sought his victims within a limited geographical location, it seems that his victim selection was first influenced by personal victim characteristics versus simply features of the residential area. This assumption is based on the fact that, arguably, there were numerous types of women (e.g., of different age, physical appearance, social status) available to Escobedo within his "hunting" area. However, most of his victims were relatively young, attractive, and easy to access, because most of them did not have an adult man living in their residence. Thus, although he could have targeted any number of women within his general geographical region, he repeatedly sought victims who exhibited similar personal characteristics.

The next component to be considered in the case of Escobedo is Component 3b, because it includes factors related to residential location and definitional crime properties of the power-reassurance rapist. For the power-reassurance rapist, there are arguably two definitional crime properties that affect this rapist's victim selection. First, because the power-reassurance rapist has feelings of self-doubt and insecurity, he seeks out victims who, by means of the assault, will help him overcome such feelings. Therefore, the rapist wants to successfully complete the rape. To fail in the course of the assault would only exacerbate his negative feelings. Thus, he is likely to seek victims that he can easily have access to, those who he can control, those who he personally finds attractive, and so on. Second, on the basis of their commonly used "surprise" approach, power-reassurance rapists are more likely to carry out rapes in the victims' homes. Essentially, the "surprise" approach necessitates knowledge of victims' routine activities, familiarity with the geographical location in which the rapes occur, and knowledge of or experience with breaking into residences.

However, all of this does not exclude a power-reassurance rapist from selecting victims on the basis of factors addressed in Component 3a. Nevertheless, because all of Escobedo's victims were approached and assaulted in their homes, it is not necessary to detail the effects of routine activities and lifestyle choices on Escobedo's selection of victims. Although it is true that a person's lifestyle choices and routine activities may affect his or her preference of residence type or location, Escobedo did not specifically focus on lifestyle or routine activity factors in the selection of his victims. Rather, his victim selection seems to have been based primarily on personal characteristics or micro-level factors and features of the potential victim's residential location.

The first factor in Component 3b is low surveillance. According to information provided in the victim chart, it seems that Escobedo may have selected dwellings that were not easily seen or observed by others. For example, in the case of one victim, Escobedo actually deterred from his usual modus operandi and actually burst through a victim's door. This approach may have been rather risky for Escobedo, yet it was noted that the door of this particular victim's apartment was surrounded by trees, thus making the doorway less easily observed. In addition, in the case of at least one other victim, it was noted that her house was secluded by shrubs. Finally, Escobedo often approached his victims at night or during early morning hours when visibility is decreased and the potential for being seen by neighbors is lower. Also, because Escobedo alluded authorities for a five-year period during which time he continually engaged in voyeuristic behavior, it would seem probable that he had to make use of various physical features (i.e., both natural and man-made) to assist in avoiding detection.

The next factor to be considered is low security. The most obvious factor related to low security in the Escobedo case is that several of the victims left doors and windows unlocked, thus permitting their assailant to enter their homes with increased ease. In at least eleven of the thirty victims included in the victim chart, there was no sign of forced entry. In six of the cases, it was specifically noted that Escobedo entered victims' homes through unlocked doors and windows. In one additional case, he entered through a window that, before the assault, he had unlocked and placed a pencil in the track of the window so that it would close and still appear locked to the victim. Also, in one case a victim had a faulty alarm system, and in another case the victim's husband had disabled the alarm before leaving the house for a jog. Thus, it is apparent that lack of appropriate security measures contributed to Escobedo's victim selection.

The next factor included in Component 3b to be applied to the case is high accessibility. Accessibility refers to whether Escobedo could physically access his victims. This factor is related to several issues. First, by seeking out victims in his local geographical area, Escobedo often had victims readily available to him. Essentially, by being close enough so that he could watch his potential victims and take advantage of them at times during which they were particularly vulnerable, many of the women were highly accessible to Escobedo. Again, in relation to the lack of security measures, by victims leaving doors and windows unlocked they ensured that their assailant could easily access them. In addition, in relation to routine activities, Escobedo typically attacked his victims while they slept. Given that sleep is a routine daily activity that most individuals do at night, Escobedo recognized that initiating the rapes during late night and early morning hours increased the accessibility of his potential victims, because they were quite likely to be home, and guardianship was quite likely to be low.

This leads to the next factor of low guardianship. Again, because Escobedo often attacked his victim during regular sleep hours, the chances of him being seen by victims' neighbors or other onlookers were decreased. However, on two occasions Escobedo was seen by neighbors fleeing the scene of a rape. Low guardianship can also be related to the type of residential setting. Again, Escobedo primarily targeted victims who lived in apartment complexes. As previously noted, individuals who opt to live in apartments often live there for relatively short periods of time and are likely to have fewer people living in the residence. Thus, based on such factors there is likely to be less significant interaction between neighbors, and ultimately a decrease in the level of guardianship.

In addition, another factor within Component 3b that is highly relevant to the discussion of guardianship is the factor of anonymity. As in the example of apartment complexes, because of the type of individuals who occupy such residences and the repeated flow of individuals in and out of them, there is greater anonymity among residents. In general, neighbors are often less familiar with each other and thus, not only is the likelihood of guardianship decreased, but the potential for it decreases as well. Arguably, if a person is not certain who does and who does not live in his or her apartment complex, then the person is less capable of recognizing a possible intruder. One of Escobedo's victims is a particularly good example of how the factors of anonymity and guardianship may affect victimization. This particular victim had moved into her apartment only hours before she was raped. In fact, it was during the process of moving into the apartment that Escobedo spotted her as a potential victim, and he continued to watch her through her window late into the night. Because the young woman was new to the complex, it was likely that neighbors would not necessarily suspect anything simply by Escobedo's presence, especially since they could not be certain whether or not he was actually supposed to be there.

The next factor in the component to be considered in the application of the case is high mobility. Again, this factor is related to personal characteristics and micro-level factors and was previously discussed with Component 2. For this reason, it is not necessary to review the factor in detail at this time. Rather, individuals who are highly mobile are more likely to select residential areas that suit such a lifestyle (e.g., apartments, rental communities). The factor was included in both components, because someone with a highly mobile lifestyle does not necessarily take residence in a community that coincides with such a lifestyle. In addition, an individual does not have to have a highly mobile lifestyle to take residence in a setting more suited to mobile individuals. Therefore, the factor was included in both components to suggest that persons with highly mobile lifestyles and those who simply live in communities that cater more to mobile individuals are both at increased risk for victim selection by power serial rapists.

In terms of applying the case to the concept of mobility as included in Component 3b, Escobedo tended to target those communities that are more appropriate for highly mobile individuals (e.g., apartments). However, it cannot be ignored that several of Escobedo's victims were career individuals with families who also resided in more established neighborhoods. Arguably, factors such as career and family reduce one's mobility and more established, family-type neighborhoods are less likely to include highly mobile persons. Yet, there are several other factors that may have played into Escobedo's selection of such victims, including proximity, exposure, personal characteristics, high accessibility and the like.

The next factor included in the component is high manageability. This concept refers to the offender's ability to physically manage the victim during the course of the assault. Factors related to manageability may include the victim's physical size and strength, and the presence of weapons or other individuals. In the case of Escobedo, he attempted to control all of his victims by the threat of use of a weapon. In most cases, Escobedo's physical strength and his threat of force was enough to control the victims. However, in some cases the victims did attempt to fight off their assailant. In general, the average woman is considered to be physically weaker than is the average man. Thus, on this basis alone, women may appear as more manageable targets to male offenders.

Yet in the case of Escobedo there were additional factors that contributed to his determination of manageability. First, there were occasions in which he entered victims' homes when they were not present. In some cases he stole personal items, and other times he simply awaited his victim. However, in one particular case previously addressed, Escobedo approached his victim at the front door of her apartment pretending to be selling candy. Once he used force to enter the apartment and controlled the victim, he immediately led her directly to her bedroom. Given that he was aware of the layout of her apartment, it is possible that he entered the residence before the assault. This type of behavior is not uncommon for power rapists and, during such occasions, the perpetrators typically study the layout of the residence and any factors that may jeopardize successful completion of the offense (e.g., presence of weapons).

Escobedo also most often approached his victims while they were asleep. By doing so, it was likely that he could gain control of his victims before they fully awoke and comprehended what was happening. Thus, simply the time in which he opted to commit the assault may have contributed to greater manageability. Finally, although seemingly risky, Escobedo attacked eleven out of thirty victims while at least one other person was present in the residence. In seven of these cases, the individuals present were children. Therefore, in such instances Escobedo was essentially able to use the children as techniques for controlling the victims. In some cases he made reference to the children being safe if the victim cooperated, and in other cases the victims took it on themselves to not fight off their assailant to keep his attention focused on them rather than the children. Thus, although the presence of others in the home at the time of the assault could be considered detrimental to the offender based on guardianship issues, the presence of others can also serve as a means of control.

High vulnerability is the next factor in the component, and essentially it has been addressed throughout the section. The combination of such factors as low surveillance, low security, low guardianship, and high accessibility certainly contribute to the factor of vulnerability. However, in some of Escobedo's cases, he planned his attacks to coincide with other events that increased the vulnerability of the victims. For example, one victim was attacked while her husband was out of town and another was assaulted while her husband was out for a jog. In these cases, it seems likely that he had studied the victims ahead of time such that he was aware not only of the fact that the women were married, but that their husbands were gone.

Finally, the last factor included in Component 3b is facilitation. For the victims of Escobedo, the most common form of facilitation involved windows and doors being left unsecured. Leaving windows and doors unlocked does not *cause* a rape, because the cause of the offense is related only to the offender. However, unsecured locks make it easier for potential perpetrators to access victims' homes. It is possible that although some potential victims may have been spared by locking doors and windows, when necessary, Escobedo also used force to enter a victim's residence. The use of force implies that even without facilitation on the victim's part, Escobedo had still selected a subject that he intended to assault.

Compared with the previously discussed victimization models and theories, the Power Serial Rapist Victim Selection Typological Model seems best suited to explain the case of power serial rapist Gilbert Escobedo. The typological model takes into account not only personal and micro-level factors associated with victims but also geographical issues, routine activities, lifestyle patterns, and residential areas. In addition, the model not only includes issues associated with victimology and victimization but also addresses criminological issues and offender factors. Unlike the previous approaches that provided typologies of victims or models for understanding victimization, the present scheme does both. First, it demonstrates the flow of factors associated with victimization and also how the factors interrelate. However, it also provides a typology of those women who are most likely to be victimized by this offender type. Finally, because the typological model is crime and offender specific, it offers a more detailed understanding of the crime of power rape and of the power rapist. Consistent with the intention behind the creation of our scheme, the Power Serial Rapist Victim Selection Typological Model is a more comprehensive, integrated and, thus, more practical model than its predecessors.

CASE APPLICATION SUMMARY

This chapter applied the case of power serial rapist Gilbert Escobedo to several preexisting victimization approaches, as well as to the Power Serial Rapist Victim Selection Typological Model. The purpose of the case application was to compare and contrast the usefulness of the various approaches and models. Specifically, the case study illustrated how our own scheme provides a more thorough understanding of victim selection techniques for the power serial rapist than other existing approaches to victimization. Although each approach was discussed separately, efforts were made to point out similarities and differences between and among the numerous theories and models by way of data offered primarily in the victim chart (Figure 2). However, the Power Serial Rapist Victim Selection Typology was discussed in greatest detail. In this context, we endeavored to provide a more thorough understanding of the victim selection techniques used by Gilbert Escobedo, the Ski Mask Rapist.

In the last chapter, we explore a number of future implications stemming from our model and its general application. Along these lines, we examine three noteworthy areas of forensic psychology including applied professional practice, criminal justice administration, and public policy. This commentary is especially important because it suggests several protean areas ripe for additional and much-needed inquiry, impacting clinical programming, institutional management, and ongoing empirical research.

Figure 2

VICTIM RAPE CHART:
VICTIMS OF POWER-REASSURANCE RAPIST
GILBERT ESCOBEDO

Victim's age	Type of residence & residence description	Method of entry	Time/ duration of assault	Personal characteristics of Victim	Others in residence at time of assault	Miscellaneous
25	Condo; residents mostly white collar workers; majority young	Unknown, but no forced entry	2 AM/2 hr	Attrative	2 roommates upstairs	Asleep when attacked
22	Unknown	Unlocked sliding glass door	3 PM/15 or 20 min	Unknown	Young child	Babysitting for a family in their home at time of offense
17	Apartment	Pretended to sell candy; entered w/force	Afternoon/ duration unknown	Unknown	None	Rapist knew where her bedroom was
21	Unknown	Unlocked window	Unknown	Unknown	2 roommates	Asleep when attacked
39	House	possibly through sliding glass door	1 AM/ duration unknown	Married; mother	2 teenage children	Asleep when attacked; husband out of town; For Sale sign on house
29	Unknown	Unknown	Time unknown/ 1–1/2 hr	Secretary; married; physically strong	None	Husband not home
36	House; upperclass community	Unknown	10:15 AM/ short duration	Married	Maid inside house; pool man outside	Husband was a doctor; wealthy

Victim's age	Type of residence & residence description	Method of entry	Time/ duration of assault	Personal characteristics of Victim	Others in residence at time of assault	Miscellaneous
36	Unknown	Unknown	Unknown	Separated; mother	3 yr old and 5yr old daughhters in bed with victim at time of assault	
25	Apartment	Unknown	Unknown	Department store buyer	Unknown	
25	Unknown	Open window	Time unknown/2 hr	Administrative aide	None	
24	Unknown	Unknown	Unknown	Sales clerk	None	
27	Apartment	Unknown	2:45 pm/ duration unknown	Night sales clerk	None	
* Unknown	House	Unknown	Unknown	Unknown	None	Considered a rape attempt; rapist was hiding in house when women arrived home
38	House; affluent community; house secluded by shrubs; faulty alarm system	Unknown	Unknown	Interior designer; divorced; mother	2 children in house; daughter asleep beside her	
*21	Condo	Unknown	Unknown	Assistant office manager	None	Attempted rape; occurred one block from a previous assault

Victim's age	Type of residence & residence description	Method of entry	Time/ duration of assault	Personal characteristics of Victim	Others in residence at time of assault	Miscellaneous
36	Townhouse; very familiar w/ neighbors; watched over community	Pencil placed under window to prevent it from locking	1:00 AM/ duration unknown	Single; mother	Young son and daughter in home	Rapist stated "i've seen yhou at work and followed you home.:
24	Apartment	Unknown	3:10 AM/ 1_hrs	Telephone operator; living with boyfriend	None	
27	House; upper-middle class community	Bedroom window	Early morning/ duration unknown	Unknown	None	
* Unknown	House	No entry	Late night/ duration unknown	Unknown	Husband in house	Caught peering through bedroom window
*28	Condo	Deadbolt pried open	Time unknown/ no assault	Model	None	Victim returned home to find door ajar; items stolen, including portfolio; lingerie scattered in bedroom
27	Unknown	Climbed through open window	9:20 PM/ duration unknown	Airline employee	None	Victim watching tv in living room when rapist entered living room window; she had received obscene phone calls in which male caller described her in detail

Victim's age	Type of residence & residence description	Method of entry	Time/duration of assault	Personal characteristics of Victim	Others in residence at time of assault	Miscellaneous
49	Luxury apartment complex	Unknown	3:00 AM/ 1_hr	Divorced; lived alone; very attrative	None	
Unknown	House	Front door unlocked and alarm off	5:32/7 min	Unknown	Two children asleep in home	Husband had just left for an early jog and turned off house alarm; this rape occurred within hours of prior rape
41	Unknown	Unknown	Unknown	Unknown	Unknown	
25	Apartment	Unknown	Unknown	Unknown	Unknown	
Unknown	Apartment .	Unknown	3:009/3:30 AM	Single; mother; administrative assistant	Daughter asleep in other room	
31	Condo	Unlocked patio door	1:30 AM/ duration unknown	Mid-level executive; recent breakup w/ serious boyfriend	None	
26	Unknown	Unknown	Unknown	Aerobics instructor	Unknown	
22	Apartment	Unknown	Early morning hours/ duration unknown	Secretary	None	Moved into the apartment only hours before rape; was watched through window prior to assault
* 21	Apartment; entranceway surrounded by trees	Bust through front door	Evening or night/no assault	Student	None	Targeted victim called police and rapist fled

* indicates that the victim was not sexually assaulted

Chapter 7

FUTURE IMPLICATIONS AND CONCLUSIONS

OVERVIEW

This study yields important implications for the field of forensic psychology, particularly when dealing with both the power serial rapist and the offender's victims. The field of forensic psychology is essentially composed of three domains: (1) applied psychology; (2) criminal justice administration; and (3) public policy (Arrigo, 2001). The applied domain deals with the clinical aspects of working with forensic populations such as assessment, diagnosis, and treatment. The criminal justice administration domain uses forensic psychological theory, research, and practice to oversee the direction of criminal justice institutions including jails, prisons, law enforcement agencies, and so on. Finally, the public policy domain draws on theory, research, and practice to inform policy making and to implement policy decisions that affect various forensic populations, as well as several crime, law, and justice institutions and/or settings.

APPLIED FORENSIC PSYCHOLOGY

Psychological Assessment

The study of victim selection is analogous to dissecting the crime within the mind of the perpetrator. Although victim selection is only one possible facet of a crime, it is certainly an important element that can provide invaluable clues into the way the offender perceives and processes the world around him or her. However, studying the victim selection techniques of the power serial rapist does not mean that the uncovered information is limited only to that particular offender type. Rather, understanding even one specific aspect in the decision-making process of such an offender may provide broader information about cognitive processes in general.

Information uncovered through the current research may help identify warning signs of individuals who are at high risk for offending, who are potentially dangerous, or who are at serious risk of being victimized. Study findings regarding characteristics of both victim and offender could be incorporated into a standard assessment interview to identify potentially dangerous aspects of an individual's behavior. For example, the reader may recall that according to the NCAVC study regarding serial rapists, sixty-eight percent of the rapists reported beginning window peeping in childhood or adolescence. In addition, several rapists stated that they used voyeuristic behaviors in the selection of their victims (Hazelwood, Reboussin, & Warren, 1989). Therefore, during an assessment if a clinician discovers that his or her client takes part in voyeuristic or other "nuisance offenses," the clinician may wish to further investigate this behavior. On the basis of previous serial rapist research, it is possible that such an individual may escalate to more serious and/or violent offenses. Voyeurism may be only one potential victim selection technique. However, knowledge of other such techniques may prove useful to clinicians during assessment interviews, particularly when dangerousness is at issue.

Victim selection research also provides an important link in assessing clients who have been victimized or determining those who are at risk for potential victimization. By understanding those factors that may contribute to an individual being victimized, a clinician may be able to ascertain what aspects of a client's behavior are problematic. For example, past research has indicated that many rapists will seek out women who are submissive and/or polite, because such women are perceived as vulnerable and thus easier victims. This type of information in combination with knowledge of the risks surrounding various lifestyles and geographical locations can allow a clinician to identify problems a client may not otherwise consider. For example, a young, single, female student who lives in a neighborhood of mostly unmarried individuals may not see her lack of assertiveness as an issue she needs to address. However, a clinician with an understanding of victimology and victim selection may recognize that the combination of such lifestyle factors puts the client at a higher risk for criminal victimization. Thus, issues such as assertiveness and awareness may become of greater significance.

Diagnosis

Many diagnoses not only rely on behavioral aspects but cognitive ones as well (e.g., lack of remorse, feelings of inferiority). Because the study of victim selection attempts to uncover a particular cognitive process, it may be possible to obtain information that would be useful for diagnostic purposes. For example, if an offender has extreme feelings of inadequacy, he may not be able (or willing) to voice such feelings. However, the types of victims he selects may offer important clues into his psychological makeup. Suppose this offender selects women who are smaller, weaker, less attractive, or less educated. Such victim selection criteria may signify that the offender's own inadequacies cause him to seek out women whom he feels are inferior or who will not be able to reject him. This type of information could prove useful to a clinician in determining possible diagnoses. Overall, although the current victim selection study may not be a significant diagnostic tool, it may offer evidence into the way an individual perceives himself or herself. However, understanding the cognitive process that an offender uses in selecting, finding, and obtaining his or her victims may provide invaluable insight into the criminal's mind.

Intervention

Victim Treatment

The field of victimology has always contended that no individual is ever responsible for his or her victimization. This position has especially held true for sexual assault victims as an attempt to repudiate accusations by society members and law enforcement officials who have at times attributed fault to the victim. Although such blamelessness of victims was promoted in the 1970's, victimology has since begun to focus more on victims as having a role in criminal acts. This idea was exemplified by such concepts as the rational-choice perspective that contends that some criminals do make decisions regarding the selection of their victims.

Although it could be justifiably argued that such a position would make victims feel denounced, this view actually empowers many victims (Davis et al., 1997). There are victims who feel that by understanding those factors that may have contributed to their victimization, they can better adapt and make specific changes to help decrease their chances of being victimized again. The creation of the victim selection typological model may not only provide an educational tool for all rape victims to help them alter potentially dangerous factors in their lives, it may also provide a therapeutic tool to help them better come to terms with their victimization.   .

Offender Treatment

Arguably, there is a clearer understanding of the offender when there is an understanding of the offender's victim(s). By creating the typological model, there is an increased awareness of the power serial rapist's thought processes and behaviors. By understanding those elements of an individual that entices or attracts a power serial rapist, it may also be possible to better comprehend the reasoning behind this offender's crimes. Although rapists are among the most difficult type of sex offender to treat, any knowledge that can be obtained regarding this offender can be of benefit to treatment or correctional professionals. The information obtained in this study regarding the power serial rapist and his victim selection adds a new "brick" to the literature foundation regarding both this particular offender and to victims in general. Furthermore, this study may assist future researchers in performing more empirical research, particularly qualitative, to acquire the perpetrator's own perspective of his use and execution of victim selection techniques.

Nevertheless, the current study may be beneficial in the treatment of all types of offenders. The concept of victim selection essentially refers to a decision-making process in which an offender selects an *appropriate* victim based on criteria that he or she deems necessary for successful completion of the crime. Although not all offenders make use of a victim selection process, many offenders rely on what may be referred to as criminal thinking. Rather than using rational thought processes to maintain a productive and law-abiding lifestyle, many offenders focus on ways to manipulate, con, and take advantage of others. Their mind set is often one of opportunity and their cognitive processes deviate from individuals who rely on moral consciousness, responsibility, and reason.

By investigating the cognitive processes that underlie victim selection, it may be possible to uncover cognitive errors that are often a part of criminal thinking. By understanding how offenders determine vulnerability, opportunity, and formulate the commission of their crime, it may be possible to intercede using cognitive therapy techniques. By better understanding the manner in which offenders view themselves, their victims, and their crimes, it may be possible to provide more appropriate therapeutic techniques.

Prevention

As previously noted, there may be aspects of an individual's behavior that act as warning signs of potential danger. For example, this danger could be in the form of an offender who will escalate in violence or in the form of an individual who is putting himself or herself at serious risk of victimization. Through an understanding of the criteria that the power serial rapist uses when selecting his victims, it may be possible to take preventive measures in dealing with both the offender and the likely victims.

For example, using the proposed typological model, a clinician may be able to identify types of locations, activities, or individuals that are potential targets of the power serial rapist. By understanding the significance of such targets, a clinician may be able to work toward decreasing the possibility of future rapes or other sexual assaults by addressing these factors. For example, knowing the victim selection techniques of the power serial rapist would inform the clinician of the offender's perception of vulnerability, inferiority, power, and so on. By dealing with and having the offender deal with these issues openly, it may be possible to decrease the need for the rape behavior. It is important to understand that offenders may not be consciously aware of the motivations of their offending. However, if a clinician understands the concepts of victim selection, he or she may be able to ascertain aspects of the offender's behavior that even the offender himself has not yet recognized. Although the preceeding example applied only to the power serial rapist, victim information in relation to other types of offenders (e.g., pedophiles, domestic violence offenders, burglars) may also prove useful for preventive work.

Victim selection research also provides a powerful tool in doing preventive work with past and/or potential victims. Whether the issue is rape or other types of criminal victimization, understanding what makes an individual a highly likely crime target is significant. The issue of vulnerability is a key factor, yet not all individuals realize what the concept of vulnerability includes. Some people may think only in terms of physical size or strength, but as demonstrated by past victimization research, vulnerability comes in many forms. Informing individuals of how factors such as geographical location, occupation, dwelling type, and so on affect the risk of victimization provides people with the ability to better protect themselves and each other. The prevention of victimization begins with an understanding of how a victim is defined within the mind of the offender.

CRIMINAL JUSTICE ADMINISTRATION

Offender Apprehension

Profiling

The development of a victim selection typological model carries implications for the apprehension of offenders. Offender typologies are a common source of information in psychological profiling, which serves as a forensic tool in assisting crime investigations. Psychological profiles are essentially estimates of the type of individual who may have committed a particular crime based on factor patterns found in similar past offenses. The use of such profiles may not only alert law enforcement officials to the physical and personality characteristics of such offenders but of behavioral characteristics as well. Although the study and use of psychological profiling has increased within the past fifteen years, the victim has often been neglected as a component in creating profiles (Holmes & Holmes, 1996). Nevertheless, the more information obtained on the crime victim, the greater the profiling results will be in targeting possible perpetrators. Overall, rape cases alone account for twenty-five percent of profiling requests submitted to the FBI's Criminal Personality Profiling Program (Holmes & Holmes, 1996).

Law enforcement agencie's understanding and use of a victim selection typology that focuses specifically on serial rape may assist in producing faster and more accurate profiles for tracking and apprehending this type of offender. By understanding the types of victims that certain offenders target, investigators can use crime victim information to better identify, or profile, the type of offender they are seeking. Because serial offenders have a number of victims, the compilation of extensive victim information in these cases makes for a more solid framework from which to apply a victim typology. Using a victim typology can assist investigators in ascertaining the category of offender they are seeking (e.g., a sadistic vs. anger rapist), and then a criminal typology can be used to elicit a profile of more characteristic information on the perpetrator.

Tracking

The Victim Selection Typological Model may also assist law enforcement officials in tracking power serial rapists by providing clues as to the location(s) where the offender may rape again. With knowledge of the geographical and physical locations that are targeted by such offenders, law enforcement agents can intensify efforts in locales that best fit the typology. For example, the power-assertive rapist tends to use the "con" method of approach. This method involves the offender approaching his potential victim in an open manner (e.g., through conversation, asking for directions). However, once she is in his control, he will then turn aggressive and attack (Hazelwood, 1995). This type of offender may target bars, clubs, or other local gathering places or may seek hitchhikers on major roadways.

On the other hand, the power-reassurance rapist tends to use the "surprise" method of approach. For this method the rapist attacks an unsuspecting victim (e.g., while a victim is sleeping) (Hazelwood, 1995). This approach is based on the presumption that the rapist pre-selected his victim and had knowledge of her daily routines (e.g., hours of sleeping, when victim is alone). This type of offender would perhaps be more readily found in residential settings (e.g., housing or apartment dwellings), where he could search for suitable targets and learn the area layout for easy access and escape. Therefore, the use of such information, as provided by a victim selection typology, would allow law enforcement officials to investigate in a more effective manner by narrowing their investigations to areas that fit the methods of the offender type they are seeking.

Apprehending

For certain types of offenses, the use of an undercover law enforcement officer as a decoy may serve as a method of apprehension. Yet without an understanding of the type of victim an offender is seeking, the use of a decoy may prove futile. It may be a reasonable assumption that any female officer could pose as a potential rape victim to aid in the apprehension of a rapist. However, such an assumption does not take into account the fact that some rapist types (e.g., power rapists) look for particular criteria when searching for their victims.

For example, a decoy was used in a past case of a serial rapist who was at large in a metropolitan area. Investigators concluded that the rapist was approaching all of his victims in the same local park area. A female officer was sent undercover to sit in the park in hopes of attracting the offender. However, the female officer was never approached even after sitting in the park for several hours each day. The perpetrator was eventually apprehended and the female officer then asked him why he never approached her in the park. Although the offender had admitted to spotting the women in the park days before, he stated that he could tell by the way she carried herself that she was not a victim. In that particular case, knowing the area in which the various victims had been approached assisted investigators in tracking the offender and targeting a particular locale for possible apprehension. However, more in-depth knowledge regarding personal characteristics (e.g., demeanor) of the previous victims may have allowed for the officers to create a more *attractive* decoy. Therefore, understanding the specifics of victim selection may allow for better methods of apprehension.

Crime Prevention

Law enforcement agencies can also use the victim selection typological model for victim profiling, which is an investigative tool that is still in its infancy. By referring to the typological model, investigators can enhance prediction of the types of women, situations, and locales most commonly associated with the power rapist's method of attack.

By identifying those factors that increase a woman's probability of being victimized, potential victims can be alerted and educated to aid in protecting themselves. Law enforcement agencies' dissemination of such information in areas where a reported serial rapist may be at large may serve to make women in that locale more cautious in their daily activities. Furthermore, the general distribution of this information can serve as an educational tool to increase all women's awareness of their own ability to protect themselves from the vulnerability of rape. Thus, the introduction of the typological model may not only enhance the psychological profiling of serial rapists but may also encourage the application and future creation of such models to aid and enhance victim profiling in investigative endeavors.

PUBLIC POLICY

The use of a victim typology model in criminal cases can only be successful if ample and accurate victim information is gathered by law enforcement officials after the reporting of a crime. This information should extend beyond a victim statement and evidentiary facts. In-depth information should be gathered from the victim regarding such factors as her daily activities, travel routes, social activities, and so on. Ideally, in cases of serial rape more extensive victim information should be obtained so investigators can make comparisons between case findings. The increased use of victim typologies and/or victim profiling by law enforcement agencies could potentially lead to new policies concerning the collection and review of victim information. There could also be policy implementation on the public dissemination of potential victim information in cases in which a reported perpetrator has not yet been apprehended.

Again, victim selection research may provide indicators of potentially dangerous behavior particularly in regard to offenders. Awareness of the behavioral aspects involved in seeking out victims may alert clinicians and/or law enforcement officials of perpetrators who are likely to escalate in number of offenses, degree of violence, and so on. This type of information may be especially useful in the creation of criminal statutes. For example, nuisance sexual offenses (e.g., voyeurism, exhibitionism) in and of themselves may be deemed harmless and therefore receive a lesser penalty. However, these types of

behaviors in combination with other factors may prove to be dangerous signs of an offender whose criminal tendencies will become
increasingly more serious. Victim selection research may allow for the
creation of laws that help to prevent sexual perpetrators from escalat-
ing in their offenses by targeting particular types of offenders for more
in-depth analysis and treatment. Although the current research focuses on the crime of rape, future victim selection studies regarding other
types of offenses may also be useful in creating statutory law that aids
in crime prevention and public protection.

Finally, on the basis of ecological and community factors associated
with this type of offense (e.g., area visibility, guardianship), a victim
selection typological model may also help inform community planning. For example, builders and planners may begin to recognize the
importance of physical accessibility. This refers to such factors as location or layout of a potential crime area that may enhance or impede
the commission of a crime. For example, the location of doors and
windows on a home, and thus the ease of entering and exiting a
dwelling, may be important determinants of an offense. In addition,
the placement of fences or hedges may make certain areas less visible
to others and, therefore, a more accessible and attractive target. Based
on these concepts and data regarding the serial rapist, physical accessibility is arguably an important factor of victim selection in power
serial rapes. Therefore, understanding ecological factors associated
with victim selection may not only yield community changes to deter
power rapists but other offender types as well (e.g., burglars, vandals)

CONCLUSIONS

This book introduced the reader to a victim selection typological
model predicated on the offense behaviors of the power serial rapist.
The investigation began by introducing the reader to the concept of
victim selection and its importance in both the fields of victimology
and criminology. In addition, arguments were made as to the usefulness of the overall project.

In Chapter 2, the reader was then introduced at length to existing
research within the rape and victimology literature. Along these lines,
we canvassed and analyzed the crime of rape. This included a brief
historical overview of the offense, a discussion of various types of rape,

a summary of rapist typologies, and, finally, research focused solely on serial rapists. Next, we systematically addressed the field of victimology. Again, a historical overview of the field was presented, including the various orientations and approaches that have contributed to the discipline. In addition, we examined the victim-offender relationship.

In Chapter 3, we reviewed several leading victimization models and theories. We explored several victim typologies and other approaches to understanding victimization. Each scheme was described in its original form, and relevant research pertaining to it was discussed. Throughout this analysis, attempts were made to link the behaviors of the power serial rapist to each identified approach.

In Chapter 4, we focused on method, subdividing the chapter into three main sections. In the first section, we explained why a critique of existing victimization approaches was warranted, reviewed previous efforts along these lines, and laid the (selection criteria) foundation for our own typological inquiry. In the second section, we engaged in the critique, examining the victim typologies of Von Hentig, Mendelsohn, and Fattah, and the power rape category created by Groth. Although not based on a typological approach per se, the lifestyle model, the routine activities approach, the opportunity theory scheme, and the social ecology model were also assessed, given their relevance in the creation of our own victim selection typology. In the third section, we explained our heuristic method, commenting on the relevance and usefulness of its selection for purposes of our inquiry.

Chapter 5 presented the Power Serial Rapist Typological Model. It was diagramed and described in detail. The description discussed not only individual factors within components of the model but also addressed how such factors and components were interrelated. In this context, research contributions from criminology and victimology were integrated

In Chapter 6, the case of power serial rapist Gilbert Escobedo was applied to the preexisting victimization approaches, as well as to our own typological model. This assessment was a deliberate attempt to determine the explanatory and predictive capabilities of any one model, chiefly focusing on the insights of our own typology. Along these lines, we indicated why our proposed model was preferable when explaining the victim selection techniques of the power serial rapist.

In Chapter 7 we outlined a series of implications for the field of forensic psychology, given our typological model. We tentatively explored three domains of relevant inquiry: (1) applied (forensic) psychology; (2) criminal justice administration and management, (3) and law and public policy. Each of these areas, although speculatively reviewed, suggested viable areas of inquiry, impacting future clinical treatment, organizational and policy management, and empirical research.

Overall, the goal of our research was to inform the reader about the importance of understanding the concept of victim selection. This was done through the creation of an offender-specific victim selection typological model. Our intent was to demonstrate how our typology was more comprehensive, integrated, and, thus, practical than other victimization approaches currently found within the literature. Given the limits we identified after the application of all existing victimization models to the case of Gilbert Escobedo, and given the strengths identified through the application of our model to the case of the Ski Mask rapist, we maintain that our typology offers greater explanatory and predictive capability than its predecessors. Thus, we contend that our research objective was realized.

In summary, victim selection is an important facet to comprehending criminal acts, the victim, and the offender. Although not all offenders make use of victim selection techniques, those who do (unwittingly) provide data enabling investigators to further explore and understand their criminal behavior. We hope that this mostly conceptual study will be used as a basis from which to engage in future empirical research on victim selection. In addition, however, we hope that the Power Serial Rapist Victim Selection Typological Model finds its way into the very real and difficult work engaged in by forensic mental health practitioners, law enforcement officials, and all those victims harmed (and potentially devastated) by the power serial rapist.

REFERENCES

Amir, M. (1976). Victim precipitated forcible rape. *The Journal of Criminal Law, Criminology, and Police Science, 58*(4), 493–502.

Amir, M. (1971). *Patterns in forcible rape.* Chicago: University of Chicago Press.

Arrigo, B.A. (1993). An experientially–informed feminist jurisprudence: Rape and the move toward praxis. *Humanity & Society, 17*(1), 28–47.

Arrigo, B.A. (2001). Reviewing graduate training models in forensic psychology: Implications for practice. *Journal of Forensic Psychology Practice, 1*(1), 9–31.

Babbie, E. (1992). The Practice of Social Research (6th ed.). Belmont, CA: Wadsworth.

Blazicek, D.L. (1979). The criminal's victim: A theoretical note on the social psychology of victim selection. *Journal of Crime and Justice, 1*, 113–131.

Brownmiller, S. (1975). *Against our will.* New York: Simon and Schuster.

Bureau of Justice Statistics (1984). *Criminal victimization in the United States,* 1982. Washington D.C.: U.S. Department of Justice.

Burgess, A. (Ed.) (1985). *Rape and sexual assault.* New York: Garland Publishing, Inc.

Burgess, A.W., & Holstrom, L.L. (1974). Rape trauma syndrome. *American Journal of Psychiatry, 131*, 982–986.

Byrne, J.M., & Sampson, R.J. (1986). Key issues in the social ecology of crime. In J.M. Byrne, & R.J. Sampson (Eds.), *The social ecology of crime.* New York: Springer-Verlag.

Chappell, D., Geis, R., & Geis, G. (Eds.) (1977). *Forcible rape: The crime, the victim and the offender.* New York: Columbia University Press.

Chappell, D., Geis, G. & Fogarty M. (1974). Forcible Rape: Bibliography. *Journal of Criminal Law & Criminology 65*, 248–262

Chappell, D., & James, J. (1986). Victim selection and apprehension from the rapists perspective: A preliminary investigation. In K. Miyazawa & M. Ohya (Eds.), *Victimology in comparative perspective.* Tokyo: Seibundo Publishing Co.

Clarke, R., & Felson, M. (1993). Introduction: Criminology, routine activity and rational choice. In R. Clarke & M. Felson (Eds.), *Routine activity and rational choice advances in criminological theory,* vol. 5. New Brunswick: Transaction Publishers.

Cohen, L.E., & Felson, M. (1979). Social change and crime rate trends: A routine activities approach. *American Sociological Review, 44*, 588–608.

Cohen, L.E., Klugel, J.R. & Land, K.C. (1981). Social inequality and predatory victimization: An exposition and test of a formal theory. *American Sociological Review, 46* (Oct.), 505–525.

Cohen, M.L., Garofalo, R., Boucher, R.J., & Seghorn, T.K. (1971). The psychology of rapists. *Seminars in Psychiatry, 3,* 307–327.

Cohen, M.L., & Seghorn, T.K. (1980). The psychology of the rape assailant. In W.J. Curran, A.L. McGarry, & C.S. Petty (Eds.), *Modern legal medicine, psychiatry, and forensic science.* Philadelphia: F.A. Davis Company.

Cohen, M.L., Seghorn, T.K., & Calmas, W. (1969). Sociometric study of the sex offender. *Journal of Abnormal Psychology, 74,* 249–255.

Cornish, D.B., & Clarke, R.V. (Eds.). (1986). *The reasoning criminal: Rational choice perspectives on offending.* New York: Springer-Verlag.

Creswell, J. W. (1998). *Qualitative inquiry and research design: Choosing among five traditions.* Thousand Oaks, CA: Sage Publications.

Crutchfield, R.D., Geerken, M.R., & Gove, W.R. (1982). Crime rate and social integration: The impact of metropolitan mobility. *Criminology, 20* (3&4), 467–478.

Davis, R.C., Taylor, B.G., & Titus, R.M. (1997). Victims as agents. In R.C. Davis, A.J. Lurigio, & W.G. Skogan, (Eds.), *Victims of crime* (2nd ed.). Thousand Oaks, CA: Sage Publications.

Deming, M.B., Eppy, A. (1981). The sociology of rape. *Sociology and Social Research, 65*(4), 357–380.

Drapkin, S, & Viano, E., (Eds.). (1974). *Victimology.* Lexington, MA: Lexington Books.

Dunn, C.S. (1980). Crime area research. In D.E. Georges-Abeyie, & K.D. Harries (Eds.), *Crime: A spatial perspective.* New York: Columbia University Press.

Fattah, E.A. (1967). Towards a criminological classification of victims. *International Criminal Police Review,* 209.

Fattah, E.A. (1979). Some recent theoretical developments in victimology. *Victimology: An International Journal, 4*(2), 198–213.

Fattah, E.A. (1991). *Understanding criminal victimization.* Scarborough, Ontario: Prentice-Hall Canada Inc.

Fattah, E.A. (1992). Victims and victimology: The facts and the rhetoric. In E.A. Fattah (Ed.), *Towards a critical victimology.* New York: Macmillan.

Fattah, E.A. (1993). The rational choice/opportunity perspectives as a vehicle for integrating criminological and victimological theories. In R. Clarke & M. Felson (Eds.), *Routine activity and rational choice advances in criminological theory,* vol. 5. New Brunswick: Transaction Publishers.

Fattah, E.A. (1995). *La victimolige au carrefour entre la science et l'ideologie. Revue Internationale de Criminologie et de Police Technique, 2,* 131–139.

Fattah, E.A. (1997). Toward a victim policy aimed at healing, not suffering. In R.C. Davis, A.J. Lurigio, & W.G. Skogan, (Eds.), *Victims of Crime* (2nd ed.). Thousand Oaks, CA: Sage Publications.

Feild, H., & Barnett, N. (1977). Forcible rape: An updated bibliography. *The Journal of Criminal Law & Criminology,* 68(1), 146–159.

Felson, M. (1986). Linking criminal choices, routine activities, informal control and criminal outcomes. In D.B. Cornish & R.V. Clarke (Eds.), *The reasoning criminal: Rational choice perspectives on offending.* New York: Springer-Verlag.

Felson, M. (1992). Routine activities and crime prevention: Armchair concepts and practical action. *Studies on Crime and Crime Prevention, 1,* 31–40.

Felson, M. (1994). *Crime and everyday life.* Thousand Oaks, CA: Pine Forge Press.

Felson, M., & Clarke, R. (1995). Routine precautions, criminology, and crime prevention. In H. Barlow (Ed.), *Crime and public policy: Putting theory to work.* Boulder, CO: Westview Press.

Felson, R.B. (1997). Routine activities and involvement in violence as actor, witness, or target. *Violence and Victims, 12*(3), 209–221.

Garofalo, J. (1986). Lifestyles and victimization: An update. In E.A. Fattah (Ed.), *From crime policy to victim policy: Reorientating the justice system.* London: McMillan.

Garofalo, J. (1987). Reassessing the lifestyle model of criminal victimization. In M.R. Gottfredson & T. Hirschi (Eds.), *Positive criminology.* Newbury Park, CA: Sage Publications.

Gates (1978), Introduction, (pp. 9–27). In J. R. Chapman & M. Gates (Eds), *Victimization of women.* Beverly Hills, CA: Sage Publications.

Gebhard, P.H., Gagnon, J.H., Pomeroy, W.B., & Christenson, C.V. (1965). *Sex offenders: An analysis of types.* New York: Harper & Row.

Geis, G. (1977). Forcible rape: an introduction. In D. Chappell, R. Geis, & G. Geis (Eds.), *Forcible rape: The crime, the victim, and the offender.* New York: Columbia University Press.

Georges-Abeyie, D.E. & Harries, K.D. (1980). *Crime: A spatial perspective.* New York: Columbia University Press.

Giorgi, A. (1992). The idea of human science. *The Humanistic Psychologist, 20* (2&3), 202–217.

Gottfredson, M.R. (1981). On the etiology of criminal victimization. *Journal of Criminal Law and Criminology, 72,* 714–726.

Groth, N., & Birnbaum, H.J. (1979). *Men who rape: The psychology of the offender.* New York: Plenum.

Groth, N., & Burgess, A. (1980, July). Male rape: Offenders an victims. *American Journal of Psychiatry, 137*(7), 806–810.

Groth, N., Burgess, A., & Holstrom, L. (1977). Rape: Power, anger, and sexuality. *American Journal of Psychiatry, 134*(11), 1239–1243.

Groth, N.A., & Hobson, W.F. (1983). The dynamics of sexual assault. In L.B. Schlesinger & E. Revitch (Eds.), *Sexual dynamics of anti–social behavior.* Springfield, IL: Charles C Thomas.

Guralnik, D.B. (1980). *Webster's new world dictionary of the American language* (2nd ed.). New York: Simon & Schuster.

Guttmacher, M.S., & Weihofen, H. (1952). *Psychiatry and the law.* New York: W.W. Norton & Company.

Hawley, A. (1950). *Human ecology: A theory of community structure.* New York: Ronald.

Hazelwood & A.W. Burgess, (Eds.), *Practical aspects of rape investigation: A multidisciplinary approach* (2nd ed.). New York: CRC Press.

Hazelwood, R., & Burgess A. (1987). An introduction to the serial rapist: Research by the FBI. *FBI Law Enforcement Bulletin,* Sept., 16–24.

Hazelwood, R. (1995). Analyzing the rape and profiling the offender. In R.R. Hazelwood, R., Reboussin, R., & Warren, J. (1989). Serial rape: Correlates of increased aggression and the relationship of offender pleasure to victim resistance. *Journal of Interpersonal Violence, 4*(1), 65–78.

Hazelwood, R., & Warren, J. (1989a). The serial rapist: His characteristics and victims (Part 1). *FBI Law Enforcement Bulletin,* Jan., 10–17.

Hazelwood, R., & Warren, J. (1989b). The serial rapist: His characteristics and victims (Conclusion). *FBI Law Enforcement Bulletin,* Feb., 18–25.

Hazelwood, R., & Warren, J. (1990). Rape: The criminal behavior of the serial rapist. *FBI Law Enforcement Bulletin,* Feb., 11–16.

Hickman, S.E., & Muehlenhard, C.L. (1997). College women's fears and precautionary behaviors relating to acquaintance rape and stranger rape. *Psychology of Women Quarterly, 21,* 527–547.

Hindelang, M.J. (1976). *Criminal victimization in eight American cities: A descriptive analysis of common theft and assault.* Cambridge, MA: Ballinger Publishing Company.

Hindelang, M., Gottfredson, M., & Garofalo, J. (1978). *Victims of personal crime: An empirical foundation for a theory of personal victimization.* Cambridge, MA: Ballinger Publishing Co.

Hodge, S., & Canter, D. (1998). Victims and perpetrators of male sexual assault. *Journal of Interpersonal Violence, 13*(2), 222–239.

Holmes, R.M. (1991). *Sex crimes.* Newbury Park, CA: Sage Publications.

Holmes, R.M., & Holmes, S.T. (1996). *Profiling violent crimes: An investigative tool* (2nd ed.). Thousand Oaks, CA: Sage Publications.

Johnson, C., Johnson, D., Rucker, L., Bumby, K., & Donaldson, S. (1996). Sexual coercion reported by men and women in prison. *The Journal of Sex Research, 33* (1), 67–76.

Kennedy, L.W., & Forde, D.R. (1990). Routine activities and crime: An analysis of victimization in Canada. *Criminology, 28*(1), 137–152.

Knight, R., & Prentky, R. (1987). The developmental antecedents and adult adaptations of rapist subtypes. *Criminal Justice and Behavior, 14,* 403–426.

Knight, R., & Prentky, R. (1990). Classifying sexual offenders: The development and corroboration of taxonomic models. In W.L. Marshall, D.R. Laws, & H.E. Barbaree (Eds.), *Handbook of sexual assault: Issues, theories, and treatment of the offender.* New York: Plenum Press.

Knight, R., Rosenberg, R., & Schneider, B.A. (1985). Classification of sexual offenders: Perspectives, methods, and validation. In A. Burgess (Ed.), *Rape and sexual assault: A research handbook.* New York: Garland Publishing, Inc.

Kopp, S.B. (1962). The character structure of sex offenders. *American Journal of Psychotherapy, 16,* 64–70.

Koss, M.P., Dinero, T.E., Seibel, C.A., & Cox, S.L. (1988). Stranger and acquaintance rape: Are there differences in the victim's experience? *Psychology of Women Quarterly, 12,* 1–24.

Laub, J.H. (1997). Patterns of criminal victimization in the United States. In R.C. Davis, A.J. Lurigio, & W.G. Skogan (Eds.), *Victims of crime* (2nd ed.). Thousand Oaks, CA: Sage Publications.

LeBeau, J.L. (1987a). Patterns of stranger and serial rape offending: Factors distinguishing apprehended and at large offenders. *The Journal of Criminal Law & Criminology, 78*(2), 309–326.

LeBeau, J.L. (1987b). The journey to rape: Geographic distance and the rapist's method of approaching the victim. *Journal of Police Science and Administration, 15*(2), 129–136.

Macrae, C.N., & Shepherd, J.W. (1989). Sex differences in the perception of rape victims. *Journal of Interpersonal Violence, 4*(3), 278–288.

McGuire, W.J. (1997). Creative Hypothesis Generating in Psychology. Some useful Heuristics. *Annual Review of Psychology 48*, 1–30

Mendelsohn, B. (1956). *Victimologie. Revue Internationale Criminal Police Technique, 10*(2), 73–78.

Mendelsohn, B. (1974). The origin of the doctrine of victimology. In S. Drapkin & E. Viano (Eds.), *Victimology*. Lexington, MA: Lexington Books.

Mawby, R.I. & Walklate, S. (1994). *Critical Victimology: International Perspectives*. London: Sage.

Miethe, T.D., Stafford, M.C., & Long, J.S. (1987). Social differentiation in criminal victimization: A test of routine activities/lifestyle theories. *American Sociological Review, 52*, 184–194.

Miers, D. (1989). Positivist victimology. A critique. *International Review of Victimology, 1*, 3–25.

Milgram, S. (1974). *Obedience to authority: An experimental view*. New York: Harper & Row.

Nagel, W.H. (1974). The notion of victimology in criminology. In S. Drapkin & E. Viano (Eds.), *Victimology*. Lexington, MA: Lexington Books.

Neff, J. (1995). *Unfinished murder: The capture of a serial rapist*. New York: Simon & Schuster, Inc.

Nichols, W.W. (1980). Mental maps, social characteristics, and criminal mobility. In D.E. Georges-Abeyie, & K.D. Harries (Eds.), *Crime: A spatial perspective*. New York: Columbia University Press.

Pitch, T. (1985). Critical criminology, the construction of social problems, and the question of rape. *International Journal of the Sociology of Law, 13*, 35–46.

Polaschek, D.L., Ward, T., & Hudson, S.M. (1997). Rape and rapists: Theory and treatment. *Clinical Psychology Review, 17*(2), 117–144.

Prentky, R., Cohen, M., & Seghorn, T. (1985). Development of a rational taxonomy for the classification of rapists: The Massachusetts treatment center system. *Bulletin of the American Academy of Psychiatry and the Law, 13*(1), 39–70.

Rengert, G. (1980). Spatial aspects of criminal behavior. In D.E. Georges-Abeyie, & K.D. Harries (Eds.), *Crime: A spatial perspective*. New York: Columbia University Press.Resnick, P.A., & Nishith, P. (1997). Sexual assault. In R. Davis, A. Lurigio, & W. Skogan (Eds.), *Victims of crime* (2nd ed.). Thousand Oaks, CA: Sage Publications.

Richards, L. (1991). A theoretical analysis of nonverbal communication and victim selection for sexual assault. *Clothing and Textiles Research Journal*, 9(4), 55–64.

Richards, L., Rollerson, B., & Phillips, J. (1991). Perceptions of submissiveness: Implications for victimization. *Journal of Psychology, 125*(4), 407–411.

Riedel, M. (1993). *Stranger violence: A theoretical inquiry.* New York: Garland Publishing, Inc.

Roncek, D.W. (1981). Dangerous places: Crime and residential environment. *Social Forces, 60*(1), 75–96.

Rossmo, D.K. (1997). Geographic profiling. In J.L., Jackson, & D.A., Bekerian (Eds.), *Offender profiling: Theory, research and practice.* New York: John Wiley & Sons.

Russell, D.E.H. (1982). *Rape in Marriage.* Bloomington, IN: Indiana University Press.

Sampson, R.J. (1983). Structural density and criminal victimization. *Criminology, 21*(2), 276–293.

Sampson, R.J. (1985). Neighborhood and crime: The structural determinants of personal victimization. *Journal of Research in Crime and Delinquency, 22*(1), 7–40.

Sampson, R.J. (1987). Personal Violence by Stangers: An Extension and Test of the Opportunity Model of Predatory Victimization. *Journal of Criminal Law and Criminology, 78*(2), 327–356.

Sampson, R.J., & Lauritsen, J.L. (1994). Violent victimization and offending: Individual-, situational-, and community-level risk factors. In A.J. Reiss, & J.A. Roth (Eds.), *Understanding and preventing violence: Social influences* (Vol. 3). Washington, D.C.: National Academy Press.

Sampson, R., & Wooldredge, J. (1987). Linking the micro- and macro-level dimensions of lifestyle-routine activity and opportunity models of predatory victimization. *Journal of Quantitative Criminology, 3,* 371–393.

Scarce, M. (1997). *Male on male rape: The hidden toll of stigma and shame.* New York: Plenum Press.

Schafer, S. (1968). *The Victim and His Criminal.* New York: Random House.

Schafer, S. (1974). The beginnings of "victimology." In S. Drapkin & E. Viano (Eds.), *Victimology.* Lexington, MA: Lexington Books.

Shaw, C.R. (1929). *Delinquency areas.* Chicago: University of Chicago Press.

Shaw, C.R., & McKay, H.D. (1931). *Report on the causes of crime, vol. 2, National Commission on Law Observance and Enforcement.* Washington, D.C.: U.S. Government Printing Office.

Shaw, C.R., & McKay, H.D. (1942). *Juvenile delinquency and urban areas.* Chicago: University of Chicago Press.

Short, J.F., Jr. (1990). *Delinquency and society.* Englewood Cliffs, N.J.: Prentice-Hall.

Silverman, R.A. (1974). Victim typologies: Overview, critique, and reformulation. In S. Drapkin & E. Viano (Eds.), *Victimology.* Lexington, MA: Lexington Books.

Smith, S.J. (1982). Victimisation in the inner city. *British Journal of Criminology, 72*(2), 386–402.

Stake, R.E. (1998). Case studies. In N.K., Denzin & Y.S., Lincoln (Eds.), *Strategies of Qualitative Inquiry.* Thousand Oaks, CA: Sage Publications.

Stevens, D.J. (1994). Predatory rapists and victim selection techniques. *The Social Science Journal,* 31(4), 421–433.

Strauss, A., & Corbin, J. (1998). Grounded theory methodology: An overview. In N.K. Denzin & Y.S. Lincoln (Eds.), *Strategies of qualitative inquiry* (pp. 158–183). Thousand Oaks, CA: Sage Publications.

Swindle, H. (1997). *Trespasses: Portrait of a serial rapist.* New York: Penguin.

Terry, R.L., & Doerge, S. (1979). Dress, posture, and setting as additive factors in subjective probabilities of rape. *Perceptual and Motor Skills, 48*, 903–906.

Ullman, S.E. (1998). Does offender violence escalate when rape victims fight back? *Journal of Interpersonal Violence, 13*(2), 179–192.

U.S. Department of Justice, Bureau of Justice Statistics, *Criminal victimization in the United States*, 1995, NCJ–171129, Washington, DC: U.S. Department of Justice (1998).

Von Hentig, H. (1948). *The criminal and his victim.* New Haven: Yale University Press.

Walklate, S. (1994). *Victimology: The Victim and the Criminal Justice Process.* London/Boston: Unwin. Hyman.

Warren, J., Reboussin, R., & Hazelwood, R.R. (1995). *The geographic and temporal sequencing of serial rape.* NIJ–91–IJ–R027, Washington, D.C.: U.S. Department of Justice.

Wisan, G. (1979). The treatment of rape in criminology textbooks. *Victimology, 4*(1), 86–99.

Wolfgang (1958). *Patterns in criminal homicide.* Glen Ridge, NJ: Patterson Smith.

Young, M. (1997). Victims rights and services. In R. Davis, A. Lurigio, & W. Skogan (Eds.), *Victims of crime* (2nd ed.) (pp. 27–52). Thousand Oaks, CA: Sage Publications.

INDEX

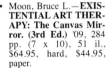
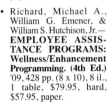
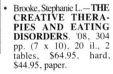